Microsoft Press

P9-AQC-816

Designing
Relational
Database
Systems

Rebecca M. Riordan

PUBLISHED BY
Microsoft Press
A Division of Microsoft Corporation
One Microsoft Way
Redmond, Washington 98052-6399

Library of Congress Cataloging-in-Publication Data
Riordan, Rebecca
    Designing Relational Database Systems / Rebecca Riordan.
        p.   cm.
    Includes index.
    ISBN 0-7356-0634-X
    1. Relational databases.   2. Database design.   I. Title.
    QA76.9.D3R548 1999
    005.75'6--dc21   99-40791
                                                                        CIP

Printed and bound in the United States of America.

1 2 3 4 5 6 7 8 9 WCWC 4 3 2 1 0 9

Distributed in Canada by Penguin Books Canada Limited.

A CIP catalogue record for this book is available from the British Library.

Microsoft Press books are available through booksellers and distributors worldwide. For further information about international editions, contact your local Microsoft Corporation office or contact Microsoft Press International directly at fax (425) 936-7329. Visit our Web site at mspress.microsoft.com.

ActiveX, Microsoft, Microsoft Press, Outlook, PowerPoint, Visual Basic, Visual SourceSafe, Visual Studio, and Windows are either registered trademarks or trademarks of Microsoft Corporation in the United States and/or other countries. Other product and company names mentioned herein may be the trademarks of their respective owners.

The example companies, organizations, products, people, and events depicted herein are fictitious. No association with any real company, organization, product, person, or event is intended or should be inferred.

The table on pages 72–73 is adapted and reprinted with permission from *Inside Microsoft SQL Server 6.5* by Ron Soukup (Microsoft Press, 1998).

Acquisitions Editor: Eric Stroo
Project Editor: Alice Turner

TABLE OF CONTENTS

FOREWORD

Finally, here is a book that builds a bridge between academic database theory and creating databases in the real world. The book also provides essential information you need to take your database applications from design to implementation, such as up-to-date suggestions for fast-track database project documentation, for GUI-based user interface design for database applications, and for user training and documentation.

If you're building real-world databases to solve real-world problems, you'll find thorough, rigorous, and highly practical information about the craft of building database solutions. A plethora of real-world examples based on common SQL implementations is provided. Even true database geeks who "know it all" will find this book is a good refresher on current theory and practice.

Have you ever wondered what a theta-join is? Or where you might use one? If you've never had formal database training and wonder what you might be missing, or just want to impress your coworkers with your rigorous theoretical database training, you'll find in this book a lot of *practical* information and techniques that arise from relational theory—information that you might not have learned even after years of experience.

Have you had a thorough academic training but want to know how to apply it in real-world scenarios? The departmental database conversion is due next week and the database system chosen for you doesn't implement the relational divide operator you desperately need for a key report. Here, you'll find out exactly what popular SQL implementations do and don't support, and discover techniques that fill the gap between theory and practice.

Ensuring that your completed design solves a real-world problem is often harder and more critical than the specifics of implementation. The second part of the book draws from Rebecca's hard-won experience building critical database applications for customers around the world. It provides practical advice and guidelines for working with your customers to ensure that you meet their real needs rather than what they think they need. It fills the gap between design and implementation by examining trade-offs between, for example, single-tier, two-tiered, and n-tiered architectures, and recent Internet innovations. It goes

on to present administrative, security, and auditing topics, which are issues all too often left unaddressed until too late in the project.

The book doesn't stop with the database design. Practical and pragmatic suggestions on managing project life cycle (and other buzzwords), and how to develop and communicate your evolving design with users and programmers, are presented. A variety of modern user interfaces for database applications are outlined with their pros and cons, as well as which specific Microsoft Windows controls map well to specific data types. Chapter 16, "Maintaining Database Integrity," is one of the most realistic, pragmatic, and user-focused treatments I've seen in any text. Rebecca's extensive database application building experience really shines through here. Last, but not least, the book provides a great description of how to help and train your users to succeed with your application by using modern techniques such as ToolTips, and tried and true, and perhaps forgotten, techniques like audible feedback and short-cut keys.

In summary, this book is a practical, pragmatic, and highly knowledgeable treatment of building real database applications in today's high-paced software development world, written by someone who's been there and done it. Anyone trying to build database applications will find it useful. Anyone trying to map database theory to practice will find it enlightening. And to top it all off, it's written in a fun, refreshing style that makes it light and entertaining to read—something I would have thought impossible for a book about databases!

Michael Mee

Acknowledgments

My name may be on the front cover of this book, but the book wasn't written by a single person—writing it required the support of the population of a small village. Not only would this book never have made it to the shelves without their help, but it is a much better book than it would have been without their unfailing generosity.

So, in order of appearance, I would like to express my gratitude to the following people:

First, my family: my husband, Mark Riordan, who for some obscure reason remains convinced that I can do anything; my father, Harlow Wright, for making me believe it just might be true; and most of all my mother, Diana Wright, for seeing to it that I kept laughing no matter what happened.

Mike Mee, who first told me this book was a good idea and was kind enough to write the Foreword.

Eric Stroo, who managed to keep his patience with a disorganized and appallingly undisciplined first-time author.

The individuals who were kind enough to read my scribbles in their early stages and give me the benefit of their great expertise: Dev Ashish, Jim Ferguson, Kim Jacobson, and Annette Marc.

Alice Turner, my wonderful editor, who understood what I had set out to do, shined light on my obscurities, gave my meanderings structure, and still found time to provide moral support above and beyond the call of duty.

Rob Nance, who managed to turn a bunch of scribbled sketches into finished illustrations.

Keri Hardwick, who came to my rescue at the eleventh hour. A friend in need…

I would also like to thank the regular contributors to the *comp.databases.ms-access* newsgroup, whose patience, generosity, and technical wizardry never cease to amaze me.

Finally, let me go on record: THE MISTAKES ARE MINE.

Thank you all,
Rebecca Riordan

INTRODUCTION

Relational databases are tricky beasts. Other kinds of commercial software are infinitely easier to understand. Word processors are really just high-tech typewriters, and it's pretty clear that the backspace key beats that little jar of white stuff cold. Spreadsheets present a familiar enough paradigm, even to non-accountants, and e-mail is close enough to the postal system for the model to be comprehensible.

Databases are different. Other kinds of software have a real-world analogy. Sometimes, as in the Windows desktop, the analogy is a little tenuous, but the analogies are close enough; you can get there from here. But relational databases are completely artificial. They're like geometry; they can be used to build models of the real world, but they don't exist in the real world. When was the last time you poured some wine for you and your sweetie and went out on the front porch to watch the geometry frolic on the lake?

Now, I'm talking about databases here, not tables. Tables exist aplenty, from the telephone book to the dictionary. But relational databases? Nope. Uh-uh. You're not going to find them frolicking on the lake, either. The card files at the library, which contain author, title, and subject files, come close to being a database, but they're still separate sets of data that are only correlated by the good graces of the local librarian.

This book is about designing database systems. My intention is to give you the knowledge you need to take a messy, complex, real-world situation and turn it into an effective database design. After reading the book, you still won't be able to watch the databases frolic on the lake, but if I've done my job well you'll be able to design and implement a relational model of the fish, the seagulls, and the effects of the plankton on them both.

The book is divided into three sections. Part 1, Relational Database Theory, covers the fundamental principles of the relational model. This is where the really ugly, theoretical stuff is. But don't worry; it will get easier. Part 2, Designing Relational Database Systems, examines the analysis and design process—what you should do to get from the real world to a reliable database system design.

Part 3 discusses the most important aspect of a database system from a user's point of view: the user interface.

Although we'll talk about implementation issues in the next few hundred pages, this isn't a "how to program" book. There are a few coding examples, but I've kept them to a minimum, and you should be able to follow them even if you've never seen a programming language before. The database examples are based on the Northwind sample database that comes with Microsoft Access. (The version of Northwind that comes with SQL Server 7 is very similar.) By the time you've finished this book, you'll have picked up most of what you need to get started building database systems, and you'll be ready to turn to one of the sources listed in the Bibliography for the finer points of programming style. And you'll be confident that your data architecture is sound and unlikely to get you into trouble later in your project.

USING THE COMPANION CD

At the back of this book, you will find the companion CD for *Designing Relational Database Systems*. The CD contains Microsoft white papers and Microsoft Knowledge Base articles relating to database design, a set of Microsoft Word documents and templates for creating design documents, and a sample database system for managing the design process.

White Papers and Knowledge Base Articles

MSDN, Microsoft TechNet, and Microsoft Knowledge Base provide a number of white papers and technical articles pertaining to various aspects of database design. A number of these are included on the companion CD in the Papers folder, organized by book chapter. For a complete list of white papers and articles, see the Readme.txt file on the CD.

Design Forms

The CD includes a number of forms that you can use during the design process. They are provided as both Word documents and Word templates.

Using the Word Documents

You might want hard copies of the forms for use during discussions with clients (or just for scribbling on at your desk). Copies of each of the forms are included in the Forms folder. You can print from Microsoft Word 97 or Microsoft Word 2000. If you don't have Word, you can use the Microsoft Word Viewer, included on the CD, to view and print the forms. For information on installing the documents, see the Readme.txt file on the CD.

Using the Word Templates

The forms are also included as Word templates in the Forms folder. Follow the steps outlined in the Readme.txt file on the CD to install the templates on your system.

If you choose to copy the templates to your system Templates folder, you can create a new document based on them by choosing New from the File menu and selecting the appropriate template from the tab you have created. You can also modify the templates for your specific needs by adding your company logo, for instance, or changing the format of the documents to suit your house style.

Sample Database

In the Access 97 Database and Access 2000 Database folders on the accompanying CD, you will find a sample Microsoft Access database system that models the design process. It is provided in Access 97 and Access 2000 formats.

The database system is structured according to the design principles outlined in this book. Although the system is functional as it stands, you should treat it more as a starting point than a functional system and adapt the processes to your own organization and way of working.

In addition to changing the general "look and feel" of the system—adding a company logo to the reports, for example—you might want to consider making some of the changes outlined below.

System Scope

The system as it stands does not include the design of the database schema. If you are not using schema tools provided by your database engine, you might want to consider including this functionality. If you *do* add the schema to the design database, you might also consider automatically generating the physical database. Alternatively, you could have the system create SQL scripts or code snippets to perform the database creation.

The system doesn't include any facility for performing cost benefit analysis, which might be appropriate in your environment.

If you are working on large or complex systems with a development team of more than two or three people, you should include some form of version management in the system, either by expanding its scope or by integrating it with a version control system. You will probably also want to consider splitting the front-end and back-end components of the database if you are going to make it available on a network. The Access Database Splitter Wizard makes this easy to do.

The system currently displays only the attribute constraints that have been defined for each attribute. Since attributes also inherit the constraints of the domains on which they're declared, you might want to consider explicitly showing these domain constraints on a form or report.

Data Model

The system doesn't currently track any information regarding the customers for whom you will be developing systems. While it probably wouldn't be appropriate to attempt to turn this into a customer management system, you might want to consider tracking at least some basic customer information such as name and contact information.

All the tables use an AutoNumber type field as a primary key, which allows duplicate entity names. Depending on your environment (and your feeling about AutoNumbers), you might want to consider using the entity names as the primary key instead.

Domain definitions are currently system-wide. You might want to add a ProjectID attribute to the domain entity to allow domains to be specific to a single project. Also note that the user interface is somewhat misleading in that the Reference Tables command button on the Projects form implies that all these tables are specific to the Project, when in fact they are global.

The system currently allows domains to be declared only against logical data types. You might want to consider allowing domains to be declared against other domains as well.

A Final Note

The database was created with the expectation that it would be extensively modified. To this end, the implementation is as simple as possible (given the complexity of the data model) so that it can be easily understood without the need of technical documentation. It is *not* intended to be an example of good programming style.

System Requirements

To use the Access database, you will need Access 97 or Access 2000.

To use the Word forms electronically, and to use the Word templates, you will need Word 97 or Word 2000. If you do not have Word, you can use the Word Viewer included on the CD to print the forms.

Support

Every effort has been made to ensure the accuracy of this book and the contents of the companion CD. Microsoft Press provides corrections for books through the World Wide Web at the following address:

http://mspress.microsoft.com/support

If you have comments, questions, or ideas regarding this book or the companion CD, please send them to Microsoft Press using either of the following methods:

Postal Mail:

Microsoft Press
Attn: Designing Relational Database Systems Editor
One Microsoft Way
Redmond, WA 98052-6399

E-mail:

MSINPUT@MICROSOFT.COM

Please note that product support is not offered through the above mail addresses. The CD contains a database in Microsoft Access 97 and Microsoft Access 2000 formats. For support on Microsoft Access, go to *http://support.microsoft.com/support/*.

Relational
Database Theory

1

Basic Concepts

So, what is this mythical creature called a relational database? Briefly, it's a tool for storing and manipulating information efficiently and effectively—"efficiently and effectively" in the sense that data is protected from accidental loss or corruption, that it doesn't use more resources (human or computer) than necessary, and that it can be retrieved in sensible ways within acceptable performance constraints. The database itself is the physical implementation of a relational model, which is a way of describing some aspect of the real world according to a set of rules first proposed by Dr. E. F. Codd in the late 1960s.

In theory, a relational database could be coded from scratch, but in reality you'll normally use the services of a database management system (DBMS). A DBMS is sometimes called a relational database management system (RDBMS), but technically a DBMS must meet some 300 rules to qualify as relational, and to the best of my knowledge no commercially available system fully qualifies. The two database management systems we'll be examining in this book are Microsoft Access and Microsoft SQL Server.

I've said that a relational database is the physical implementation of a relational model (the data model), and it's important to keep these two concepts distinct. While it's almost impossible to completely ignore the constraints of the implementation environment during the design phase, best practice dictates that the original model be as "pure" as possible. Although you might already know that for performance reasons you're going to have to make certain trade-offs during implementation, you can, and should, ignore these decisions during data modeling. An example of this is storing calculated fields (such as OrderTotal) in a base table, which is a *major* no-no in relational design but a common technique in practice. Whatever you choose to do with your implementation, your model should not include the calculated field.

What Is a Database?

Database terminology is almost as slippery as the term "object-oriented programming." The word "database" can be used to describe everything from a single set of data, such as a telephone list, to a complex set of tools, such as SQL Server, and a whole lot in between. This lack of precision isn't a bad thing, necessarily—it's just the nature of language—but it's not particularly useful for our purposes, so I'll try to be a bit more precise here. Figure 1-1 shows the relationships between the terms discussed below.

Although relational databases don't have real-world analogies, most are intended to model some aspect of the real world. I'll call that bit of the real world the *problem space*. The problem space, by its nature, is messy and complex—if it weren't, we wouldn't need to build a model of it. But it is critical to the success of your project to limit the database system you're designing to a specific, well-defined set of objects and interactions; only by doing so can you make sensible decisions about the scope of your system.

I'll use the term *data model* to mean the conceptual description of the problem space. This includes the definition of entities, their attributes (a Customer, for example, is an entity, and it might have the attributes Name and Address), and the entity constraints (such as, the CustomerName cannot be empty). The data model also includes a description of the relationships between entities and any constraints on those relationships—for example, managers are not allowed to have more than five individuals reporting to them. It does not include any reference to the physical layout of the system.

The definition of the physical layout—the tables and views that will be implemented—is the *database schema* or just *schema*. It's the translation of the conceptual model into a physical representation that can be implemented using a database management system. Note that the schema is still conceptual, not physical. The schema is nothing more than the data model expressed in the terms that you will use to describe it to the database engine—tables and triggers and such creatures. One of the benefits of using a database engine is that you don't ever have to deal with the physical implementation; you can largely ignore B-trees and leaf nodes.

Once you've explained to the database engine what you want the data to look like, using either code or an interactive environment such as Microsoft Access, the engine will create some physical objects (usually, but not always, on a hard disk someplace) and you'll store data in them. The combination of structure and data is what I'll refer to as a *database*. This database includes the physical tables; the defined views, queries, and stored procedures; and the rules the engine will enforce to protect the data.

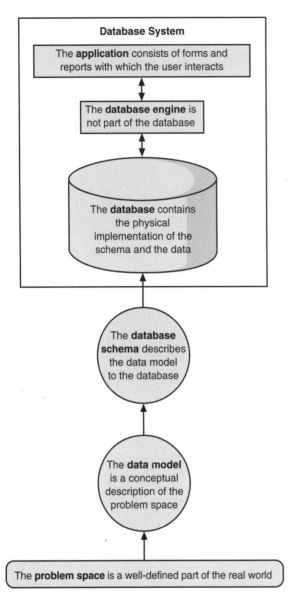

Figure 1-1. *Relational database terminology.*

The term "database" does *not* include the *application,* which consists of the forms and reports with which your users will interact, nor does it include any of the bits and pieces—things such as middleware or Microsoft Transaction Server—used to stick the front and back ends together. The term "database" also

excludes the database engine. Thus, an Access .mdb file is a database, while Microsoft Jet is a database engine. Actually, an .mdb file can contain other things besides the database—forms and reports, for example—but that's a topic we'll discuss later.

To describe all these components—the application, the database, the database engine, and the middleware—I'll use the term *database system*. All of the software and data that goes into making a production system is part of the database system.

Database Tools

Although this book focuses on design rather than implementation, abstract theory isn't of much value unless you know how to apply it; so in this book, we'll be talking a lot about building relational databases using the tools provided by Microsoft. There are a lot of these tools, and Microsoft seems to introduce a new one every time you turn around, so let's take a minute now to look at what all these gadgets are and how they fit together. Figure 1-2 shows the tools we'll be discussing. It's easiest to think about these tools in terms of what we, as developers, need to translate a system from an abstract model to a live production system, and this is how they're grouped in the figure.

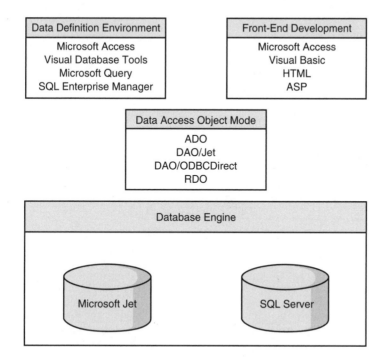

Figure 1-2. *The database tools discussed in this book.*

Database Engines

At the lowest level are the database engines. These are sometimes called "back ends," but that's a bit sloppy since the term "back end" really refers to a specific physical architecture, as we'll see in Chapter 10. These are the gadgets that will handle the physical manipulation of data—storing it to disk and feeding it back on demand. We'll be looking at two: the Jet database engine and SQL Server. You may be surprised not to see Microsoft Access here. Access uses the Jet database engine to manipulate data stored in .mdb files and can link to and manipulate data stored in any ODBC data source, including SQL Server. Access has always used the Jet database engine, although Microsoft didn't expose the engine as a separate entity until the release of Microsoft Visual Basic 3. With the introduction of support for ODBCDirect in Access 97 and support for SQL Server in Access 2000, Microsoft has begun to uncouple the Access front-end tools from the Jet database engine, and I expect this trend to continue in future releases. (But don't quote me.)

The Jet database engine and SQL Server, although very different, are both wonderful tools for storing and manipulating data. The difference between them lies in their architectures and the problems they are intended to address. Microsoft Jet is a "desktop" database engine, intended for small-sized to medium-sized systems. SQL Server, on the other hand, uses a client/server architecture and is intended for medium-sized to huge systems, scalable to potentially thousands of users running mission-critical applications. (Note please that this does *not* imply that the Jet database engine is appropriate only for trivial systems.) We'll be looking at the differences between the two database engines throughout this book and discussing the trade-offs between the two architectures in Chapter 10.

Data Access Object Models

Both Access and Visual Basic provide simple mechanisms for binding form controls directly to a data source, avoiding the necessity for dealing directly with the database engine. For various reasons that we'll be looking at, however, this is not always either possible or appropriate. In these instances, it's most effective to use a data object model to manipulate the data in code.

A data access object model is a kind of glue between the programming environment and the database engine; it provides a set of objects with properties and methods that can be manipulated in code. Microsoft (currently) provides three data access object models: Data Access Objects (DAO), which comes in two flavors, DAO/Jet and DAO/ODBCDirect; Remote Data Objects (RDO), used primarily for accessing open database connectivity (ODBC) data sources; and Microsoft ActiveX Data Objects (ADO), which is intended to replace both DAO and RDO in the near future.

DAO, the oldest of the three, is the native interface to the Jet database engine. RDO is similar to DAO but is optimized for accessing ODBC data sources such

as SQL Server and Oracle. ADO uses a smaller object hierarchy than the other two, consisting of only four primary objects, and provides some significant extensions to the model—for example, its support for disconnected recordsets and data shaping.

Since this book deals primarily with design rather than implementation, we won't be discussing the trade-offs between these models in any depth. William Vaughn's *Hitchhiker's Guide to Visual Basic and SQL Server* and various white papers available at the Microsoft Web site are your best sources for a discussion of these issues. (By the way, there are alternatives to data access object models, such as the Visual Basic Library for SQL Server (VBSQL) and OLE DB, but we won't be looking at them here.)

Front-End Development Tools

Microsoft Jet and SQL Server handle the physical aspects of manipulating data for us, but we need some way to tell them how to structure the data. Microsoft provides a plethora of methods for doing this, but we'll be looking at only two in detail: Access and Microsoft Visual Database Tools. The other methods provide roughly the same capabilities, but these are the two I prefer. Of course, once you understand the principles, you can use whichever tools best get the job done for you.

It's also possible to define the structure of your database using code, and we'll look at how you go about doing this, although under normal circumstances I don't recommend it. Unless for some reason you need to alter the structure of the data during the run-time use of your application (and with the possible exception of temporary tables, I'm highly suspicious of this practice), the interactive tools are quicker, easier, and a lot more fun to use.

Once the physical definition of your database is in place, you'll need tools to create the forms and reports your users will interact with. We'll be looking primarily at two of these: Access and Visual Basic. We'll take a quick look at Internet browsers in Chapter 10, but HTML itself is outside the scope of this book.

The Relational Model

The relational model is based on a collection of mathematical principles drawn primarily from set theory and predicate logic. These principles were first applied to the field of data modeling in the late 1960s by Dr. E. F. Codd, then a researcher at IBM, and first published in 1970.[1] The relational model defines the way data can be represented (data structure), the way data can be protected (data integrity), and the operations that can be performed on data (data manipulation).

---

1. E. F. Codd, "A Relational Model of Data for Large Shared Data Banks," *Communications of the ACM*, Vol. 13, No. 6 (June 1970).

The relational model is not the only method available for storing and manipulating data. Alternatives include the hierarchical, network, and star models. Each of these models has its advocates, and each has its advantages for certain kinds of tasks. The relational model is not particularly well-suited for handling hierarchical data, for instance, a problem the star model was specifically designed to address. But because of its efficiency and flexibility, the relational model is by far the most popular database technique and is the one discussed in this book. Both the Microsoft Jet database engine and Microsoft SQL Server implement the relational model.

In general terms, relational database systems have the following characteristics:

- All data is conceptually represented as an orderly arrangement of data into rows and columns, called a *relation*.

- All values are *scalar*. That is, at any given row/column position in the relation there is one and only one value.

- All operations are performed on an entire relation and result in an entire relation, a concept known as *closure*.

If you've worked with Microsoft Access databases at all, you'll recognize a "relation" as a "recordset" or, in SQL Server terms, as a "result set." Dr. Codd, when formulating the relational model, chose the term "relation" because it was comparatively free of connotations, unlike, for example, the word "table." It's a common misconception that the relational model is so called because relationships are established between tables. In fact, the name is derived from the relations on which it's based.

Notice that the model requires only that data be *conceptually* represented as a relation; it doesn't specify how the data should be physically implemented. This separation of the conceptual and physical representations, although it seems obvious now, was a major innovation 30 years ago when database programming generally meant writing machine code to physically manipulate the data storage devices.

In fact, relations need not have a physical representation at all. A given recordset might map to an actual physical table someplace on a disk, but it can just as well be based on columns drawn from half a dozen different tables, with a few calculated fields—which aren't physically stored anywhere—thrown in for good measure. A relation is a relation provided that it's arranged in row and column format and its values are scalar. Its existence is completely independent of any physical representation.

The principle of closure—that both base tables and the results of operations are represented conceptually as relations—enables the results of one operation to be used as the input to another operation. Thus, with both the Jet database

engine and SQL Server we can use the results of one query as the basis for another. This provides database designers with functionality similar to a subroutine in procedural development: the ability to encapsulate complex or commonly performed operations and reuse them wherever necessary.

For example, you might have created a query called FullNameQuery that concatenates the various attributes representing an individual's name into a single calculated field called FullName. You can create a second query using FullNameQuery as a source that uses the calculated FullName field just like any field that's actually present in the base table. There is no need to recalculate the name.

The requirement that all values in a relation be scalar can be somewhat treacherous. The concept of "one value" is necessarily subjective, based as it is on the semantics of the data model. To give a common example, a "Name" might be a single value in one model, but another environment might require that that value be split into "Title", Given Name", and "Surname", and another might require the addition of "Middle Name" or "Title of Courtesy". None of these is more or less correct in absolute terms; it depends on the use to which the data will be put.

Relational Terminology

Figure 1-3 shows a relation with the formal names of the basic components marked. Those of you who know something about relational design will recognize that the relation is not in normal form. That's okay; it still qualifies as a relation because it's arranged in row and column format and its values are scalar.

Tuple   Attribute

SupplierName:CompanyName	Product:ProductName	UnitPrice:Currency
Leka Trading	Singaporean Hokkien Fried Mee	$14.00
Cooperativa de Quesos 'Las Cabras'	Queso Cabrales	$21.00
Formaggi Fortini s.r.l.	Mozzarella di Giovanni	$34.80
G'day, Mate	Manjimup Dried Apples	$53.00
Mayumi's	Tofu	$23.25
New England Seafood Cannery	Jack's New England Clam Chowder	$9.65
New Orleans Cajun Delights	Louisiana Fiery Hot Pepper Sauce	$21.05
G'day, Mate	Manjimup Dried Apples	$53.00
New Orleans Cajun Delights	Louisiana Fiery Hot Pepper Sauce	$21.05
PB Knäckebröd AB	Gustaf's Knäckebröd	$21.00
Pasta Buttini s.r.l.	Ravioli Angelo	$19.50

Heading ← (points to header row)
Body ← (points to data rows)

Figure 1-3. *The components of a relation.*

The entire structure is, as we've said, a *relation*. Each row of data is a *tuple* (rhymes with "couple"). Actually, each row is an n-tuple, but the "n-" is usually dropped. The number of tuples in a relation determines its *cardinality*. In this case, the relation has a cardinality of 11. Each column in the tuple is called an *attribute*. The number of attributes in a relation determines its *degree*. The example relation has a degree of 3.

The relation is divided into two sections, the *heading* and the *body*. The tuples make up the body, while the heading is composed of, well, the heading. Note that the label for each attribute is composed of two terms separated by a colon— for example, UnitPrice:Currency. The first part of the label is the name of the attribute, while the second part is its domain. The *domain* of an attribute is the "kind" of data it represents—in this case, currency. A domain is *not* the same as a data type. We'll be discussing this issue in detail in the next section. The specification of domain is often dropped from the heading.

The body of the relation consists of an unordered set of zero or more tuples. There are some important concepts here. First, the relation is unordered. Record numbers do *not* apply to relations. Relations have no intrinsic order. Second, a relation with no tuples (an empty relation) still qualifies as a relation. Third, a relation is a set. The items in a set are, by definition, uniquely identifiable. Therefore, for a table to qualify as a relation, each record must be uniquely identifiable and the table must contain no duplicate records.

If you've read the Access or SQL Server documentation, you might be wondering why you've never seen any of these words before. They're the formal terminology used in the technical literature, not the terms used by Microsoft. I've included them just so you won't be embarrassed at cocktail parties (at least not about n-tuples of third degree, anyway). Remember that relations are purely conceptual; once instantiated in the database, they become *recordsets* in Microsoft Jet and *result sets* in SQL Server, while for both Microsoft Jet and SQL Server an attribute becomes a *field* and a tuple becomes a *record*. The correspondences are pretty much one-to-one, but remember that relations are conceptual and recordsets and result sets are physical.

The Data Model

The most abstract level of a database design is the *data model,* the conceptual description of a problem space. Data models are expressed in terms of entities, attributes, domains, and relationships. The remainder of this chapter discusses each of these in turn.

Entities

It's difficult to provide a precise formal definition of the term entity, but the concept is intuitively quite straightforward: an *entity* is anything about which the system needs to store information.

When you begin to design your data model, compiling an initial list of entities isn't difficult. When you (or your clients) talk about the problem space, most of the nouns and verbs used will be candidate entities. "Customers buy products. Employees sell products. Suppliers sell us products." The nouns "Customers," "Products," "Employees," and "Suppliers" are all clearly entities.

The events represented by the verbs "buy" and "sell" are also entities, but a couple of traps exist here. First, the verb "sell" is used to represent two distinct events: the sale of a product to a customer and the purchase of a product by the organization. That's fairly obvious in this example, but it's an easy trap to fall into, particularly if you're not familiar with the problem space.

The second gotcha is the inverse of the first: two different verbs ("buy" in the first sentence and "sell" in the second) are used to describe the same event, the purchase of a product by a customer. Again, this isn't necessarily obvious unless you're familiar with the problem space. This problem is often trickier to track down than the first. If a client is using different verbs to describe what appears to be the same event, they might in fact be describing different kinds of events. If the client is a tailor, for example, "customer buys suit" and "customer orders suit" might both result in the sale of a suit, but in the first case it's a prêt-à-porter sale and in the second it's bespoke. These are very different processes that might need to be modeled differently.

In addition to interviewing clients to establish a list of entities, it's also useful to review any documents that exist in the problem space. Input forms, reports, and procedures manuals are all good sources of candidate entities. You must be careful with documents, however. Printed documents have a great deal of inertia: input forms particularly are expensive to print and frequently don't keep up with changes to policies and procedures. If you stumble across an entity that's never come up in an interview, don't assume the client just forgot to mention it. Chances are that it's a legacy item that's no longer pertinent to the organization. You'll need to check.

Once you've developed an initial list of candidate entities, you need to review them for completeness and consistency. Again, you need to find duplicates and distinct entities that are masquerading as the same entity. A useful tool in this process is the concept of entity subtypes. To return to our example of the tailor, "prêt-à-porter" and "bespoke" both represent the purchase of an item of clothing, but they're different *kinds* of purchases. In other words, Sale and Order are both subtypes of the entity Purchase.

Attributes that are common to both types of Purchase are assigned to the super-type, in this case, Purchase, and attributes specific to a subtype—PretAPorter or Bespoke in this instance—are factored out to that subtype. This allows both kinds of events to be treated as generic Purchases when that is appropriate (as when calculating total sales) or as specific kinds of Purchases (as when comparing subtypes).

Sometimes you might discover that the entity subtypes don't actually have distinct attributes, in which case it's more convenient to make TypeOfSale (or TypeOfCustomer, or TypeOfWhatever) an attribute of the supertype rather than modeling the subtypes as distinct entities. With our tailoring example for be-spoke sales you might need to know the cloth and color selected, whereas for prêt-à-porter sales you might need to track the garment manufacturer. In this case, you would use subtypes to model these entities. If, however, you only need to know that a sale was bespoke or prêt-à-porter, a TypeOfSale attribute would be simpler to implement.

Subtypes are usually mutually exclusive, but this is by no means always the case. Consider an employee database. All employees have certain attributes in com-mon (hire date, department, and telephone extension), but only some will be salespeople (with specific attributes for commission rate and target) and only a few will join the company softball team. There's nothing preventing a salesperson from playing basketball, however.

Most entities model objects or events in the physical world: customers, prod-ucts, or sales calls. These are *concrete entities*. Entities can also model abstract concepts. The most common example of an *abstract entity* is one that models the relationship between other entities—for example, the fact that a certain sales representative is responsible for a certain client or that a certain student is en-rolled in a certain class.

Sometimes all you need to model is the fact that a relationship exists. Other times you'll want to store additional information about the relationships, such as the date on which it was established or some characteristic of the relation-ship. The relationship between cougars and coyotes is competitive, that between cougars and rabbits is predatory, and it's useful to know this if you're planning an open-range zoo.

Whether relationships that do not have attributes ought to be modeled as sepa-rate entities is a matter of some discussion. I don't think anything is gained by doing so, and it complicates the process of deriving a database schema from the data model. However, understand that relationships are as important as entities are in the data model.

Attributes

Your system will need to keep track of certain facts about each entity. These facts are referred to as the entity's attributes. If your system includes Customer entities, for example, you'll probably want to know the names and addresses of the customers and perhaps the businesses they're in. If you're modeling an event such as a Service Call, you'll probably want to know who the customer was, who made the call, when it was made, and whether the problem was resolved.

Determining the attributes to be included in your model is a semantic process. You must make your decisions based on what the data means and how it will be used. Let's look at one common example: an address. Do you model the address as a single entity (the Address) or as a set of entities (HouseNumber, Street, City, State, ZipCode)? Most designers (myself included) would tend to automatically break the address up into a set of attributes on the general principle that structured data is easier to manipulate, but this is not necessarily correct and certainly not straightforward.

Let's take, for instance, a local amateur musical society. It will want to store the addresses of its members in order to print mailing labels. Since all the members live in the same city, there is no reason to ever look at an address as anything other than a blob: a single, multiline chunk of text that gets spat out on demand.

But what about a mail-order company that does all its business on the Internet? For sales tax purposes, the company needs to know the states in which its customers reside. While it's possible to extract the state from the single text field used by the musical society, it isn't easy; so it makes sense in this case to at least model the state as a separate attribute. What about the rest of the address? Should it be composed of multiple attributes, and if so, what are they? Be aware that while addresses in the United States conform to a fairly standard pattern, modeling them is probably not as simple as it appears.

You might think that a set of attributes {HouseNumber, Street, City, State, ZipCode} might be adequate. But then you need to deal with apartment numbers and post office boxes and APO addresses. What do you do with an address to be sent in care of someone else? And of course the world is getting smaller but not less complex, so what happens when you get your first customer outside the United States? Not only do you need to know the country and adjust the zip code, but the arrangement of the attributes might need to change. In most of Europe, for example, the house number follows the street name. That's not too bad, it's easy enough to map that when you're entering data, but how many of your users would know that in the address 4/32 Griffen Avenue, Bondi Beach, Australia, 4/32 means Apartment 4, Number 32?

The point here is not so much that addresses are hard to model, although they are, but rather that you can't make any assumptions about how you should model any specific kind of data. The complex schema that you develop for handling international mail order is completely inappropriate for the local musical society.

Matisse is reputed to have said that a painting was finished when nothing could be either added or subtracted. Entity design is a bit like that. How do you know when you've reached that point? The unfortunate answer is that you can never know for certain. At the current state of technology, there isn't any way to develop a provably correct database design. You can prove that some designs have flaws, but you can't prove that any given design doesn't. You can't, if you will, prove your innocence. How do you tackle this problem? There are no rules, but there are some strategies.

The first strategy is: start with the result and don't make the design any more complex than it needs to be.

What questions does your database have to answer? In our first example, the musical society, the only question was "Where do I mail a letter to this person?", so a single-attribute model was sufficient. The second example, the mail order company, also had to answer "In what state does this person live?", so we needed a different structure to provide the results.

You need to be careful, of course, that you try to provide the flexibility to handle not just the questions your users are asking now but also the ones you can foresee them asking in the future. I'd be willing to bet, for instance, that within a year of implementing the musical society system the society will come back asking you to sort the addresses by zip code so that they can qualify for bulk mail discounts.

You should also be on the lookout for questions the users would ask if they only knew they could, particularly if you're automating a manual system. Imagine asking a head librarian how many of the four million books in the collection were published in Chicago before 1900. He or she would point you to the card file and tell you to have fun. Yet this is trivial information to request from a well-designed database system.

One of the hallmarks of good designers is the thoroughness and creativity with which they solicit potential questions. Inexperienced analysts are frequently heard to remark that the users don't know what they want. Of course they don't; it's *your* job to help them discover what they want.

There's a trap here, however. Often, the trade-off for flexibility is increased complexity. As we saw with the address examples, the more ways you want to slice and dice the data the more exceptions you have to handle, and there comes a point of diminishing returns.

This leads me to strategy two: find the exceptions. There are two sides to this strategy: first that it is important to identify all the exceptions, and second that you must design the system to handle as many exceptions as you can without confusing users. To illustrate what this means, let's walk through another example: personal names.

If your system will be used to produce correspondence, it's crucial that you get the name right. (Case in point: any unsolicited mail arriving at my house addressed to *Mr.* R. M. Riordan doesn't even get opened.) Most names are pretty straightforward. Ms. Jane Q. Public consists of the Title, FirstName, MiddleInitial, and LastName, right? Wrong. (You saw this coming, didn't you?) In the first place, FirstName and LastName are culturally specific. It's more correct to use GivenName and Surname. Next, what happens to Sir James Peddington Smythe, Lord Dunstable? Is Peddington Smythe his Surname or is Peddington his MiddleName, and what do you do about the "Lord Dunstable" part? And the singer Sting? Is that a GivenName or a Surname? And what will happen to The Artist Formerly Known as Prince? Do you really care?

That last question isn't as flippant as it sounds. A letter addressed to Sir James Peddington Smythe probably won't offend anyone. But the gentleman in question is not Sir Smythe; he's Sir James, or maybe Lord Dunstable. Realistically, though, how many of your clients are lords of a realm? The local musical society is not going to thank you for giving them a membership system with a screen like the one in Figure 1-4.

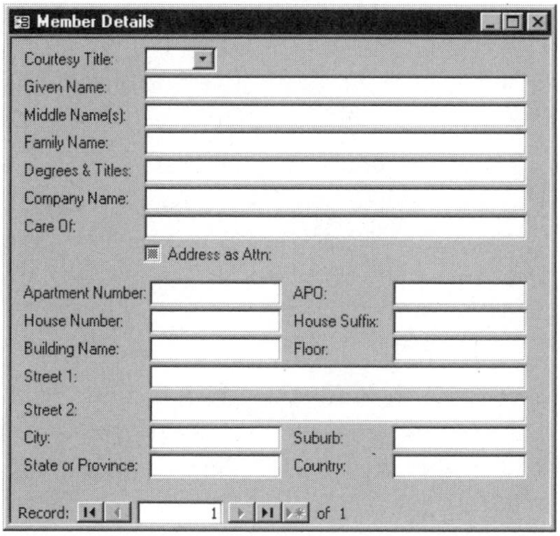

Figure 1-4. *An overly complex address screen.*

So be aware that there's a trade-off between flexibility and complexity. While it's important to catch as many exceptions as possible, it's perfectly reasonable to eliminate some of them as too unlikely to be worth the cost of dealing with them.

Distinguishing between entities and attributes is sometimes difficult. Again, addresses are a good example, and again, your decision must be based on the problem space. Some designers advocate the creation of a single address entity used to store all the addresses modeled by the system. From an implementation viewpoint, this approach has certain advantages in terms of encapsulation and code reuse. From a design viewpoint, I have some reservations.

It's unlikely that addresses for employees and customers will be used in the same way. Mass mailings to employees, for example, are more likely to be done via internal mail than the postal service. This being the case, the rules and requirements are different. That awful data entry screen shown in Figure 1-4 might very well be justified for customer addresses, but by using a single address entity you're forced to use it for employees as well, where it's unlikely to be either necessary or appreciated.

Domains

You might recall from the beginning of this chapter that a relation heading contains an AttributeName:DomainName pair for each attribute. I said then that a domain definition specifies the *kind* of data represented by the attribute. More particularly, a domain is the set of all possible values that an attribute may validly contain.

Domains are often confused with data types, but this is inaccurate. Data type is a physical concept while domain is a logical one. "Number" is a data type, and "Age" is a domain. To give another example, "StreetName" and "Surname" might both be represented as text fields, but they are obviously different *kinds* of text fields; they belong to different domains.

Domain is also a broader concept than data type in that a domain definition includes a more specific description of the valid data. Take, for example, the domain DegreeAwarded, which represents the degrees awarded by a university. In the database schema, this attribute might be defined as Text[3], but it's not just any three-character string, it's a member of the set {BA, BS, MA, MS, PhD, LLD, MD}.

Of course, not all domains can be defined by simply listing their values. Age, for example, contains a hundred or so values if we're talking about people, but tens of thousands if we're talking about museum exhibits. In such instances it's useful to define the domain in terms of the rules which can be used to determine the membership of any specific value in the set of all valid values.

For example, PersonAge could be defined as "an integer in the range 0 to 120," whereas ExhibitAge might simply be "an integer equal to or greater than 0."

"Ah," I can hear you saying to yourself. "Domain is the combination of the data type and the validation rule." Well, if you think of them this way you won't go too far wrong. But remember, validation rules are part of the data integrity, not part of the data description. For example, the validation rule for a zip code might refer to the State attribute, whereas the domain of ZipCode is "a six-digit string."

Note that all these definitions make some reference to the kind of data stored (number or string). This looks a whole lot like a data type, but it isn't really. Data types, as I've said, are physical; they're defined and implemented in terms of the database engine. It would be a mistake developing the data model to define a domain as varchar(30) or a Long Integer, which are engine-specific descriptions.

For any two domains, if it makes sense to compare attributes defined on them (and, by extension, to perform relational operations such as joins, which we'll discuss in Chapter 5), then the two domains are said to be *type-compatible*. For example, given the two relations in Figure 1-5, it would be perfectly sensible to link them on EmployeeID = SalespersonID—you might do this to obtain a list of invoices for a given employee, for example. The domains EmployeeID and SalespersonID are type-compatible. Trying to combine the relations on EmployeeID = OrderDate will probably not result in a meaningful answer, even if the two domains were defined on the same data type.

Orders

OrderID	Customer	SalespersonID	OrderDate
10248	Vins et alcools Chevalier	5	04-Aug-94
10249	Toms Spezialitäten	6	05-Aug-94
10250	Hanari Carnes	4	08-Aug-94
10251	Victuailles en stock	3	08-Aug-94
10252	Suprêmes délices	4	09-Aug-94

Employees

EmployeeID	LastName	FirstName	Title
1	Davolio	Nancy	Sales Representative
2	Fuller	Andrew	Vice President, Sales
3	Leverling	Janet	Sales Representative
4	Peacock	Margaret	Sales Representative
5	Buchanan	Steven	Sales Manager
6	Suyama	Michael	Sales Representative

Figure 1-5. *The Employees and Orders relations.*

Unfortunately, neither the Jet database engine nor SQL Server provides strong intrinsic support for domains, beyond data types. And even within data types, neither engine performs strong checking; both will quietly convert data behind the scenes. For example, if you've defined EmployeeID as a long integer in the

Employees table and InvoiceTotal as a currency value in the Invoices table in the Microsoft Access Northwind sample database, you can create a query linking the two tables with the criteria WHERE EmployeeID = InvoiceTotal, and Microsoft Jet will quite happily give you a list of all employees who have an EmployeeID that matches the total value of an invoice. The two attributes are not type-compatible, but the Jet database engine doesn't know that.

So why bother with domains at all? Because, as we'll see in Part 2, they're extremely useful design tools. "Are these two attributes interchangeable?" "Are there any rules that apply to one but don't apply to the other?" These are important questions when you're designing a data model, and domain analysis helps you think about them.

Relationships

In addition to the attributes of each entity, a data model must specify the relationships between entities. At the conceptual level, *relationships* are simply associations between entities. The statement "Customers buy products" indicates that a relationship exists between the entities Customers and Products. The entities involved in a relationship are called its *participants*. The number of participants is the *degree* of the relationship. (The degree of a relationship is similar to, but not the same as, the degree of a relation, which is the number of attributes.)

The vast majority of relationships are binary, like the "Customers buy products" example, but this is not a requirement. Ternary relationships, those with three participants, are also common. Given the binary relationships "Employees sell products" and "Customers buy products," there is an implicit ternary relationship "Employees sell products to customers." However, specifying the two binary relationships does not allow us to identify which employees sold which products to which customers; only a ternary relationship can do that.

A special case of a binary relationship is an entity that participates in a relationship with itself. This is often called the bill of materials relationship and is most often used to represent hierarchical structures. A common example is the relationship between employees and managers: any given employee might both *be* a manager and *have* a manager.

The relationship between any two entities can be one-to-one, one-to-many, or many-to-many. One-to-one relationships are rare, most often being used between supertype and subtype entities. To return to our earlier example, the relationship between an employee and that employee's salesperson details is one-to-one.

One-to-many relationships are probably the most common type. An invoice includes many products. A salesperson creates many invoices. These are both examples of one-to-many relationships.

Although not as common as one-to-many relationships, many-to-many relationships are also not unusual and examples abound. Customers buy many products, and products are bought by many customers. Teachers teach many students, and students are taught by many teachers. Many-to-many relationships can't be directly implemented in the relational model, but their indirect implementation is quite straightforward, as we'll see in Chapter 3.

The participation of any given entity in a relationship can be *partial* or *total*. If it is not possible for an entity to exist unless it participates in the relationship, the participation is total; otherwise, it is partial. For example, Salesperson details can't logically exist unless there is a corresponding Employee. The reverse is not true. An employee might be something other than a salesperson, so an Employee record can exist without a corresponding Salesperson record. Thus, the participation of Employee in the relationship is partial, while the participation of Salesperson is total.

The trick here is to ensure that the specification of partial or total participation holds true for all instances of the entity for all time. It's not unknown for companies to change suppliers for a product, for example. If the participation of Products in the "Suppliers provide products" relation has been defined as total, it won't be possible to delete the current supplier without deleting the other product details.

Entity Relationship Diagrams

The Entity Relationship model, which describes data in terms of entities, attributes, and relations, was introduced by Peter Pin Shan Chen in 1976.[2] At the same time, he proposed a method of diagramming called Entity Relationship (E/R) diagrams, which has become widely accepted. E/R diagrams use rectangles to describe entities, ellipses for attributes, and diamonds to represent relationships, as shown in Figure 1-6.

The nature of the relationship between entities (one-to-one, one-to-many, or many-to-many) is represented in various ways. A number of people use 1 and M or 1 and ∞ (representing infinity) to represent one and many. I use the "crow's foot" technique shown in Figure 1-6, which I find more expressive.

The great advantage of E/R diagrams is that they're easy to draw and understand. In practice, though, I usually diagram the attributes separately, since they exist at a different level of detail.

Generally, one is either thinking about the entities in the model and the relationships between them or thinking about the attributes of a given entity, but rarely thinking about both at the same time.

---

2. Peter Pin Shan Chen, "The Entity Relationship Model—Toward a Unified View of Data?", ACM TODS 1, No. 1 (March 1976).

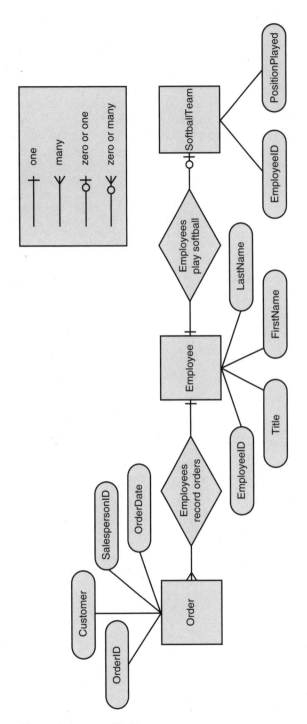

Figure 1-6. *An E/R diagram.*

SUMMARY

In this chapter, we've looked at the components of a database system and laid the foundations for the rest of the book. We began by describing the *problem space* as some well-defined part of the real world. The *conceptual data model* is a description of the problem space in terms of *entities, attributes,* and the *domains* on which they are defined. The physical layout of the data model is the *database schema,* which is instantiated as a *database.* Finally, the *database engine* handles the physical manipulation of the database on behalf of the *application,* which consists of the forms and reports with which users interact.

In the next chapter, we'll examine the structure of a database in more detail as we explore the principles of normalization.

2

Database Structure

This chapter discusses the first facet of designing relational database models: the structure of the relations themselves. The primary goal of this design phase is simple: to ensure that the model is capable of answering every question that might reasonably be asked of it. Secondarily, you want to minimize redundancy and the problems associated with it.

Redundancy is a bad idea not only because it wastes resources but also because it makes life a lot harder. Take, for example, the recordset shown in Figure 2-1, representing a company's invoices. (Assume, for the moment, that this recordset is a base table that is explicitly stored in the database, not the result of a query.)

OrderID	EmployeeName	HireDate	TelephoneExtension	CompanyName	ProductName	Quantity
10358	Buchanan Steven	10/17/93	3453	La maison d'Asie	Sasquatch Ale	10
10607	Buchanan Steven	10/17/93	3453	Save-a-lot Markets	Mozzarella di Giovanni	12
10714	Buchanan Steven	10/17/93	3453	Save-a-lot Markets	Zaanse koeken	50
10437	Callahan Laura	3/5/94	2344	Wartian Herkku	Perth Pasties	15
10383	Callahan Laura	3/5/94	2344	Around the Horn	Konbu	20
10773	Davolio Nancy	5/1/92	5467	Ernst Handel	Gorgonzola Telino	70
10325	Davolio Nancy	5/1/92	5467	Königlich Essen	Mozzarella di Giovanni	40
10773	Davolio Nancy	5/1/92	5467	Ernst Handel	Rhönbräu Klosterbier	7
10992	Davolio Nancy	5/1/92	5467	The Big Cheese	Mozzarella di Giovanni	2
10916	Davolio Nancy	5/1/92	5467	Rancho grande	Ravioli Angelo	20
10727	Fuller Andrew	8/14/92	3457	Reggiani Caseifici	Gnocchi di nonna Alice	10
10727	Fuller Andrew	8/14/92	3457	Reggiani Caseifici	Raclette Courdavault	10
10597	King Robert	1/2/94	465	Piccolo und mehr	Guaraná Fantástica	35
10642	King Robert	1/2/94	465	Simons bistro	Sir Rodney's Scones	30
10523	King Robert	1/2/94	465	Seven Seas Imports	Gravad lax	18
10956	Leverling Janet	4/1/92	3355	Antonio Moreno Taquería	Singaporean Hokkien Fried Mee	20
10856	Leverling Janet	4/1/92	3355	Antonio Moreno Taquería	Chang	20
10644	Leverling Janet	4/1/92	3355	Wellington Importadora	Spegesild	21
10554	Peacock Margaret	5/3/93	5176	Ottilies Käseladen	Tarte au sucre	20
10554	Peacock Margaret	5/3/93	5176	Ottilies Käseladen	Tunnbröd	20
10867	Suyama Michael	10/17/93	428	Lonesome Pine Restaurant	Perth Pasties	3
10356	Suyama Michael	10/17/93	428	Die Wandernde Kuh	Gorgonzola Telino	30
10701	Suyama Michael	10/17/93	428	Hungry Owl All-Night Grocers	Lakkalikööri	35
10271	Suyama Michael	10/17/93	428	Split Rail Beer & Ale	Geitost	24

Figure 2-1. *This recordset has redundant data.*

You can see that HireDate and TelephoneExtension values are listed several times for each employee. Now, this has a couple of consequences. First, it means that every time you enter a new invoice you have to reenter values into these two fields. And, of course, every time you enter something you have another

chance to get it wrong. For example, given the recordset shown in Figure 2-2, how do you know whether Steven Buchanan was hired in 1989 or 1998? Second, the structure prevents you from storing the hire date or phone number for a new employee until that employee has made a sale. Third, if the invoices for a given year are archived and removed from the database, the hire date and phone number information will be lost.

OrderID	EmployeeName	HireDate	TelephoneExtension	CompanyName	ProductName	Quantity
10358	Buchanan Steven	10/17/89	3453	La maison d'Asie	Sasquatch Ale	10
10607	Buchanan Steven	10/17/98	3453	Save-a-lot Markets	Mozzarella di Giovanni	12
10714	Buchanan Steven	10/17/98	3453	Save-a-lot Markets	Zaanse koeken	50

Figure 2-2. *Duplicate data can result in inconsistencies.*

These kinds of problems, usually called *update anomalies*, are even worse if the redundant data is stored in more than one relation. Consider the example shown in Figure 2-3. (Again, assume that these are base tables, not query results.) If the phone number of Around the Horn changes, you must change it in the Customer recordset and also remember to update every instance in the Invoice recordset.

Customers relation

CustomerID	CompanyName	Phone
ALFKI	Alfreds Futterkiste	030-0074321
ANATR	Ana Trujillo Emparedados y helados	(5) 555-4729
ANTON	Antonio Moreno Taquería	(5) 555-3932
AROUT	Around the Horn	(171) 555-7788
BERGS	Berglunds snabbköp	0921-12 34 65

Invoices relation

OrderID	CompanyName	Phone
10952	Alfreds Futterkiste	030-0074321
10952	Alfreds Futterkiste	030-0074321
10625	Ana Trujillo Emparedados y helados	(5) 555-4729
10625	Ana Trujillo Emparedados y helados	(5) 555-4729
10625	Ana Trujillo Emparedados y helados	(5) 555-4729
10856	Antonio Moreno Taquería	(5) 555-3932
10558	Around the Horn	(171) 555-7788
10558	Around the Horn	(171) 555-7788
10558	Around the Horn	(171) 555-7788
10558	Around the Horn	(171) 555-7788
10572	Berglunds snabbköp	0921-12 34 65
10875	Berglunds snabbköp	0921-12 34 65
10875	Berglunds snabbköp	0921-12 34 65
10875	Berglunds snabbköp	0921-12 34 65

Figure 2-3. *The same duplicate data can exist in multiple recordsets.*

It's not so much that this is impossible or even difficult to do. The problem is remembering to do it. And even if *you* never forget anything, how will you ensure that the maintenance programmer modifying your system six months

from now will know there are redundancies of this kind, much less remember (or know how) to handle them appropriately? It's better, much better, to avoid the redundancies and the resulting problems altogether.

You need to make sure that the redundant attributes you're considering really are redundant. Consider the example in Figure 2-4. At first glance, you might think that the UnitPrice attributes in these two relations are redundant. But they actually represent two distinct values. The UnitPrice attribute in the Products relation represents the current selling price. The UnitPrice attribute in the Orders relation represents the price at the time the item was sold. Tofu, for example, is listed at a UnitPrice of $18.60 in the Orders relation and $23.25 in the Products relation. The fact that Tofu currently sells for $23.25 doesn't change the fact that it was sold for $18.60 at some point in the past. The two attributes are defined on the same domain, but they are logically distinct.

Products relation

ProductID	ProductName	UnitPrice
11	Queso Cabrales	$21.00
14	Tofu	$23.25
22	Gustaf's Knäckebröd	$21.00
41	Jack's New England Clam Chowder	$9.65
42	Singaporean Hokkien Fried Mee	$14.00
51	Manjimup Dried Apples	$53.00
57	Ravioli Angelo	$19.50
65	Louisiana Fiery Hot Pepper Sauce	$21.05
66	Louisiana Hot Spiced Okra	$17.00
72	Mozzarella di Giovanni	$34.80

Orders relation

OrderID	ProductName	UnitPrice	Quantity	OrderDate
10248	Singaporean Hokkien Fried Mee	$9.80	10	04-Aug-94
10248	Queso Cabrales	$14.00	12	04-Aug-94
10248	Mozzarella di Giovanni	$34.80	5	04-Aug-94
10249	Tofu	$18.60	9	05-Aug-94
10249	Manjimup Dried Apples	$42.40	40	05-Aug-94
10250	Manjimup Dried Apples	$42.40	35	08-Aug-94
10250	Louisiana Fiery Hot Pepper Sauce	$16.80	15	08-Aug-94
10250	Jack's New England Clam Chowder	$7.70	10	08-Aug-94
10251	Ravioli Angelo	$15.60	15	08-Aug-94
10251	Louisiana Fiery Hot Pepper Sauce	$16.80	20	08-Aug-94
10251	Gustaf's Knäckebröd	$16.80	6	08-Aug-94

Figure 2-4. *Seemingly identical data might not actually be redundant.*

The ability of a data model to answer the questions asked of it is largely determined by its completeness (obviously, no database system can provide data it doesn't contain) and only secondarily by its structure. But the *ease* with which questions can be answered is almost exclusively the result of the structure. The principle here is that it is easy to combine attributes and relations but very difficult to take them apart, as illustrated in Figure 2-5.

EmployeeID	TitleOfCourtesy	FirstName	LastName	Title
1	Ms.	Nancy	Davolio	Sales Representative
2	Dr.	Andrew	Fuller	Vice President, Sales
3	Ms.	Janet	Leverling	Sales Representative
4	Mrs.	Margaret	Peacock	Sales Representative
5	Mr.	Steven	Buchanan	Sales Manager

EmployeeID	FullName
1	Ms. Nancy Davolio, Sales Representative
2	Dr. Andrew Fuller, Vice President, Sales
3	Ms. Janet Leverling, Sales Representative
4	Mrs. Margaret Peacock, Sales Representative
5	Mr. Steven Buchanan, Sales Manager

Figure 2-5. *Concatenating information is easy, but extracting it from composite fields is hard.*

To return to the name example from Chapter 1, given the two relations shown in Figure 2-5, the FullName can be easily derived from the top relation with the statement:

```
TitleOfCourtesy & " " & FirstName & " " & LastName & _
   ", " & Title
```

But retrieving only the LastName from the FullName field shown in the bottom relation would require manipulating the string:

```
Function GetLastname(FullName) As String
   Dim lastname As String

   'strip off the Title
   lastname = Left(FullName, InStr(FullName, ",") - 1)
   'strip off the TitleOfCourtesy
   lastname = Right(lastname, Len(lastname) - _
      InStr(lastname, " "))
   'strip off FirstName
   lastname = Right(lastname , Len(lastname ) - _
      InStr(lastname , " "))

   GetLastname = lastname

End Function
```

This technique is also vulnerable to variations in the contents of the FullName field; the name "Billy Rae Jones" is going to return "Rae Jones", when what you probably wanted was "Jones". Further, producing a list in the format LastName, FirstName could get very ugly.

The second principle involved in creating a data model that can effectively answer the questions asked of it is to avoid situations where answering the question requires evaluating the same information from multiple fields. Take the relations shown in Figures 2-6 and 2-7, for example, both of which model student enrollments. To answer the question "Which students are studying Biology this year?" using the first relation, you would have to search for the value "Biology" in six fields. The SQL SELECT statement would look like this:

```
SELECT StudentID FROM Enrollments WHERE Period1 = "Biology"
    OR Period2 = "Biology" OR Period3 = "Biology"
    OR Period4 = "Biology" OR Period5 = "Biology"
    OR Period6 = "Biology";
```

Using the second structure requires searching only a single field, Class:

```
SELECT StudentID FROM Enrollments WHERE Class = "Biology";
```

They both work, but the second one is obviously easier and less error-prone to code, not to mention easier to think about.

Enrollments relation

StudentID	FirstName	LastName	Period1	Period2	Period3	Period4	Period5	Period6
1	Nancy	Davolio	Biology	French	English	History	Chemistry	Physical Education
2	Andrew	Fuller	Physical Educa	Biology	French	English	Chemistry	History
3	Janet	Leverling	Physical Educa	Biology	French	English	Chemistry	History
4	Margaret	Peacock	French	Physical Educa	History	English	Biology	Chemistry
5	Steven	Buchanan	Biology	French	Physical Educa	History	English	Chemistry
6	Michael	Suyama	French	Physical Educa	Biology	History	English	Chemistry
7	Robert	King	History	French	English	Biology	Chemistry	Physical Education

Figure 2-6. *This structure makes certain questions difficult to answer.*

Enrollments relation

StudentID	FirstName	LastName	Period	Class
1	Nancy	Davolio	1	Biology
2	Andrew	Fuller	1	Physical Education
3	Janet	Leverling	1	Physical Education
4	Margaret	Peacock	1	French
5	Steven	Buchanan	1	Biology
6	Michael	Suyama	1	French
7	Robert	King	1	History
1	Nancy	Davolio	2	French
2	Andrew	Fuller	2	Biology
3	Janet	Leverling	2	Biology
4	Margaret	Peacock	2	Physical Education
5	Steven	Buchanan	2	French
6	Michael	Suyama	2	Physical Education
7	Robert	King	2	French
1	Nancy	Davolio	3	English
2	Andrew	Fuller	3	French

Figure 2-7. *This structure has more records, but it's easier to formulate queries against it.*

Avoiding redundancy and making it easy to retrieve the data are all you need to know about data modeling; the rest is just an attempt to formalize these two basic principles. But if you've ever done much (or any) data modeling, you'll know that, simple as they might be, these principles can be very slippery to apply. They're like a paper clip: the answer is perfectly obvious once you've seen it, but a little hard to come up with the first time you're faced with a bunch of loose paper and a bit of wire.

Basic Principles

The principles of normalization discussed in the rest of this chapter are tools for controlling the structure of data in the same way that a paper clip controls sheets of paper. The normal forms (we'll discuss six) specify increasingly stringent rules for the structure of relations. Each form extends the previous one in such a way as to prevent certain kinds of update anomalies.

Bear in mind that the normal forms are not a prescription for creating a "correct" data model. A data model could be perfectly normalized and still fail to answer the questions asked of it; or, it might provide the answers, but so slowly and awkwardly that the database system built around it is unusable. But if your data model is normalized—that is, if it conforms to the rules of relational structure— the chances are high that the result will be an efficient, effective data model. Before we turn to normalization, however, you should be familiar with a couple of underlying principles.

Lossless Decomposition

The relational model allows relations to be joined in various ways by linking attributes. The process of obtaining a fully normalized data model involves removing redundancy by dividing relations in such a way that the resultant relations can be recombined without losing any of the information. This is the principle of *lossless decomposition*. For example, given the relation shown in Figure 2-8, you can derive the two relations shown in Figure 2-9.

OrderID	OrderDate	RequiredDate	CompanyName	Address	City	PostalCode
10248	04-Aug-94	01-Sep-94	Vins et alcools Chevalier	59 rue de l'Abbaye	Reims	51100
10249	05-Aug-94	16-Sep-94	Toms Spezialitäten	Luisenstr. 48	Münster	44087
10250	08-Aug-94	05-Sep-94	Hanari Carnes	Rua do Paço, 67	Rio de Janeiro	05454-876
10251	08-Aug-94	05-Sep-94	Victuailles en stock	2, rue du Commerce	Lyon	69004
10252	09-Aug-94	06-Sep-94	Suprêmes délices	Boulevard Tirou, 255	Charleroi	B-6000

Figure 2-8. *An unnormalized relation.*

Customers relation

CustomerID	CompanyName	Address	City	PostalCode
ALFKI	Alfreds Futterkiste	Obere Str. 57	Berlin	12209
ANATR	Ana Trujillo Emparedados y helados	Avda. de la Constitución 2222	México D.F.	05021
ANTON	Antonio Moreno Taquería	Mataderos 2312	México D.F.	05023
AROUT	Around the Horn	120 Hanover Sq.	London	WA1 1DP
BERGS	Berglunds snabbköp	Berguvsvägen 8	Luleå	S-958 22

Invoices relation

OrderID	CustomerID	OrderDate	RequiredDate
10248	VINET	8/4/94	9/1/94
10249	TOMSP	8/5/94	9/16/94
10250	HANAR	8/8/94	9/5/94
10251	VICTE	8/8/94	9/5/94
10252	SUPRD	8/9/94	9/6/94

Figure 2-9. *The relation in Figure 2-8 can be divided into these two relations without losing any information.*

Using two relations eliminates the redundant addresses but still allows you to a find customer's address simply by looking up the CustomerNumber, which is stored in both the Customers and Invoices recordsets.

Candidate Keys and Primary Keys

In Chapter 1, I defined a relation body as an unordered set of zero or more tuples and pointed out that by definition each member of a set is unique. This being the case, for any relation there must be some combination of attributes that uniquely identifies each tuple. This set of one or more attributes is called a *candidate key*.

There might be more than one candidate key for any given relation, but it must always be the case that each candidate key uniquely identifies each tuple, not just for any specific set of tuples but for all possible tuples for all time. The inverse of this principle must also be true, by the way. Given any two tuples with the same candidate key, both tuples must represent the same entity. The implication of this statement is that you cannot determine a candidate key by inspection. Just because some field or combination of fields is unique for a given set of tuples, you cannot guarantee that it will be unique for *all* tuples, which it must be to qualify as a candidate key. Once again, you must understand the semantics of the data model.

Consider the Invoices relation shown in Figure 2-9. The CustomerID is unique in the example, but it's extremely unlikely that it will remain that way—and almost certainly not the intention of the company! Despite appearances, the semantics of the model tell us that this field is *not* a candidate key.

By definition, all relations must have at least one candidate key: the set of all attributes comprising the tuple. Candidate keys can be composed of a single attribute (a *simple key*) or of multiple attributes (a *composite key*). However, an additional requirement of a candidate key is that it must be irreducible, so the set of all attributes is not *necessarily* a candidate key. In the relation shown in Figure 2-10, the attribute CategoryID is a candidate key, but the set {CategoryID, CategoryName}, although it is unique, is not a candidate key, since the CategoryName attribute is unnecessary.

CategoryID	CategoryName	Description
1	Beverages	Soft drinks, coffees, teas, beers, and ales
2	Condiments	Sweet and savory sauces, relishes, spreads, and seasonings
3	Confections	Desserts, candies, and sweet breads
4	Dairy Products	Cheeses
5	Grains/Cereals	Breads, crackers, pasta, and cereal
6	Meat/Poultry	Prepared meats
7	Produce	Dried fruit and bean curd
8	Seafood	Seaweed and fish

Figure 2-10. *Candidate keys must be irreducible, so CategoryID qualifies, but {CategoryID, CategoryName} does not.*

It is sometimes the case—although it doesn't happen often—that there are multiple possible candidate keys for a relation. In this case, it is customary to designate one candidate key as a *primary key* and consider other candidate keys *alternate keys*. This is an arbitrary decision and isn't very useful at the logical level. (Remember that the data model is purely abstract.) To help maintain the distinction between the model and its physical implementation, I prefer to use the term "candidate key" at the data model level and reserve "primary key" for the implementation.

NOTE When the only possible candidate key is unwieldy—it requires too many fields or is too large, for example—you can use a data type that both the Microsoft Jet database engine and Microsoft SQL Server provide for creating artificial keys with values that will be generated by the system. Called AutoNumber fields in Microsoft Jet and Identity fields in SQL Server, fields based on this data type are terrifically useful tools, provided you don't try to make them mean anything. They're just tags. They aren't guaranteed to be sequential, you have very little control over how they're generated, and if you try to use them to mean anything you'll cause more problems than you solve.

Although choosing candidate keys is a semantic process, don't assume that the attributes you use to identify an entity in the real world will make an appropriate candidate key. Individuals, for example, are usually referred to by their names, but a quick look at any phone book will establish that names are hardly unique.

Of course, the name must provide a candidate key when combined with some other set of attributes, but this can be awkward to determine. I once worked in an office with about 20 people, of whom two were named Larry Simon and one was named Lary Simon. They were "Short Lary," "German Larry," and "Blond Larry"; that's height, nationality, and hair color combined with name, hardly a viable candidate key. In situations like this, it's probably best to use a system-generated ID number, such as an AutoNumber or Identity field, but remember, don't try to make it *mean* anything!

Functional Dependency

The concept of *functional dependency* is an extremely useful tool for thinking about data structures. Given any tuple T, with two sets of attributes $\{X_1...X_n\}$ and $\{Y_1...Y_n\}$ (the sets need not be mutually exclusive), then set Y is functionally dependent on set X if, for any legal value of X, there is only one legal value for Y.

For example, in the relation shown in Figure 2-10 every tuple that has the same values for {CategoryID} will have the same value for {CategoryName, Description}. We can therefore say that the attribute CategoryID *functionally determines* {CategoryName, Description}. Note that functional dependency doesn't necessarily work the other way: knowing a value for {CategoryName, Description} won't allow us to determine the corresponding value for {CategoryID}.

You can indicate the functional dependency between sets of attributes as shown in Figure 2-11. In text, you can express functional dependencies as X → Y, which reads "X functionally determines Y."

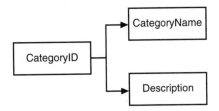

Figure 2-11. *Functional dependency diagrams are largely self-explanatory.*

Functional dependency is interesting to academics because it provides a mechanism for developing something that starts to resemble a mathematics of data modeling. You can, for example, discuss the reflexivity and transitivity of a functional dependency if you are so inclined.

In practical application, functional dependency is a convenient way of expressing what is a fairly self-evident concept: given any relation, there will be some set of attributes that is unique to each tuple, and knowing those it is possible to determine those attributes that are not unique.

If {X} is a candidate key, then all attributes {Y} must necessarily be functional dependent on {X}; this follows from the definition of candidate key. If {X} is not a candidate key and the functional dependency is not trivial (that is, {Y} is not a subset of {X}), then the relation will necessarily involve some redundancy, and further normalization will be required. In a sense, data normalization is the process of ensuring that, as shown in Figure 2-11, all the arrows come *out* of candidate keys.

First Normal Form

A relation is in first normal form if the domains on which its attributes are defined are scalar. This is at once both the simplest and most difficult concept in data modeling. The principle is straightforward: each attribute of a tuple must contain a single value. But what constitutes a single value? In the relation shown in Figure 2-12, the Items attribute obviously contains multiple values and is therefore not in first normal form. But the issue is not always so clear cut.

OrderID	CustomerID	OrderDate	Items	OrderTotal
1	CACTU	1/1/99	3 Zaanse koeken, 1 Tarte au sucre	$89.70
2	BSBEV	1/5/98	4 Mozzarella di Giovanni	$139.20
3	SUPRD	5/2/99	3 Ravioli Angelo, 6 Tofu	$198.06

Figure 2-12. *The Items attribute in this relation is not scalar.*

We saw some of the problems involved in determining whether an attribute is scalar when we looked at the modeling of names and addresses in Chapter 1. Dates are another tricky domain. They consist of three distinct components: the day, the month, and the year. Ought they be stored as three attributes or as a composite? As always, the answer can be determined only by looking to the semantics of the problem space you're modeling.

If your system uses the date exclusively, or even primarily, as a single value, it is scalar. But if your system must frequently manipulate the individual components of the date, you might be better off storing them as separate attributes.

You might not care about the day, for example, but only the month and year. Or you might care only about the month and day, but not the year. This isn't often the case, but it happens.

Date arithmetic is tedious to perform, so you'll most often use an attribute defined on the DateTime data type to offload the majority of the work to the development environment. However, this can get you into trouble if you're doing comparisons on a single component. This is particularly true if you're ignoring the time component of a field. For example, if you set the value of a DateCreated field to the result of the VBA function Now, which returns both date and time, and then later attempt to compare it to the value returned by Date(), which returns the date only, you might get incorrect results. Even if you never display the time to users, it is being stored, and obviously "1/1/1999 12:30:19 AM" isn't the same as "1/1/1999".

Another place people frequently have problems with nonscalar values is with codes and flags. Many companies assign case numbers or reference numbers that are calculated values, usually something along the lines of REF0010398, which might indicate that this is the first case opened in March 1998. While it's unlikely that you'll be able to alter company policy, it's not a good idea to attempt to manipulate the individual components of the reference number in your data model.

It's far easier in the long run to store the values separately: {Ref#, Case#, Month, Year}. This way, determining the next case number or the number of cases opened in a given year becomes a simple query against an attribute and doesn't require additional manipulation. This has important performance implications, particularly in client/server environments, where extracting a value from the middle of an attribute might require that each individual record be examined locally rather than offloaded to the database server.

Another type of nonscalar attribute that causes problems for people is the bit flag. In conventional programming environments, it's common practice to store sets of Boolean values as individual bits in a word, and then to use bitwise operations to check and test them. Windows API programming relies heavily on this technique, for example. In conventional programming environments, this is a perfectly sensible thing to do. In relational data models, it is not. Not only does the practice violate first normal form, but you can't actually do it, since neither the Jet database engine nor SQL Server versions of the SQL language provide bitwise operators. You can accomplish this using custom functionality in the database application, but only in Microsoft Access (Microsoft Visual Basic doesn't support custom functions in queries), and it forces the query to be processed locally.

Unfortunately, this is the kind of constraint that frequently gets imposed on you for historical reasons, but if you've any choice in the matter, don't encode more than one piece of information in a single attribute. If you're using legacy information, you can always unpack the data and store both versions in the recordset.

There's another kind of nonscalar value to be wary of when checking a relation for first normal form: the repeating group. Figure 2-13 shows an Invoice relation. Someone, at some point, decided that customers are not allowed to buy more than 5 items. I wonder if they checked that decision with the sales manager first? Seriously, this is almost certainly an artificial constraint imposed by the system, not the business. Artificial system constraints are evil, and in this case, just plain wrong as well.

OrderID	CustomerID	Item1	Qty1	Item2	Qty2	Item3	Qty3	Item4	Qty4	Item5	Qty5
1	ANTON	Queso Cabrales	4	Tofu	3	Ravioli Angelo	1	0	0	0	0
2	BLAUS	Louisiana Fiery Hot Pepper Sauce	2		0		0		0		0

Figure 2-13. *This data model restricts the number of items a customer can purchase.*

Another example of a repeating group is shown in Figure 2-14. This isn't as obvious an error, and many successful systems have been implemented using a model similar to this. But this is really just a variation of the structure shown in Figure 2-13 and has the same problems. Imagine the query to determine which products exceeded target by more than 10 percent any time in the first quarter.

Product	Year	TargetJan	ActualJan	TargetFeb	ActualFeb	TargetMar	ActualMar
Aniseed Syrup	1999	$1,000.00	$1,300.00	$0.00	$0.00	$0.00	$0.00
Chai	1999	$4,000.00	$2,000.00	$0.00	$0.00	$0.00	$0.00
Chang	1999	$3,000.00	$8,022.00	$0.00	$0.00	$0.00	$0.00
Chef Anton's Cajun Seasoning	1999	$7,000.00	$7,300.00	$0.00	$0.00	$0.00	$0.00
Chef Anton's Gumbo Mix	1999	$3,000.00	$3,231.00	$0.00	$0.00	$0.00	$0.00

Figure 2-14. *This is a repeating group.*

Second Normal Form

A relation is in second normal form if it is in first normal form and in addition all its attributes are dependent on the entire candidate key. The key in Figure 2-15, for example, is {ProductName, SupplierName}, but the SupplierPhoneNumber field is dependent only on the SupplierName, not on the full composite key.

ProductName	SupplierName	CategoryName	SupplierPhoneNumber
Chai	Exotic Liquids	Beverages	(171) 555-2222
Chang	Exotic Liquids	Beverages	(171) 555-2222
Aniseed Syrup	Exotic Liquids	Condiments	(171) 555-2222
Chef Anton's Cajun Seasoning	New Orleans Cajun Delights	Condiments	(100) 555-4822
Chef Anton's Gumbo Mix	New Orleans Cajun Delights	Condiments	(100) 555-4822

Figure 2-15. *All the attributes in a relation should depend on the whole key.*

We've already seen that this causes redundancy, and that the redundancy can, in turn, result in unpleasant maintenance problems. A better model would be that shown in Figure 2-16.

Products relation

ProductID	ProductName	CategoryName
1	Chai	Beverages
2	Chang	Beverages
3	Aniseed Syrup	Condiments
4	Chef Anton's Cajun Seasoning	Condiments
5	Chef Anton's Gumbo Mix	Condiments

Suppliers relation

SupplierID	SupplierName	SupplierPhoneNumber
1	Exotic Liquids	(171) 555-2222
2	New Orleans Cajun Delights	(100) 555-4822
3	Grandma Kelly's Homestead	(313) 555-5735
4	Tokyo Traders	(03) 3555-5011
5	Cooperativa de Quesos 'Las Cabras'	(98) 598 76 54
6	Mayumi's	(06) 431-7877
7	Pavlova, Ltd.	(03) 444-2343
8	Specialty Biscuits, Ltd.	(161) 555-4448
9	PB Knäckebröd AB	031-987 65 43

Figure 2-16. *These two relations are in second normal form.*

Logically, this is an issue of not trying to represent two distinct entities, Products and Suppliers, in a single relation. By separating the representation, you're not only eliminating the redundancy, you're also providing a mechanism for storing information that you couldn't otherwise capture. In the example in Figure 2-16, it becomes possible to capture information about Suppliers before obtaining any information regarding their products. That could not be done in the first relation, since neither component of a primary key can be empty.

The other way that people get into trouble with second normal form is in confusing constraints that happen to be true at any given moment with those that are true for all time. The relation shown in Figure 2-17, for example, assumes that a supplier has only one address, which might be true at the moment but will not necessarily remain true in the future.

SupplierID	Address	City	Region	PostalCode
1	49 Gilbert St.	London		EC1 4SD
2	P.O. Box 78934	New Orleans	LA	70117
3	707 Oxford Rd.	Ann Arbor	MI	48104
4	9-8 Sekimai	Tokyo		100
5	Calle del Rosal 4	Oviedo	Asturias	33007
6	92 Setsuko	Osaka		545
7	74 Rose St.	Melbourne	Victoria	3058
8	29 King's Way	Manchester		M14 GSD
9	Kaloadagatan 13	Göteborg		S-345 67
10	Av. das Americanas 12.890	São Paulo		5442
11	Tiergartenstraße 5	Berlin		10785
12	Bogenallee 51	Frankfurt		60439
13	Frahmredder 112a	Cuxhaven		27478
14	Viale Dante, 75	Ravenna		48100
15	Hatlevegen 5	Sandvika		1320
16	3400 - 8th Avenue	Bend	OR	97101
17	Brovallavägen 231	Stockholm		S-123 45
18	203, Rue des Francs-Bourgeois	Paris		75004
19	Order Processing Dept.	Boston	MA	02134
20	471 Serangoon Loop, Suite #402	Singapore		0512
21	Lyngbysild	Lyngby		2800
22	Verkoop	Zaandam		9999 ZZ
23	Valtakatu 12	Lappeenranta		53120
24	170 Prince Edward Parade	Sydney	NSW	2042
25	2960 Rue St. Laurent	Montréal	Québec	H1J 1C3

Figure 2-17. *Suppliers might have more than one address.*

Third Normal Form

A relation is in third normal form if it is in second normal form and in addition all nonkey attributes are mutually independent. Let's take the example of a company that has a single salesperson in each state. Given the relation shown in Figure 2-18, there is a dependency between Region and Salesperson, but neither of these attributes is reasonably a candidate key for the relation.

OrderID	CompanyName	Region	Salesperson
10389	Bottom-Dollar Markets	BC	Margaret Peacock
10290	Comércio Mineiro	SP	Laura Callahan
10347	Família Arquibaldo	SP	Laura Callahan
10386	Família Arquibaldo	SP	Laura Callahan
10423	Gourmet Lanchonetes	SP	Laura Callahan
11061	Great Lakes Food Market	OR	Michael Suyama
10528	Great Lakes Food Market	OR	Michael Suyama
10785	GROSELLA-Restaurante	DF	Nancy Davolio
10268	GROSELLA-Restaurante	DF	Nancy Davolio
10253	Hanari Carnes	RJ	Janet Leverling
10925	Hanari Carnes	RJ	Janet Leverling
10981	Hanari Carnes	RJ	Nancy Davolio
11052	Hanari Carnes	RJ	Janet Leverling
10415	Hungry Coyote Import Store	OR	Michael Suyama
10375	Hungry Coyote Import Store	OR	Michael Suyama
10394	Hungry Coyote Import Store	OR	Michael Suyama

Figure 2-18. *Although mutually dependent, neither Region nor Salesperson should be a candidate key.*

It's possible to get really pedantic about third normal form. In most places, for example, you can determine a PostalCode value based on the City and Region values, so the relation shown in Figure 2-19 is not strictly in third normal form.

CompanyName	Address	City	Region	PostalCode
Alfreds Futterkiste	Obere Str. 57	Berlin		12209
Ana Trujillo Emparedados y helados	Avda. de la Constitución 2222	México D.F.		05021
Antonio Moreno Taquería	Mataderos 2312	México D.F.		05023
Around the Horn	120 Hanover Sq.	London		WA1 1DP
Berglunds snabbköp	Berguvsvägen 8	Luleå		S-958 22
Blauer See Delikatessen	Forsterstr. 57	Mannheim		68306
Blondel père et fils	24, place Kléber	Strasbourg		67000
Bólido Comidas preparadas	C/ Araquil, 67	Madrid		28023
Bon app'	12, rue des Bouchers	Marseille		13008
Bottom-Dollar Markets	23 Tsawassen Blvd.	Tsawassen	BC	T2F 8M4

Figure 2-19. *This relation is not in strict third normal form.*

The two relations shown in Figure 2-20 are technically more correct, but in reality the only benefit you're gaining is the ability to automatically look up the PostalCode when you're entering new records, saving users a few keystrokes. This isn't a trivial benefit, but there are probably better ways to implement this functionality, ones that don't incur the overhead of a relation join every time the address is referenced.

CompanyName	Address	City	Region
Bottom-Dollar Markets	23 Tsawassen Blvd.	Tsawassen	BC
Comércio Mineiro	Av. dos Lusíadas, 23	São Paulo	SP
Família Arquibaldo	Rua Orós, 92	São Paulo	SP
Gourmet Lanchonetes	Av. Brasil, 442	Campinas	SP
Great Lakes Food Market	2732 Baker Blvd.	Eugene	OR
GROSELLA-Restaurante	5ª Ave. Los Palos Grandes	Caracas	DF
Hanari Carnes	Rua do Paço, 67	Rio de Janeiro	RJ
HILARIÓN-Abastos	Carrera 22 con Ave. Carlos Soublette #8-35	San Cristóbal	Táchira
Hungry Coyote Import Store	City Center Plaza	Elgin	OR
Island Trading	Garden House	Cowes	Isle of Wight

City	Region	PostalCode
Tsawassen	BC	T2F 8M4
São Paulo	SP	05432-043
São Paulo	SP	05442-030
Campinas	SP	04876-786
Eugene	OR	97403
Caracas	DF	1081
Rio de Janeiro	RJ	05454-876
San Cristóbal	Táchira	5022
Elgin	OR	97827
Cowes	Isle of Wight	PO31 7PJ

Figure 2-20. *These two relations are in third normal form.*

As with every other decision in the data modeling process, when and how to implement third normal form can only be determined by considering the semantics of the model. You'll create a separate relation only when the entity is important to the model, or the data changes frequently, or you're certain there

are technical implementation advantages. Postal codes do change, but not often; and they aren't intrinsically important in most systems.

Further Normalization

The first three normal forms were included in Codd's original formulation of relational theory, and in the vast majority of cases they're all you'll need to worry about. Just remember the jingle I learned in grad school: "The key, the whole key, and nothing but the key, so help me Codd."

The further normal forms—Boyce/Codd, fourth, and fifth—have been developed to handle special cases, most of which are rare.

Boyce/Codd Normal Form

Boyce/Codd normal form, which is considered a variation of third normal form, handles the special case of relations with multiple candidate keys. In fact, for Boyce/Codd normal form to apply, the following conditions must hold true:

- The relation must have two or more candidate keys.

- At least two of the candidate keys must be composite.

- The candidate keys must have overlapping attributes.

The easiest way to understand Boyce/Codd normal form is to use functional dependencies. Boyce/Codd normal form states, essentially, that there must be no functional dependencies *between* candidate keys. Take, for example, the relation shown in Figure 2-21. The relation is in third normal form (assuming supplier names are unique), but it still contains significant redundancy.

SupplierID	SupplierName	ProductID	Quantity	UnitPrice
5	Cooperativa de Quesos 'Las Cabras'	11	12	$14.00
14	Formaggi Fortini s.r.l.	72	5	$34.80
20	Leka Trading	42	10	$9.80
6	Mayumi's	14	9	$18.60
24	G'day, Mate	51	40	$42.40

Figure 2-21. *This relation is in third normal form but not in Boyce/Codd normal form.*

The two candidate keys in this case are {SupplierID, ProductID} and {SupplierName, ProductID}, and the functional dependency diagram is shown in Figure 2-22.

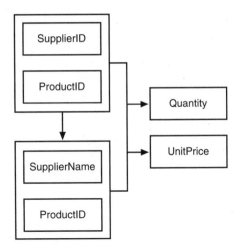

Figure 2-22. *This is the functional dependency diagram of the relation in Figure 2-21.*

As you can see, there is a functional dependency {SupplierID}→{SupplierName}, which is in violation of Boyce/Codd normal form. A correct model is shown in Figure 2-23.

Suppliers relation

SupplierID	SupplierName
20	Leka Trading
5	Cooperativa de Quesos 'Las Cabras'
14	Formaggi Fortini s.r.l.
6	Mayumi's
24	G'day, Mate

Products relation

SupplierID	ProductID	Quantity	UnitPrice
20	42	10	$9.80
5	11	12	$14.00
14	72	5	$34.80
6	14	9	$18.60
24	51	40	$42.40

Figure 2-23. *This model is a fully normalized version of Figure 2-21.*

Violations of Boyce/Codd normal form are easy to avoid if you pay attention to what the relation is logically *about*. If Figure 2-21 is about Products, the supplier information shouldn't be there (and vice versa, of course).

Fourth Normal Form

Fourth normal form provides a theoretical foundation for a principle that is intuitively obvious: independent repeating groups should not be combined in a single relation. By way of example, let's assume that the own-brand products sold by Northwind Traders come in multiple package sizes, that they are sourced from multiple suppliers, and that all suppliers provide all pack sizes. A completely unnormalized version of the Products relation might look like Figure 2-24.

ProductName	SupplierName	PackSize
Chai	Exotic Liquids	8 oz, 16 oz, 32 oz
Chef Anton's Cajun Seasoning	New Orleans Cajun Delights	8 oz, 16 oz, 32 oz
Pavlova	Pavlova, Ltd.	8 oz, 16 oz, 32 oz

Figure 2-24. *This is an unnormalized relation.*

Now, the first step in normalizing this relation is to eliminate the nonscalar PackSize attribute, resulting in the relation shown in Figure 2-25.

ProductName	SupplierName	PackSize
Chai	Exotic Liquids	16 oz
Chai	Exotic Liquids	12 oz
Chai	Exotic Liquids	8 oz
Chef Anton's Cajun Seasoning	New Orleans Cajun Delights	16 oz
Chef Anton's Cajun Seasoning	New Orleans Cajun Delights	12 oz
Chef Anton's Cajun Seasoning	New Orleans Cajun Delights	8 oz
Pavlova	Pavlova, Ltd.	16 oz
Pavlova	Pavlova, Ltd.	12 oz
Pavlova	Pavlova, Ltd.	8 oz

Figure 2-25. *This version of the relation shown in Figure 2-24 is in Boyce/Codd normal form.*

Surprisingly, Figure 2-25 is in Boyce/Codd normal form, since it is "all key." But there are clearly redundancy problems, and maintaining data integrity could be a nightmare. The resolution to these problems lies in the concept of *multivalued dependency pairs* and fourth normal form.

A multivalued dependency pair is two mutually independent sets of attributes. In Figure 2-24, the multivalued dependency is {ProductName} $\twoheadrightarrow$ {PackSize} | {SupplierName}, which is read "Product multidetermines PackSize and Supplier." Fourth normal form states, informally, that multivalued dependencies must be divided into separate relations, as shown in Figure 2-26. Formally, a relation is in fourth normal form if it is in Boyce/Codd normal form and in addition all the multivalued dependencies are also functional dependencies out of the candidate keys.

ProductName	PackSize
Chai	16 oz
Chai	12 oz
Chai	8 oz
Chef Anton's Cajun Seasoning	16 oz
Chef Anton's Cajun Seasoning	12 oz
Chef Anton's Cajun Seasoning	8 oz
Pavlova	16 oz
Pavlova	12 oz
Pavlova	8 oz

ProductName	SupplierName
Chai	Exotic Liquids
Chai	Exotic Liquids
Chai	Exotic Liquids
Chef Anton's Cajun Seasoning	New Orleans Cajun Delights
Chef Anton's Cajun Seasoning	New Orleans Cajun Delights
Chef Anton's Cajun Seasoning	New Orleans Cajun Delights
Pavlova	Pavlova, Ltd.
Pavlova	Pavlova, Ltd.
Pavlova	Pavlova, Ltd.

Figure 2-26. *Relations containing multivalued dependencies should be decomposed.*

The important thing to understand about fourth normal form is that it comes into play only if there are multiple values for the attributes. If each product in the example above had only a single pack size or a single supplier, fourth normal form would not apply. Similarly, if the two sets of attributes are not mutually independent, the relation is most likely in violation of second normal form.

Fifth Normal Form

Fifth normal form addresses the extremely rare case of *join dependencies*. A join dependency expresses the cyclical constraint "if Entity1 is linked to Entity2, and Entity2 is linked to Entity3, and Entity3 is linked back to Entity1, then all three entities must *necessarily* coexist in the same tuple."

To translate this into something resembling English, it would mean that if {Supplier} supplies {Product}, and {Customer} ordered {Product}, and {Supplier} supplied *something* to {Customer}, then {Supplier} supplied {Product} to {Customer}. Now, in the real world this is not a valid deduction. {Supplier} could have supplied anything to {Customer}, not necessarily {Product}. A join dependency exists only if there is an additional constraint that states that the deduction is valid.

It is not sufficient, in this situation, to use a single relation with the attributes {Supplier, Product, Customer} because of the resulting update problems. Given the relationship shown in Figure 2-27, for example, inserting the tuple {"Ma Maison", "Aniseed Syrup", "Berglunds snabbköp"} requires the insertion

of a second tuple, {"Exotic Liquids", "Aniseed Syrup", "Berglunds snabbköp"}, since a new link, "Aniseed Syrup" to "Berglunds snabbköp" has been added to the model.

Supplier	Product	Customer
Exotic Liquids	Aniseed Syrup	Alfreds Futterkiste
Exotic Liquids	Chef Anton's Cajun Seasoning	Berglunds snabbköp

Figure 2-27. *This relation is not in fifth normal form.*

Decomposing the relation into three distinct relations (SupplierProduct, ProductCustomer, and SupplierCustomer) eliminates this problem but causes problems of its own; in re-creating the original relation, all three relations must be joined. Interim joins of only two relations will result in invalid information.

From a system designer's point of view, this is a terrifying situation, since there's no intrinsic method for enforcing the three-table join except through security restrictions. Further, if a user should create an interim result set, the results will *seem* perfectly reasonable, and it's unlikely that the user will be able to detect the error by inspection.

Fortunately, this cyclical join dependency is so rare that the complications can be safely ignored in most situations. Where they can't, your only resource is to build the database system in such a way as to ensure the integrity of the multirelation join.

SUMMARY

In this chapter, we've examined the structure of databases in terms of the normalization process. The basic principle underlying normalization is the elimination of redundancy by way of lossless decomposition—the ability to split relations apart without losing information. This principle is formalized in the concepts of normal forms. The first three normal forms, which are the ones most commonly applied, are encapsulated in the jingle "The key, the whole key, and nothing but the key, so help me Codd." The remaining three normal forms are used only in exceptional cases.

In the next chapter, we'll examine how relations are logically linked when we explore the modeling of the relationships between entities.

3

Relationships

Chapter 2 explored the process of normalizing the data model: analyzing the entities in the problem space to develop a set of relations that capture all the relevant data efficiently and effectively. But the relations are only one part of the data model. The associations between relations and the constraints on those associations are just as important. In this chapter, we'll look at modeling relationships. As with defining relations, the basic principles are straightforward once you understand the semantics of the data model. Certain special cases don't fit neatly into the model of relationships, however, and we'll look at some of these later.

Terminology

Some basic terminology applies to relationships. The entities that are related are called *participants,* and the number of participants in a relationship is its *degree.* The vast majority of relationships are *binary,* having two participants, but *unary relationships* (a relation that is related to itself) are also common, while *ternary relationships* (with three participants) are not unknown. The examples throughout most of this chapter are binary. We'll examine unary and ternary relationships as special cases later in the chapter.

The participation of an entity in a relationship can be classified as *total participation* or *partial participation,* depending on whether the entity can exist without participating in the relationship. For example, given the two entities Customer and Order, the participation of Customer in the relationship is partial since Customer details might be entered before the customer has placed any orders. Order, on the other hand, has total participation, since an order can't be placed except by a Customer.

The same principle is sometimes used to classify the entities themselves as either *weak* (having total participation) or *regular* (having partial participation). Weak entities can exist only in relationships with other entities, while regular entities can exist in isolation. This classification is part of the Entity Relationship (E/R) diagramming method as originally described by Chen.

Of the three ways to classify a relationship—total or partial, optional or mandatory, and in terms of weak or regular entities—I have always found optionality to be the most useful. However, explicitly expressing the effect of the relationship on the entity can be helpful in large or complex systems. You can use the notation shown in Figure 3-1 in E/R diagrams to show whether an entity is weak or regular.

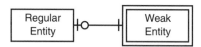

Figure 3-1. *This notation can be used to distinguish weak and regular entities.*

It's occasionally useful to divide relationships into "IsA" and "HasA" types. The concept is straightforward: entity A either *IsA* B or *HasA* B. For example, an Employee IsA SoftballTeam member; the same Employee HasA(n) Address. Of course, "is" and "has" are not always very good English terms to describe a relationship. An Employee doesn't "have" a SalesOrder, he "creates" one; but as it's clearly not the case that the Employee *is* a SalesOrder, the intellectual stretch isn't too great.

The classification of participation in a relationship is also an indication of the *optionality* of the relationship: whether or not an entity is required to participate in a given relationship. This is a rather tricky area because implementation by the database engines doesn't match the problem domain, as we'll see when we discuss the implementation of data integrity in Chapter 4.

The maximum number of instances of one entity that can be associated with an instance of another entity is what I refer to as the *cardinality* of a relationship. (Note that both degree and cardinality have slightly different meanings when applied to relationships than when applied to relations.) There are three generic flavors of cardinality: one-to-one, one-to-many, and many-to-many.

I use the notation shown in Figure 3-2 to indicate the cardinality and optionality of relationships. I find the crow's foot notation (introduced in Chapter 1) the most expressive and simplest to explain to clients. Obviously, alternative techniques are available, and you must use the one that works best for you.

Relationships are shown as lines between boxes.

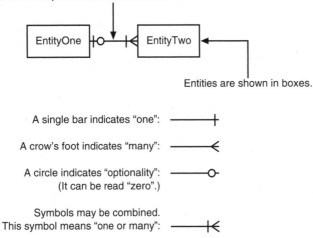

Entities are shown in boxes.

A single bar indicates "one": ——————+

A crow's foot indicates "many": ——————<

A circle indicates "optionality": ——————o
(It can be read "zero".)

Symbols may be combined.
This symbol means "one or many": ——————+<

Figure 3-2. *This notation will be used to indicate optionality and cardinality.*

Modeling Relationships

Once you've determined that a relationship exists, you must model it by including attributes from one relation (the *primary relation*) in the other (the *foreign relation*), as shown in Figure 3-3.

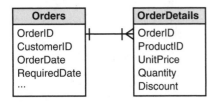

Figure 3-3. *A relationship is modeled by including attributes from the primary relation (Orders) in the foreign relation (OrderDetails).*

You'll notice some differences between this diagram and the formal E/R diagram shown in Figure 1-6 on page 21. First, the attributes are not shown as separate objects. At this level of design, you're primarily interested in the relationships between entities, not their composition. I find showing the attributes to be distracting, and it clutters up the diagram.

Second, the relationships are not labeled. I find labeling unnecessary, and because the description of the relationship changes depending on which direction you're reading it (teachers *teach* students, but students *learn from* teachers), labels can sometimes be confusing. However, although I don't label the relationships, I do sometimes indicate the attribute that will be used to implement the relation in the database schema. This can be useful, for example, if the primary entity has more than one candidate key and you want to show explicitly which one is to be used.

As I said, I've found this style of diagram useful when working with clients, and it's easy to draw by hand or by using a diagramming tool such as Visio Professional or Micrografx Flowcharter 7. But Microsoft Access, Microsoft SQL Server, and Microsoft Visual Basic all provide diagramming tools as well, and you may decide to use them in preference to, or in addition to, the technique I've shown.

The advantage of using either the Access relationships window (for a Jet database engine .mdb file) or database diagrams (for a database implemented using SQL Server) is that the diagrams become part of the database and automatically reflect changes to it. Unfortunately, this is also the greatest disadvantage of these tools. You can't build abstract diagrams; you must first build the physical tables. There is always a danger in jumping into anything that even *looks* like implementation too early in the design process, before the implementation model has been finalized.

In my own work, I often use both abstract diagrams and ones that are embedded in the database. I create abstract diagrams in the early stages of the design process, and use one of the Microsoft tools once the conceptual design has been finalized and I'm documenting the physical database schema.

Of course, you don't just copy *any* attributes from the primary relation to the foreign relation; you must choose attributes that uniquely identify the primary entity. In other words, you add the attributes that make up the candidate key in the primary relation to the foreign relation. Not surprisingly, the duplicated attributes become known as the *foreign key* in the foreign relations. In the example shown in Figure 3-3 on page 45, OrderID—the candidate key of the Orders relation—has been added to the OrderDetails relation. Orders is the primary relation, and OrderDetails is the foreign relation.

| NOTE | The candidate key/foreign key pair that models the relationship need not be the primary key of the primary table; any candidate key will serve. You should use the candidate key that makes the most sense semantically. |

The choice of primary and foreign relations isn't arbitrary. It is determined first by the cardinality of the relationship and second—when there is any doubt—by the semantics of the data model. For example, given two relations that have a one-to-many relationship, the relation on the one side is always the primary relation, while the relation on the many side is always the foreign relation. That is, a candidate key from the relation on the one side is added (as a foreign key) to the relation on the many side. We'll be looking at this issue as we examine each type of relationship in the rest of this chapter.

Sometimes you'll want to model not only the fact that a relationship exists, but also certain properties of the relationship—its duration or its commencement date, for example. In this case, it's useful to create an abstract relation representing the relationship, as shown by the Positions relation in Figure 3-4.

Figure 3-4. *Abstract relations can model the properties of relationships.*

This technique complicates the data model somewhat, and one might be tempted to simply include the relationship attributes in one of the participating relations. However, if there are a lot of attributes or a lot of relations with attributes, this can get unwieldy. More importantly, a distinct relationship entity allows you to track the history of a relationship. The model shown in Figure 3-4, for example, allows you to determine an individual's employment history, which would not have been possible had Position been made an attribute of the Employees relation.

Abstract relationship entities are also useful when you need to track the way a relationship changes over time. Figure 3-5 is an example of a State Transition diagram describing the possible legal changes in an individual's marital status.

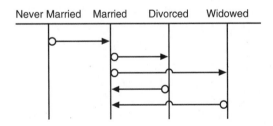

Figure 3-5. *State Transition diagrams plot the valid changes in an entity's status, in this case in an individual's marital status.*

State Transition diagrams are not difficult to understand. Each vertical line indicates a valid change in state. For example, an individual can go from married to divorced and vice versa, but not from divorced to never married. Now, if all you need to model is an individual's current marital state, you don't need to implement an abstract relationship entity to make sure only valid changes are made. But if you ever need to know that John and Mary Smith were married in 1953 and divorced in 1972, and that Mary remarried in 1975 but was widowed in 1986, then you'll need an abstract relationship entity to track that.

One-to-One Relationships

Perhaps the simplest type of relationship is the one-to-one relationship. If it's true that any instance of entity X can be associated with only one instance of entity Y, then the relationship is one-to-one. Most IsA relationships will be one-to-one, but otherwise, examples of one-to-one relationships are fairly rare in the problem domain. When choosing a one-to-one relationship between entities, you need to be sure that the relationship is either true for all time or, if it does change, that you don't care about past values. For example, say you're modeling the office space in a building. Assuming that there is one person to an office, there's a one-to-one relationship, as shown in Figure 3-6.

Figure 3-6. *There is a one-to-one relationship between Office and Employee.*

But the relationship between an employee and an office is true only at a specific moment in time. Over time, different employees will be assigned to the office. (The arrangement of offices in the building might change as well, but that's a different problem.) If you use the one-to-one relationship shown in Figure 3-6, you will have a simple, clean model of the building, but you'll have no way of determining the history of occupancy. You might not care. If you're building a system for a mail room, you need to know where to send Jane Doe's mail today, not where it would have been sent three months ago. But if you're designing a system for a property manager, you can't lose this historical information—the system will be asked to determine, for example, how often tenants change.

Although one-to-one relationships are rare in the real world, they're very common and useful abstract concepts. They're most often used to either reduce the number of attributes in a relation or model subclasses of entities. There is a physical limitation of 255 fields per table if you're using the Jet database engine, and

250 fields per table if you're using SQL Server. I'm suspicious—*very* suspicious—of any data model that exceeds these limitations. But I have occasionally seen systems, usually in science and medicine, where the entities had more than 255 genuine attributes. In these cases, you have no choice but to create a new relation with some arbitrary subset of attributes and to create a one-to-one relationship between it and the original, controlling relation.

Another problem domain that often *appears* to require that the physical limitations on table size be exceeded is the modeling of tests and questionnaires. Given a test with an arbitrary number of questions, you might be tempted to model an individual's responses as shown in Figure 3-7.

Test
StudentName
DateTaken
Answer1
Answer2
AnswerN

Figure 3-7. *This structure is sometimes used to model tests and questionnaires, but it is not ideal.*

This structure is easy to implement, but it is not generally the best solution. The answer attributes are a repeating group, and the relationship is therefore not in first normal form. A better model is shown in Figure 3-8.

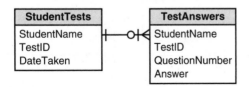

Figure 3-8. *Although more difficult to implement, this structure is preferable for modeling tests and questionnaires.*

Subclassing Entities

A more interesting use of one-to-one relationships is for entity subclassing, a concept borrowed from object-oriented programming. To see some of the benefits of subclassing entities, let's first look at a more traditional implementation. In the Microsoft Access Northwind sample database, each product is assigned to a product category, as shown in Figure 3-9.

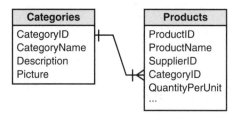

Figure 3-9. *Each product in the Northwind database is assigned to a product category.*

Having a Categories relation allows the products to be grouped for reporting purposes and might be all that is required by your problem space. But with this design, you can treat a product only as a product, not as an instance of its specific category. Any attributes defined for Products are stored for *all* products, whatever their type. This isn't a very close match to the problem domain—Beverages intrinsically have different attributes than Condiments.

You might be tempted to model the Northwind product list as shown in Figure 3-10. This model allows us to store all the specific information for each product type, one type per relation, but makes it difficult to treat a product as a product.

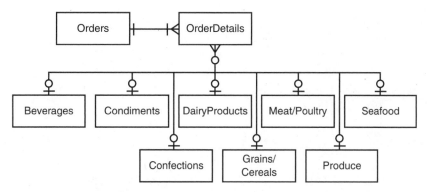

Figure 3-10. *This model allows category-specific attributes to be captured.*

Imagine, for example, the process of checking that a product code entered by a user is correct: "if the code exists in the x relation, or the y relation, or…". This is as ugly as the repeating group query in Chapter 2. Also, you might run into integrity problems with this structure if you have certain attributes that apply only to one product category (UnitsPerPackage, for example, which might pertain to Beverages but not DairyProducts) and the category of a particular product changes. What do you do in these circumstances? Throw away the old values? But what if the change was accidental, and the user immediately changes it back?

Subclassing the product entity provides the best of both worlds. You can capture information specific to certain product categories without losing the ability to treat the products as the generic type when that's appropriate, and you can defer the deletion of the no-longer-applicable information until you're certain it really *is* no longer applicable. Figure 3-11 shows a model developed using entity subclasses.

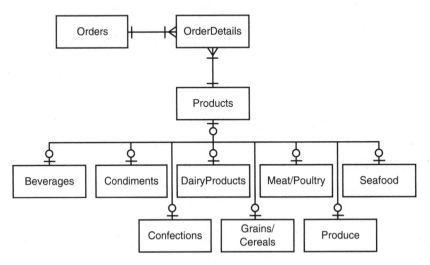

Figure 3-11. *This model uses subclassing to provide the capabilities of both previous figures.*

It must be said that while entity subclassing is an elegant solution to certain types of data modeling problems, it can be an awkward beast to implement. To take just one example, a report containing Product details would need to include conditional processing to display only the fields appropriate to the current subclass. This isn't an insurmountable task by any means, but it *is* a consideration. Under most circumstances, I wouldn't recommend that you compromise the data model to make life easier for the programmers. But there's certainly no point in adding the complexity of subclassing to the model if all you need is the ability to group or categorize entities for reporting purposes; in this situation, the structure shown in Figure 3-9 is perfectly adequate and far more sensible.

Identifying the primary and foreign relations in a one-to-one relationship can sometimes be tricky, as you must base the decision on the semantics of the data model. If you've chosen this structure in order to subclass the entity, the generic entity becomes the primary relation and each of the subclasses becomes a foreign relation.

> **NOTE**   In this situation, the foreign key that the subclasses acquire is often also the candidate key of the subclasses. There is rarely a reason for subclasses to have their own identifiers.

If, on the other hand, you're using one-to-one relationships to avoid field limitations, or the entities have a genuine one-to-one relationship in the problem space, the choice must be somewhat arbitrary. You must choose the primary relation based on your understanding of the problem space.

One thing that can help in this situation is the optionality of the relationship. If the relationship is optional on one side only (and I've never seen a model where it was optional on both sides), the relation on the optional side is the foreign relation. In other words, if only one of the entities is weak and the other regular, the regular entity is the primary relation and the weak entity is the foreign relation.

One-to-Many Relationships

The most common type of relationship between entities is one-to-many, wherein a single instance of one entity can be associated with zero, one, or many instances of another entity. The majority of the normalization techniques discussed in Chapter 2 result in relations with one-to-many relationships between them.

One-to-many relationships present few problems once they've been identified. However, it's important to be careful in specifying the optionality on each side of the relationship. It's commonly thought that only the many side of the relationship can be optional, but this isn't the case. Take, for example, the relationship shown in Figure 3-12.

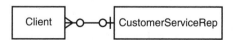

Figure 3-12. *This relationship is optional in both directions.*

The relationship between Client and CustomerServiceRep is optional in both directions. In English, this would be expressed as a "CustomerServiceRep can have zero or more clients. A client's CustomerServiceRep, *if one has been assigned,* must be present in the CustomerServiceRep relation." Specifying optionality on the one side of a one-to-many relationship has important implications for both the implementation and usability of the system. We'll discuss these issues in detail in Chapters 4 and 14, but understand here that relational theory does not require that the one side of a one-to-many relationship be mandatory.

Identifying the primary and foreign relations in a one-to-many relationship is easy. The entity on the one side of the relationship is always the primary relation; its candidate key is copied to the relation on the many side, which becomes the foreign relation. The key candidate of the primary relation often forms part of the candidate key for the relation on the many side, but it can never uniquely identify the tuples of foreign relation by itself. It must be combined with one or more other attributes to form a candidate key.

Many-to-Many Relationships

Many-to-many relationships exist aplenty in the real world. Students take many courses; any given course is attended by many students. Customers shop in many stores; a store has many customers, or so one hopes! But many-to-many relationships can't be implemented in a relational database. Instead, they are modeled using an intermediary relation that has a one-to-many relationship with each of the original participants, as shown in Figure 3-13. Such an intermediary relation is usually called a *junction table,* even when working at the data model level, where of course we're talking about relations, not tables.

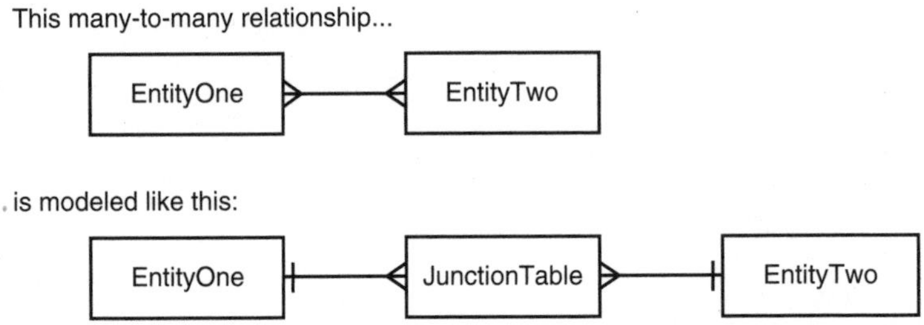

This many-to-many relationship...

. is modeled like this:

Figure 3-13. *An intermediary table is used to resolve many-to-many relationships.*

Since a many-to-many relationship is modeled as two one-to-many relationships, determining the primary and foreign relations is straightforward. As we've seen, the relation on the one side of a one-to-many relationship is always the primary relation. This means that each of the original entities will become a primary relation, and the junction table will be the foreign relation, receiving the candidate keys of the relations on each side of it.

Junction tables most often contain only the candidate keys of the two original participants, but they are really just a special case of the abstract relationship entities discussed earlier. As such, they can contain whatever additional attributes are appropriate.

Unary Relationships

All the relationships discussed so far have been binary relationships having two participants. Unary relationships have only one participant—the relation is associated with itself. The classic example of a unary relationship is Employee to Manager. One's manager is, in most cases, also an employee with a manager of his or her own.

Unary relationships are modeled in the same way as binary relationships—the candidate key of the primary relation is added to the foreign relation. The only difference is that the primary and foreign relations are the same. Thus, if the candidate key of the Employee relation is EmployeeID, declared on the EmployeeID domain, then you'd add an attribute to the relation called perhaps ManagerID, also declared on the EmployeeID domain, as shown in Figure 3-14.

| **Employees** |
| EmployeeID |
| LastName |
| FirstName |
| Title |
| TitleOfCourtesy |
| BirthDate |
| HireDate |
| Address |
| City |
| Region |
| PostalCode |
| Country |
| HomePhone |
| Extension |
| Photo |
| Notes |
| ManagerID |

Figure 3-14. *A unary relationship exists when a relation is linked to itself.*

Unary relationships can be of any cardinality. One-to-many unary relationships are used to implement hierarchies, such as the organizational hierarchy implicit in the Employee-Manager relationship. Many-to-many unary relationships, like their binary counterparts, must be modeled with a junction table. Unary relationships can also be optional on the one side, as shown in Figure 3-14. The CEOs of most organizations do not have a manager. (The stockholders don't count unless they're an independent part of the data model.)

Ternary Relationships

Ternary relationships are usually in the form *X does Y to Z*, and like many-to-many relationships they can't be directly modeled in a relational database. Unlike many-to-many relationships, however, there isn't a single recipe for modeling them.

In Figure 3-15, we can see that the Mozzarella di Giovanni purchased by Vins et alcools Chevalier is supplied by both Formaggi Fortini s.r.l. and Forêts d'érables, but there is no way to determine which of them supplied the specific cheese that was shipped to Vins et alcools Chevalier. A ternary relationship has been lost in the data model. Suppliers don't merely supply products, they supply products that are purchased by specific customers.

CustomerID	CompanyName
VINET	Vins et alcools Chevalier

Customer	OrderID	Product
VINET	10248	Queso Cabrales
VINET	10248	Singaporean Hokkien Fried Mee
VINET	10248	Mozzarella di Giovanni

ProductName	CompanyName
Mozzarella di Giovanni	Formaggi Fortini s.r.l.
Mozzarella di Giovanni	Forêts d'érables

Figure 3-15. *These relations don't indicate which supplier's cheese was purchased by Vins et alcools Chevalier.*

To understand the problem, it's useful to first examine the relationships in a more typical problem space, as shown in Figure 3-16.

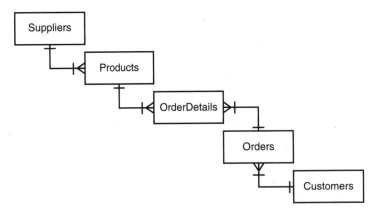

Figure 3-16. *This is the typical relationship chain for the entities participating in an order.*

In this diagram, each product is provided by only a single supplier and the ternary relationship is maintained—if you know the product, you know who supplied it. In Figure 3-17, however, each product is provided by multiple suppliers and the ternary relationship has been lost.

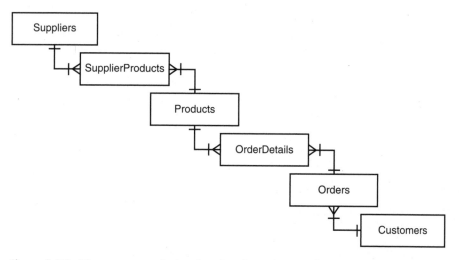

Figure 3-17. *The ternary relationship has been lost in this model.*

The key to resolving the problem is to examine the direction of the one-to-many relationships. Given any entity on the many side, you can determine the corresponding entity on the one side. Thus, given a specific OrderDetails item in Figure 3-16 you can determine the Orders item to which it belongs, and knowing the Orders item you can determine the Customers. The process works in the other direction as well, of course: knowing the OrderDetails item, you can determine the product and then the supplier.

But the reverse is not true. Having identified an entity on the one side of the relationship, you can't select a single entity on the many side. This is the problem with Figure 3-17. Knowing an OrderDetails item, you can determine the product, but knowing the product, you can't determine to which SupplierProducts entity it's linked.

An easy way to think of this is that you can't change directions from one-to-many to many-to-one more than once in a relationship chain. The chain in Figure 3-16 changes directions only once, at OrderDetails. The chain in Figure 3-17 changes directions twice, at OrderDetails and again at SupplierProducts.

The solution is to eliminate the Products entity from the chain, as shown in Figure 3-18.

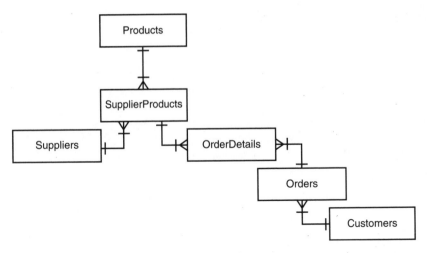

Figure 3-18. *This model preserves the ternary relationship.*

The chain now changes direction only once, at OrderDetails, and the relationship has been maintained. Notice, however, that the Products entity hasn't been eliminated. Chances are good that orders will still be placed for Products rather than for SupplierProducts, and maintaining the Products entity allows the user interface to accommodate this.

Of course, you might not care about the ternary relationships in your problem space, or there may be some other way of tracing the relationship when necessary, such as a lot number on the packaging. In this case, there is absolutely no need to model it. It's important to understand that the model in Figure 3-18 isn't intrinsically better or more correct than that in Figure 3-17. You must choose the model that best reflects the semantics of your problem space.

Relationships of Known Cardinality

Occasionally the minimum, absolute, or maximum number of tuples on the many side of a one-to-many relationship will be known in advance. There are five periods in the school day, 200 bones in the adult skeleton, and a golfer is allowed to carry only 14 clubs during tournament play.

It's always tempting to model this situation by including the candidate key of each tuple as an attribute in the relation on the one side, as shown in Figure 3-19, but there are two major problems with this approach. First, it's a repeating group, and second, it's unreliable.

StudentID:StudentNumber	FirstName:Name	LastName:Name	Period1:ClassPeriod	Period2:ClassPeriod	Period3:ClassPeriod	Period4:ClassPeriod
1	Nancy	Davolio	Biology	French	English	History
2	Andrew	Fuller	Physical Education	Biology	French	English
3	Janet	Leverling	Physical Education	Biology	French	English
4	Margaret	Peacock	French	Physical Education	History	English
5	Steven	Buchanan	Biology	French	Physical Education	History
6	Michael	Suyama	French	Physical Education	Biology	History
7	Robert	King	History	French	English	Biology

Figure 3-19. *It's tempting, but unwise, to model known cardinality like this.*

The repeating nature of the attributes is disguised in Figure 3-19 by the attribute names, but they're all defined on the same domain, ClassPeriod. Whenever you have multiple attributes defined on the same domain, chances are good that you have category or type values masquerading as attribute names.

In addition to this theoretical problem, structures like this are unreliable. It might very well be company policy, for example, that managers have a maximum of five employees reporting directly to them, but policy isn't reality. By embedding the policy in the data model, you're implementing it as a non-negotiable system constraint. I'd be willing to bet that you'll discover during initial data entry that at least one manager has six direct reports. What happens then? Will somebody suddenly have a new boss? Will the manager get entered (and maybe paid) twice? Or will the programmer who got a support call at 3 A.M. say some *very* uncharitable things about you?

Limitations on cardinality such as these must be implemented as system constraints; they shouldn't be embedded in the structure of the relations themselves. Furthermore, as we'll discuss in Chapter 16, you should think long and hard about the impact on usability before implementing limitations on cardinality at all.

SUMMARY

In this chapter, we've examined the relationships between entities in detail. We've looked at each type of binary relationship—one-to-one, one-to-many, and many-to-many—and seen how to represent them in the data model by establishing a primary relation and including its candidate key in the other relationship participant, the foreign relation. In addition, we've examined the special cases of unary and ternary relationships and seen how they can also be represented in the data model.

You've now seen all the basic components of a data model: the entities, their attributes, and the relationships between them. In Chapter 4, we'll turn to data integrity and the mechanisms available to you to maintain the consistency of the database.

4

Data Integrity

Creating a model of the entities in the problem space and the relationships between them is only part of the data modeling process. You must also capture the rules that the database system will use to ensure that the actual physical data stored in it is, if not correct, at least plausible. In other words, you must model the *data integrity*.

It's important to understand that the chances of being able to guarantee the literal *correctness* of the data are diminishingly small. Take, for example, an order record showing that Mary Smith purchased 17 hacksaws on July 15, 1999. The database system can ensure that Mary Smith is a customer known to the system, that the company does indeed sell hacksaws, and that it was taking orders on July 15, 1999. It can even check that Mary Smith has sufficient credit to pay for the 17 hacksaws. What it *can't* do is verify that Ms. Smith actually ordered 17 hacksaws and not 7 or 1, or 17 screwdrivers instead. The best the system might do is notice that 17 is rather a lot of hacksaws for an individual to purchase and notify the user to that effect. Even having the system do this much is likely to be expensive to implement, probably more expensive than its value warrants.

My point is that the system can never verify that Mary Smith did place the order as it's recorded; it can verify only that she *could have done so*. Of course, that's all any record-keeping system can do, and a well-designed database system can certainly do a better job than the average manual system—if for no other reason than its consistency in applying the rules. But no database system, and no database system designer, can guarantee that the data in the database *is* true, only that it *could* be true. It does this by ensuring that the data complies with the *integrity constraints* that have been defined for it.

Integrity Constraints

Some people refer to integrity constraints as business rules. However, business rules is a much broader concept; it includes all of the constraints on the system rather than just the constraints concerning the integrity of the data. In particular,

system security—that is, the definition of which users can do what and under what circumstances they can do it—is part of system administration, not data integrity. But certainly security is a business requirement and will constitute one or more business rules. We'll look at database security issues in Chapter 8 when we discuss system administration.

Data integrity is implemented at several levels of granularity. Domain, transition, and entity constraints define the rules for maintaining the integrity of the individual relations. Referential integrity constraints ensure that necessary relationships between relations are maintained. Database integrity constraints govern the database as a whole, and transaction integrity constraints control the way data is manipulated either within a single database or between multiple databases.

Domain Integrity

As we discussed in Chapter 1, a domain is the set of all possible values for a given attribute. A domain integrity constraint—usually just called a *domain constraint*—is a rule that defines these legal values. It might, of course, be necessary to define more than one domain constraint to describe a domain completely.

A domain isn't the same thing as a data type, and defining domains in terms of physical data types can backfire. The danger is that you will unnecessarily constrain the values—for example, by choosing an integer because you think it will be big enough rather than because 255 is the largest permitted value for the domain.

That being said, however, data types *can* be a convenient shorthand in the data model, and for this reason choosing a logical data type is often the first step in determining the domain constraints in a system. By *logical data type,* I mean "date," "string," or "image," nothing more specific than that. Dates are probably the best example of the benefits of this approach. I recommend against defining the domain TransactionDate as DateTime, which is a physical representation. However, defining it as "a date" allows you to concentrate on it being "a date between the commencement of business and the present date, inclusive" and ignore all those rather tedious rules about leap years.

Having chosen a logical data type, it might be appropriate to define the scale and precision of a numeric type, or the maximum length of string values. This is very close to specifying a physical data type, but you should still be working at the logical level. Obviously, you will not be hit by lightning if your particular shorthand for "a string value of no more than 30 characters" is char(30). But the more abstract you keep the description in the data model, the more room you'll have to maneuver later and the less likely you'll be to impose accidental constraints on the system.

The next aspect of domain integrity to consider is whether a domain is permitted to contain unknown or nonexistent values. The handling of these values is contentious, and we'll be discussing them repeatedly as we examine various aspects of database system design. For now, it's necessary to understand only that there is a difference between an unknown value and a nonexistent value, and that it is often (although not always) possible to specify whether either or both of these is permitted for the domain.

The first point here, that "unknown" and "nonexistent" are different, doesn't present too many problems at the logical level. (And please remember, always, that a data model is a *logical* construct.) My father does not have a middle name; I do not know my next-door neighbor's. These are quite different issues. Some implementation issues need not yet concern us, but the logical distinction is quite straightforward.

The second point is that, having determined whether a domain is allowed to include unknown or nonexistent values, you'll need to decide whether either of these values can be accepted by the system. To return to our TransactionDate example, it's certainly possible for the date of a transaction to be unknown, but if it occurred at all it occurred at some fixed point in time and therefore cannot be nonexistent. In other words, there must *be* a transaction date; we just might not *know* it.

Now, obviously, we can be ignorant of anything, so any value can be unknown. That's not a useful distinction. What we're actually defining here is not so much whether a value can be unknown as whether an unknown value should be stored. It might be that it's not worth storing data unless the value is known, or it might be that we can't identify an entity without knowing its value. In either case, you would prevent a record containing an unknown value in the specified field from being added to the database.

This decision can't always be made at the domain level, but it's always worth considering since doing so can make the job a little easier down the line. To some extent, your decision depends on how generic your domains are. As an example, say that you have defined a Name domain and declared the attributes GivenName, MiddleName, Surname, and CompanyName against it. You might just as well have defined these attributes as separate domains, but there are some advantages to using the more general domain definition since doing so allows you to capture the overlapping rules (and in this case, there are probably a lot of them) in a single place. However, in this case you won't be able to determine whether empty or unknown values are acceptable at the domain level; you will have to define these properties at the entity level.

The final aspect of domain integrity is that you'll want to define the set of values represented by a domain as specifically as possible. Our TransactionDate

domain, for example, isn't just the set of all dates; it's the set of dates from the day the company began trading until the current date. It might be further restricted to eliminate Sundays, public holidays, and any other days on which the company does not trade.

Sometimes you'll be able to simply list the domain values. The domain of Weekends is completely described by the set {"Saturday", "Sunday"}. Sometimes it will be easier to list one or more rules for determining membership, as we did for TransactionDate. Both techniques are perfectly acceptable, although a specific design methodology might dictate a particular method of documenting constraints. The important thing is that the constraints be captured as carefully and completely as possible.

Transition Integrity

Transition integrity constraints define the states through which a tuple can validly pass. The State-Transition diagram in Figure 4-1, for example, shows the states through which an order can pass.

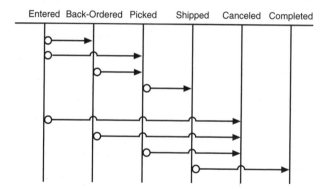

Figure 4-1. *This diagram shows the states through which an order can pass.*

You would use transitional integrity constraints, for instance, to ensure that the status of a given order never changed from "Entered" to "Completed" without passing through the interim states, or to prevent a canceled order from changing status at all.

The status of an entity is usually controlled by a single attribute. In this case, transition integrity can be considered a special type of domain integrity. Sometimes, however, the valid transitions are controlled by multiple attributes or even multiple relations. Because transition constraints can exist at any level of granularity, it's useful to consider them a separate type of constraint during preparation of the data model.

For example, the status of a customer might only be permitted to change from "Normal" to "Preferred" if the customer's credit limit is above a specified value and he or she has been doing business with the company for at least a year. The credit limit requirement would most likely be controlled by an attribute of the Customers relation, but the length of time the customer has been doing business with the company might not be explicitly stored anywhere. It might be necessary to calculate the value based on the oldest record for the customer in the Orders relation.

Entity Integrity

Entity constraints ensure the integrity of the entities being modeled by the system. At the simplest level, the existence of a primary key is an entity constraint that enforces the rule "every entity must be uniquely identifiable."

In a sense, this is *the* entity integrity constraint; all others are technically entity-level integrity constraints. The constraints defined at the entity level can govern a single attribute, multiple attributes, or the relation as a whole.

The integrity of an individual attribute is modeled first and foremost by defining the attribute against a specific domain. An attribute within a relation inherits the integrity constraints defined for its domain. At the entity level, these inherited constraints can properly be made more rigorous but not relaxed. Another way of thinking about this is that the entity constraint can specify a subset of the domain constraints but not a superset. For example, an OrderDate attribute defined against the TransactionDate domain might specify that the date must be in the current year, whereas the TransactionDate domain allows any date between the date business commenced and the current date. An entity constraint should not, however, allow OrderDate to contain dates in the future, since the attribute's domain prohibits these.

Similarly, a CompanyName attribute defined against the Name domain might prohibit empty values, even though the Name domain permits them. Again, this is a narrower, more rigorous definition of permissible values than that specified in the domain.

> **NOTE** Designers often specify the validity of empty and unknown values at the entity level rather than the domain level. In fact, some designers would argue that these constraints apply only at the entity level. There is some justification for this position, but I recommend making the domain definition as complete as possible. Certainly, *considering* empty and unknown values at the domain level does no harm and can make the process of specification (and implementation) simpler.

In addition to narrowing the range of values for a single attribute, entity constraints can also effect multiple attributes. A requirement that ShippingDate be on or after OrderDate is an example of such a constraint. Entity constraints can't reference other relations, however. It wouldn't be appropriate, for example, to define an entity constraint that sets a customer DiscountRate (an attribute of the Customer relation) based on the customer's TotalSales (which is based on multiple records in the OrderItems relation). Constraints that depend on multiple relations are database-level constraints; we'll discuss them later in this chapter.

Be careful of multiple-attribute constraints; they might indicate that your data model isn't fully normalized. If you are restricting or calculating the value of one attribute based on another, you're probably OK. An entity constraint that says "Status is not allowed to be 'Preferred' unless the Customer record is at least one year old" would be fine. But if the value of one attribute *determines* the value of another—for example, "If the customer record is older than one year, then Status = 'Preferred'"—then you have a functional dependency and you're in violation of third normal form.

Referential Integrity

In Chapter 3, we looked at the decomposition of relations to minimize redundancy and at foreign keys to implement the links between relations. If these links are ever broken, the system will be unreliable at best and unusable at worst. *Referential integrity constraints* maintain and protect these links.

There is really only one referential integrity constraint: foreign keys cannot become orphans. In other words, no record in the foreign table can contain a foreign key that doesn't match a record in the primary table. Tuples that contain foreign keys that don't have a corresponding candidate key in the primary relation are called *orphan entities*. There are three ways orphan entities can be created:

- A tuple is added to the foreign table with a key that does not match a candidate key in the primary table.

- The candidate key in the primary table is changed.

- The referenced record in the primary table is deleted.

All three of these cases must be handled if the integrity of a relationship is to be maintained. The first case, the addition of an unmatched foreign key, is usually simply prohibited. But note that unknown and nonexistent values don't count. If the relationship is declared as optional, any number of unknown and nonexistent values can be entered without compromising referential integrity.

The second cause of orphaned entities—changing the candidate key value in the referenced table—shouldn't occur very often. In fact, I would strongly recommend that changes to candidate keys be prohibited altogether wherever possible. (This would be an entity constraint, by the way: "Candidate keys are not allowed to change.") But if your model does allow candidate keys to be changed, you must ensure that these changes are made in the foreign keys as well. This is known as a *cascading update*. Both Microsoft Jet and Microsoft SQL Server provide mechanisms for easily implementing cascading updates.

The final cause of orphan foreign keys is the deletion of the tuple containing the primary entity. If one deletes a Customer record, for example, what becomes of that customer's orders? As with candidate key changes, you can simply prohibit the deletion of tuples in the primary relation if they are referenced in a foreign relation. This is certainly the cleanest solution if it is a reasonable restriction for your system. For when it's not, both the Jet database engine and SQL Server provide a simple means of cascading the operation, known as a *cascading delete*.

But in this case, you also have a third option that's a little harder to implement. At any rate, it can't be implemented automatically. You might want to reassign the dependent records. This isn't often appropriate, but it is sometimes necessary. Say, for example, that CustomerA purchases CustomerB. It might make sense to delete CustomerB and reassign all of CustomerB's orders to CustomerA.

A special kind of referential integrity constraint is the maximum cardinality issue discussed in Chapter 3. In the data model, rules such as "Managers are allowed to have a maximum of five individuals reporting to them" are defined as referential constraints.

Database Integrity

The most general form of integrity constraint is the *database constraint*. Database constraints reference more than one relation: "A Customer is not allowed to have a status of 'Preferred' unless he or she has made a purchase in the last 12 months." The majority of database constraints take this form.

It's always a good idea to define integrity constraints as completely as possible, and database integrity is no exception. You must be careful, however, not to confuse a database constraint with the specification of a work process. A *work process* is something that is done with the database, such as adding an order, whereas an integrity constraint is a rule about the contents of the database. The rules that define the tasks that are performed using the database are work process constraints, not database constraints. Work processes, as we'll see in Chapter 8, can have a major impact on the data model, but they shouldn't be made a part of it.

It isn't always clear whether a given business rule is an integrity constraint or a work process (or something else entirely). The difference might not be desperately important. All else being equal, implement the rule where it's most convenient to do so. If it's a straightforward process to express a rule as a database constraint, do so. If that gets tricky (as it often can, even when the rule is clearly an integrity constraint), move it to the front-end processing, where it can be implemented procedurally.

On the other hand, if the rule is extremely volatile and subject to frequent change, it will probably be easier to maintain if it's part of the database schema, where a single change will effect (but hopefully not *break*) all the systems referencing it.

Transaction Integrity

The final form of database integrity is *transaction integrity*. Transaction integrity constraints govern the ways in which the database can be manipulated. Unlike other constraints, transaction constraints are procedural and thus are not part of the data model per se.

Transactions are closely related to work processes. The concepts are, in fact, orthogonal, inasmuch as a given work process might consist of one or more transactions and vice versa. It isn't quite correct, but it's useful to think of a work process as an abstract construct ("add an order") and a transaction as a physical one ("update the OrderDetail table").

A transaction is usually defined as a "logical unit of work," which I've always found to be a particularly unhelpful bit of rhetoric. Essentially, a transaction is a group of actions, all of which (or none of which) must be completed. The database must comply with all of the defined integrity constraints before the transaction commences and after it's completed, but might be temporarily in violation of one or more constraints *during* the transaction.

The classic example of a transaction is the transfer of money from one bank account to another. If funds are debited from Account A but the system fails to credit them to Account B, money has been lost. Clearly, if the second command fails, the first must be undone. In database parlance, it must be "rolled back."

Transactions can involve multiple records, multiple relations, and even multiple databases. To be precise, all operations against a database are transactions. Even updating a single existing record is a transaction. Fortunately, these low-level transactions are performed transparently by the database engine, and you can generally ignore this level of detail.

Both the Jet database engine and SQL Server provide a means of maintaining transactional integrity by way of the BEGIN TRANSACTION, COMMIT TRANSACTION,

and ROLLBACK TRANSACTION statements. As might be expected, SQL Server's implementation is more robust and better able to recover from hardware failure as well as certain kinds of software failure. However, these are implementation issues and are outside the scope of this book. What is important from a design point of view is to capture and specify transaction dependencies, those infamous "logical units of work."

Implementing Data Integrity

Up until now, we've concentrated on capturing the problem space at an abstract level in the conceptual data model. In this section, we'll look at a few of the issues involved in creating the physical model of the problem space: the database schema. Moving from one level to another is primarily a change in terminology—relations become tables and attributes become fields—except for issues of data integrity. These never map quite as cleanly as one wants.

Unknown and Nonexistent Values (Again)

Earlier in this chapter, I somewhat blithely declared that domains and attributes should be examined to determine whether they are permitted to be empty or unknown without considering how these constraints might be implemented. The implementation issue (and it *is* an issue) can't be avoided once we turn to the database schema.

The soi-disant "missing information problem" has been acknowledged since the relational model was first proposed. How does one indicate that any given bit of information is either missing (the customer does have a surname, we just don't know what it is) or nonexistent (the customer doesn't have a middle name)? Most relational databases, including Microsoft Jet databases and SQL Server databases, have incorporated the null as a way of handling missing and nonexistent values.

To call the null a solution to the issue is probably excessive, as it has numerous problems. Some database experts reject nulls entirely. C. J. Date declares that they "wreck the model,"[1] and I've lost track of how many times I've heard them declared "evil." Any remarks about the complexity of handling nulls or rueful admissions to having been caught out by them *will* result in remarks along the lines of "Good. You shouldn't be using them. They should hurt."

As an alternative, the "nulls are evil" school recommends the use of specific values of the appropriate domain to indicate unknown or nonexistent values, or both. I think of this as the *conventional value approach*. The conventional

---

1. C. J. Date, *An Introduction to Database Systems*, 6th ed. (Reading: Addison-Wesley, 1995), 128

value approach has several problems. First, in many instances the chosen value *is* only conventional. A date of 9/9/1900 doesn't *really* mean the date is unknown, we just agree that's what we'll interpret it to mean. I fail to see that this approach is an improvement over the null. A null is a conventional value as well, of course, but it can't be confused with anything else, and it has the advantage of being supported by the relational model and most relational database engines.

The second, and to my mind disqualifying, problem with the conventional value approach is its impact on referential integrity. Take, for example, an optional relationship between a Customer and a Customer Service Representative (CSR), such that the CSR, if one is assigned, must be listed in the CSR table. The conventional value approach requires that a record be added to the CSR table to match the conventional value chosen to indicate that no CSR is assigned, as shown in Figure 4-2.

Customers

CustomerID	CompanyName	CSR
ALFKI	Alfreds Futterkiste	Nancy Davolio
ANATR	Ana Trujillo Emparedados y helados	Andrew Fuller
ANTON	Antonio Moreno Taquería	Anne Dodsworth
AROUT	Around the Horn	Steven Buchanan
BERGS	Berglunds snabbköp	Margaret Peacock
BLAUS	Blauer See Delikatessen	UNASSIGNED
BLONP	Blondel père et fils	Steven Buchanan
BOLID	Bólido Comidas preparadas	Nancy Davolio
BONAP	Bon app'	UNASSIGNED
BOTTM	Bottom-Dollar Markets	Robert King
BSBEV	B's Beverages	UNASSIGNED
CACTU	Cactus Comidas para llevar	Robert King
CENTC	Centro comercial Moctezuma	Laura Callahan
CHOPS	Chop-suey Chinese	Janet Leverling
COMMI	Comércio Mineiro	Michael Suyama
CONSH	Consolidated Holdings	Andrew Fuller
DRACD	Drachenblut Delikatessen	Steven Buchanan
DUMON	Du monde entier	UNASSIGNED
EASTC	Eastern Connection	Laura Callahan
ERNSH	Ernst Handel	Robert King
FAMIA	Familia Arquibaldo	Margaret Peacock
FISSA	FISSA Fabrica Inter. Salchichas S.A.	Janet Leverling
FOLIG	Folies gourmandes	UNASSIGNED
FOLKO	Folk och fä HB	Janet Leverling
FRANK	Frankenversand	Janet Leverling
FRANR	France restauration	UNASSIGNED
FRANS	Franchi S.p.A.	Janet Leverling

CSRs

EmployeeID	LastName	FirstName
1	Davolio	Nancy
2	Fuller	Andrew
3	Leverling	Janet
4	Peacock	Margaret
5	Buchanan	Steven
6	Suyama	Michael
7	King	Robert
8	Callahan	Laura
9	Dodsworth	Anne
10	UNASSIGNED	

Figure 4-2. *Conventional values require the addition of "dummy" records to maintain referential integrity.*

Now, how many CSRs does the company employ? One less than the number of CSRs listed in the table, since one of them is a dummy record. Oops. What's the average number of customers per CSR? The number of records in the Customer table minus the number of records that match the "UNASSIGNED" CSR, divided by one less than the number of records in the CSR table. Double oops.

Conventional values *are* useful, however, when you're producing reports. For example, you might want to substitute "Unknown" for Null values and "Not Applicable" for empty values. This is, of course, a very different proposition from storing these conventional values in the database, where they interfere with data manipulation, as we've seen.

Evil the null might be, and ugly it most assuredly is, but it's the best tool we have for handling unknown and nonexistent values. Just think the issue through, find alternatives where that's reasonable, and allow for the difficulties of using nulls where alternatives are *not* reasonable.

One of the problems with nulls is that, with the exception of domains declared to be string or text data types, they might be forced to do double duty. A field declared as a DateTime data type can accept only dates or nulls. If the corresponding attribute is defined as allowing both unknown and nonexistent values, and both are represented by null, there is no way to determine whether a null in any specific record represents "unknown" or "nonexistent." This problem doesn't arise for string or text data types, since you can use an empty, zero-length string for the empty value, leaving null to represent the unknown value.

In practice, this problem doesn't occur as often as one might expect. Few nontext domains permit the nonexistent value, so in these domains a null can always be interpreted as meaning unknown. For those domains that do accept a non-existent value, a sensible alternative can often be chosen to represent it. Note that I'm recommending an actual value here, not a conventional one. For example, even though a Product relation has a Weight attribute, a Service Call attribute, which obviously doesn't have a weight, can use the value zero. (Zero is a good choice to represent empty for many, but not all, numeric fields.)

The second and far more serious problem with nulls is that they complicate data manipulation. Logical comparisons become more complex, and posing certain kinds of questions can get a bit hairy. We'll look at this in detail in Chapter 5.

I don't take nulls lightly, and when there's a reasonable alternative, I'd recommend taking it. But as I've said elsewhere, and it bears repeating, don't dent the data model just to make life easier for the programmers. Think it through, but if the system requires nulls, use them.

Violation Responses

When defining the database schema, you must not only determine how a given integrity constraint might most effectively be implemented, you must also decide what action the database engine should take if the constraint is violated. In most cases, of course, the database will simply reject the offending command, posting an error in whatever method is most effective. Sometimes, however, the database can take corrective action that makes the requested change acceptable. Examples of this include the provision of a default value for attributes that do not allow empty values, or performing a cascading update or cascading delete to preserve referential integrity. We'll discuss violation responses in detail in Part 3.

Declarative and Procedural Integrity

Relational database engines provide integrity support in two ways: declarative and procedural. *Declarative integrity* support is explicitly defined ("declared") as part of the database schema. Both the Jet database engine and SQL Server provide some declarative integrity support. Declarative integrity is the preferred method for implementing data integrity. You should use it wherever possible.

SQL Server implements *procedural integrity* support by way of *trigger* procedures that are executed ("triggered") when a record is either inserted, updated, or deleted. The Jet database engine does not provide triggers or any other form of procedural integrity. When an integrity constraint cannot be implemented using declarative integrity it must be implemented in the front end.

We'll be looking at the specifics of mapping the integrity constraints defined in the data model to the physical database schema in the rest of this chapter.

Domain Integrity

SQL Server provides a limited kind of support for domains in the form of user-defined data types (UDDTs). Fields defined against a UDDT will inherit the data type declaration as well as domain constraints defined for the UDDT.

Equally importantly, SQL Server will prohibit comparison between fields declared against different UDDTs, even when the UDDTs in question are based on the same system data type. For example, even though the CityName domain and the CompanyName domain are both defined as being char(30), SQL Server would reject the expression CityName = CompanyName. This can be explicitly overridden by using the convert function CityName = CONVERT(char(30), CompanyName), but it's good that you have to think about it before comparing fields declared against different domains since these comparisons don't often make sense.

UDDTs can be created either through the SQL Server Enterprise Manager or through the system stored procedure sp_addtype. Either way, UDDTs are initially declared with a name or a data type and by whether they are allowed to accept nulls. Once a UDDT has been created, default values and validation rules can be defined for it. A SQL Server *rule* is a logical expression that defines the acceptable values for the UDDT (or for a field, if it is bound to a field rather than a UDDT). A *default* is simply that, a default value to be inserted by the system into a field that would otherwise be null because the user did not provide a value.

Binding a rule or default to a UDDT is a two-step procedure. First you must create the rule or default, and then bind it to the UDDT (or field). The "it's not a bug, it's a feature" justification for this two-step procedure is that, once defined, the rule or default can be reused elsewhere. I find this tedious since in my experience these objects are reused only rarely. When defining a table, SQL Server provides the ability to declare defaults and CHECK constraints directly, as part of the table definition. (CHECK constraints are similar to rules, but more powerful.) Unfortunately this one-step declaration is not available when declaring UDDTs, which must use the older "create-then-bind" methodology. It is heartily to be wished that Microsoft add support for default and CHECK constraint declarations to UDDTs in a future release of SQL Server.

A second way of implementing a kind of deferred domain integrity is to use lookup tables. This technique can be used in both Microsoft Jet and SQL Server. As an example, take the domain of USStates. Now theoretically you can create a rule listing all 50 states. In reality, this would be a painful process, particularly with the Jet database engine, where the rule would have to be retyped for every field declared against the domain. It's much, much easier to create a USStates lookup table and use referential integrity to ensure that the field values are restricted to the values stored in the table.

Entity Integrity

In the database schema, entity constraints can govern individual fields, multiple fields, or the table as a whole. Both the Jet database engine and SQL Server provide mechanisms for ensuring integrity at the entity level. Not surprisingly, SQL Server provides a richer set of capabilities, but the gap is not as great as one might expect.

At the level of individual fields, the most fundamental integrity constraint is of course the data type. Both the Jet database engine and SQL Server provide a rich set of data types, as shown in the table on the following page.

Logical Data Type	SQL Server Data Type	Microsoft Jet Data Type	Value Range	Storage Size
Integer	Int	Long integer	Whole numbers from −2,147,483,648 to 2,147,483,647	4 bytes
	Smallint	N/A	Whole numbers from −32,768 to 32,767	2 bytes
	Tinyint	Integer	Whole numbers from 0 to 255	1 byte
Packed decimal (exact numeric)	Decimal	Number (type varies)	Whole or fractional numbers from -10^{38-1} to 10^{38-1}	2–17 bytes
Floating point (approx. numeric)	Float (15-digit precision)	Double	Approximations of numbers from $-1.79E^{308}$ to $1.79E^{308}$ Positive range: $2.23E^{-308}$ to $1.79E^{308}$ Negative range: $-2.23E^{-308}$ to $-1.79E^{308}$	8 bytes
	Real	Single	Approximations of numbers from $-3.40E^{38}$ to $3.40E^{38}$ Positive range: $1.18E^{-38}$ to $3.40E^{38}$ Negative range: $-1.18E^{-38}$ to $-3.40E^{38}$	4 bytes
Character (fixed length)	Char	N/A	Maximum of 255 characters in Jet; 8000 characters in SQL Server 7.0 (255 in previous versions)	1 byte per character declared
Character (variable length)	Varchar	Text	Maximum of 255 characters in Jet; 8000 characters in SQL Server 7.0 (255 in previous versions)	1 byte per character stored
Monetary	Money	Currency	Numbers accurate to four decimal places, from −922,337,208,685,477.5808 to 922,337,208,685,477.5807	8 bytes

Logical Data Type	SQL Server Data Type	Microsoft Jet Data Type	Value Range	Storage Size
	Smallmoney	N/A	Numbers accurate to four decimal places, from −214,748.3648 to 214,748.3647	4 bytes
Date and Time	Datetime	Date/Time	1 January 1753 to 31 December 9999 in SQL Server; 1 January 100 to 31 December 9999 in Jet	8 bytes
	Smalldatetime	N/A	1 January 1900 to 6 June 2079	4 bytes
Binary (fixed length)	Binary	N/A	Maximum of 8000 bytes	Number of bytes declared plus 4 bytes
Binary (variable length)	Varbinary	(Supported only for linked tables)	Maximum of 8000 bytes	Number of bytes actually stored plus 4 bytes
Long Text/ Binary Long OBject	Text	Memo	Character data up to 2 GB in SQL Server, or 1 GB in a Microsoft Jet database	Amount of data stored plus 16 bytes
(BLOB)	Image	OLE Object	Binary data up to 2 GB in SQL Server, or 1 GB in a Microsoft Jet database	Amount of data stored plus 16 bytes
Boolean	Bit	Yes/No	0 or 1	1 byte, but bit columns in a table are combined in SQL Server; thus 8 or fewer columns will take 1 byte in total

As we saw in the previous section, SQL Server also allows fields to be declared against UDDTs. A UDDT field inherits the nullability, defaults, and rules that were defined for the type, but these can be overridden by the field definition. Logically the field definition should only narrow UDDT constraints, but in fact SQL

Server simply replaces the UDDT definition in the field description. It is thus possible to allow a field to accept nulls even though the UDDT against which it is declared does not.

Both SQL Server and the Jet database engine provide control over whether a field is allowed to contain nulls. When defining a column in SQL Server, one simply specifies NULL or NOT NULL or clicks the appropriate box in the Enterprise Manager.

The Jet database engine equivalent of the null flag is the Required field. In addition, the Jet database engine provides the AllowZeroLength flag which determines whether empty strings ("") are permitted in Text and Memo fields. This constraint can be implemented in SQL Server using a CHECK constraint.

Simply setting the appropriate property when defining the field sets default values in the Jet database engine. In SQL Server, you can set the Default property when creating the field or you can bind a system default to the field as described for UDDTs. Declaring the default as part of the table definition is certainly cleaner and the option I would generally recommend if you do not (or cannot) declare the default at the domain level.

Finally, both the Jet database engine and SQL Server allow specific entity constraints to be established. The Jet database engine provides two field properties, ValidationRule and ValidationText. SQL Server allows CHECK constraints to be declared when the field is defined or system rules to be bound to the field afterwards. CHECK constraints are the preferred method.

At first glance, the Jet database engine validation rules and SQL Server CHECK constraints appear to be identical, but there are some important differences. Both take the form of a logical expression, and neither is allowed to reference other tables or columns. However, a Jet database engine validation rule must evaluate to True for the value to be accepted. A SQL Server CHECK constraint must not evaluate to False. This is a subtle point: both True and Null are acceptable values for a CHECK constraint; only a True value is acceptable for a validation rule.

In addition, multiple CHECK constraints can be defined for one SQL Server field. In fact, one rule and any number of CHECK constraints can be applied to a single SQL Server field, whereas a Jet database engine field has a single ValidationRule property. The Jet database engine ValidationText property setting, by the way, is returned to the front end as an error message. Microsoft Access displays the text in a message box; it is available to Microsoft Visual Basic and other programming environments as the text of the Errors collection.

Entity constraints that reference multiple fields in a single table are implemented as table validation rules in the Jet database engine and table CHECK

constraints in SQL Server. Other than being declared in a different place, these table-level constraints function in precisely the same way as their corresponding field-level constraints.

The most fundamental entity integrity constraint is the requirement that each instance of an entity be uniquely identifiable. Remember that this is *the* entity integrity rule; all others are more properly referred to as entity-level integrity constraints. The Jet database engine and SQL Server support uniqueness constraints in pretty much the same way, but the support looks quite different. Both engines implement the constraints using indices, but SQL Server hides this from the user. Whether one explicitly creates an index (Jet database engine) or declares a constraint (SQL Server) is largely a mechanical detail.

Both the Jet database engine and SQL Server support the definition of sets of fields as being unique. Both also support the definition of a set of one or more fields as being the primary key, which implies uniqueness. There can be only one primary key for a table, although it can consist of multiple fields. There can be any number of unique constraints.

The other important difference between unique constraints and primary keys is that unique indices can contain nulls; primary keys cannot. There are some differences in the way the two engines treat nulls in unique indices. The Jet database engine provides a property, IgnoreNulls, which prevents records containing Null values in the indexed columns from being added to the index. The records are added to the table but not included in the index. This capability is not available in SQL Server.

In addition, SQL Server allows only a single record containing NULL in the index. This is logically insupportable since it treats records with NULL values as being equal, which of course they are not. A null is not equal to anything, including another null.

Interestingly, neither the Jet database engine nor SQL Server requires that a primary key be defined for a table or even that it have a unique constraint. In other words, it is possible to create tables that are not relations since tuples in relations must be uniquely identifiable but records in tables need not be. Why one would want to do this escapes me, but I suppose it's nice to know that the possibility is there if you should ever need it.

SQL Server also provides a procedural mechanism for providing entity-level integrity that the Jet database engine does not provide. *Triggers* are little bits of code (specifically, Transact-SQL code) that are automatically executed when a specific event occurs. Multiple triggers can be defined for each INSERT, UPDATE, or DELETE event, and a given trigger can be defined for multiple events.

Referential Integrity

While their support for entity integrity is substantively the same, the Jet database engine and SQL Server implement different paradigms for supporting referential integrity. SQL Server allows foreign key constraints to be declared as part of the table definition. A *foreign key constraint* establishes a reference to a candidate key in another table, the primary table. Once the reference is established, SQL Server prevents the creation of orphan records by rejecting any insertions that do not have a matching record in the primary table. Nulls are not prohibited in foreign key columns, although they can be prevented if the column participates in the primary key of the table, which is often the case. SQL Server also prohibits the deletion of records in the primary table if they have any matching foreign key values.

The Jet database engine supports referential integrity through a *Relation object* within the database. Microsoft's terminology is unfortunate here—the Jet database engine Relation object is a physical representation of the relationship between two entities. Don't confuse the Relation object with the logical relations that are defined in the data model.

The simplest way of creating Relation objects is in the Access user interface (using the Relationships command on the Tools menu), but they can also be created in code. The Data Access Object (DAO) Relation object's Table and ForeignTable properties define the two tables participating in the relationship, while the Fields collection defines the linked fields in each table.

The manner in which the Jet database engine will maintain referential integrity for the relation is governed by the Attributes property of the relation, as shown in the table below.

Attribute Constant	Description
dbRelationUnique	The relationship is one-to-one.
dbRelationDontEnforce	The relationship isn't enforced. (There is no referential integrity.)
dbRelationInherited	The relationship exists in a noncurrent database that contains the two linked tables.
dbRelationUpdateCascade	Updates will cascade.
dbRelationDeleteCascade	Deletes will cascade.

Note the attribute flags dbRelationUpdateCascade and dbRelationDeleteCascade. If the update flag is set and a referenced field is changed, the Jet database engine will automatically update the matching fields in the foreign table. Similarly, the delete flag will cause the matching records to be automatically deleted from

the foreign table. SQL Server does not have comparable automatic flags, but the cascading behavior can easily be implemented using triggers.

Other Kinds of Integrity

In the data model, we define three additional kinds of integrity: database, transition, and transaction. Some transition constraints are simple enough to be declared as validation rules. Most, however, as well as all database and transaction constraints, must be implemented procedurally. For SQL Server databases, this means using triggers. Since the Jet database engine does not support triggers, these constraints must be implemented in the front end.

SUMMARY

In this chapter, we've looked at modeling and implementing data integrity. Three kinds of integrity constraints—domain, transition, and entity—control individual relations, while referential integrity constraints ensure that the relations *between* relations are maintained. Finally, database constraints and transaction constraints control the database as a whole.

Data integrity is implemented in the database schema using a combination of declarative and procedural integrity. Declarative integrity is explicitly declared as part of the schema and is the preferred method of implementation. However, not all constraints can be implemented using declarative integrity, and where they cannot, procedural integrity must be used.

In Chapter 5, we'll examine relational algebra and the operations that can be performed on the relations in the database.

5

Relational Algebra

In the previous chapters, we have looked at defining a particular kind of relation, called a *base relation,* that will be given a physical representation in the database. The relational model also supports the creation of several kinds of derived relations. A *derived relation* is a relation that is defined in terms of other relations rather than in terms of attributes. These named relations can be base relations or other derived relations, in any combination.

In the database schema, a base relation is represented by a table. Derived relations are represented by *views* in Microsoft SQL Server and *queries* in the Microsoft Jet database engine. For the sake of linguistic simplicity, I'll use the term "view," since it's the standard relational term. I'll also use the term "recordset" generically when I mean either a view or a query.

Views are defined in terms of the relational operations that are the subject of this chapter. Microsoft Access and the SQL Server Enterprise Manager provide a graphical interface for defining views. They can also be defined in terms of SQL SELECT statements.

SQL (usually pronounced "sequel") stands for *Structured Query Language.* It is a standard language for expressing relational operations. Both the Jet database engine and SQL Server support a dialect of SQL. Not, of course, the same dialect. That would be too easy. Fortunately, the differences between the two implementations don't often affect the relational algebra that we'll be discussing in this chapter. Where the syntax differs, I'll give examples from both dialects.

The SQL SELECT statement is extremely powerful and more than a little complex. A detailed examination of it is outside the scope of this book. For our purposes, we can restrict ourselves to the basic structure, which has the following syntax:

```
SELECTV<fieldList>
FROM <recordsetList>
    <joinType> JOIN <joinCondition>
WHERE <selectionCriteria>
GROUP BY <groupByFieldList>
HAVING <selectionCriteria>
ORDER BY <orderByFieldList>
```

The <fieldList> in the SELECT clause is a list of one or more fields to be included in the recordset resulting from the statement. The fields can be actually present in the underlying recordsets, or they can be calculated. The <recordsetList> in the FROM clause is, as one might expect, a list of tables and views on which the SELECT statement is based. These are the only two clauses of the SELECT statement that must be included; all others are optional.

The JOIN clause defines the relationship between the recordsets listed in <recordsetList>. We'll be looking at joins in detail later in this chapter. The WHERE clause defines a logical expression, <selectionCriteria>, which restricts the data to be included in the resulting recordset. We'll look at restriction in detail later, as well.

The GROUP BY clause combines records having the same values in the specified list of fields to be combined into a single record. The HAVING clause is used to further restrict the fields returned after they've been combined by the GROUP BY clause. Finally, the ORDER BY clause causes the recordset to be sorted according to the fields listed in <orderByFieldList>.

Nulls and Three-Valued Logic (One More Time)

Most of the operations of relational algebra involve the use of *logical operators*, operators that usually return a *Boolean result*—that is, True or False. I say "usually" because with the addition of nulls to the relational model things get a little more complicated.

Nulls add a third value to the set of Boolean values; you must then work with True, False, and Null. Not surprisingly, these operators become known as *three-valued logic*. The three-valued truth tables for the standard logical operators are shown in Figure 5-1.

AND	True	False	Null
True	True	False	Null
False	False	False	Null
Null	Null	Null	Null

OR	True	False	Null
True	True	True	Null
False	True	False	Null
Null	Null	Null	Null

XOR	True	False	Null
True	False	True	Null
False	True	False	Null
Null	Null	Null	Null

Figure 5-1. *The three-valued And, Or, and XOr truth tables.*

As you can see, Null *op* anything, where *op* is a logical operator, results in Null. This is generally also true of the logical comparison operators, as shown in Figure 5-2.

=	True	False	Null
True	True	False	Null
False	False	True	Null
Null	Null	Null	Null

≠	True	False	Null
True	False	True	Null
False	True	False	Null
Null	Null	Null	Null

Figure 5-2. *The three-valued Equal and Not Equal truth tables.*

SQL Server, for reasons that I'm sure make sense to its designers, adds an "extension" to normal logical operations. If the option ANSI_NULLS is turned off, Null = Null evaluates to True, and Null = <value>, where <value> is anything except Null, evaluates to False. (This is undoubtedly related to the issue of allowing only a single Null value in UNIQUE indices.)

SQL provides two unary operators—IS NULL and IS NOT NULL—to specifically handle Null values. They work exactly as one might expect. The truth tables for IS NULL and IS NOT NULL are shown in Figure 5-3. Again, <value> indicates anything except Null.

	Is Null	Is Not Null
<value>	False	True
True	False	True
False	False	True
Null	True	False

Figure 5-3. *The IS NULL and IS NOT NULL truth tables.*

Relational Operators

We'll begin our examination of relational algebra with the four types of relational operators: restriction, projection, join, and divide. The first two affect a single recordset, although that recordset can, of course, be a view based on any number of other recordsets. The join operator is perhaps the most fundamental to the relational model and defines how two recordsets are to be combined. The final operator, divide, is a rarely used but occasionally handy method of determining which records in one recordset match all the records in a second recordset.

All of these operators are implemented with some form of the SQL SELECT statement. They can be combined in any way you want, subject to the system constraints regarding maximum length and complexity for the statement.

Restriction

The restriction operator returns only those records that meet the specified selection criteria. It is implemented using the WHERE clause of the SELECT statement, as follows:

```
SELECT * FROM Employees WHERE LastName = "Davolio";
```

In the Northwind database, this statement returns Nancy Davolio's employee record, since she's the only person in the table with that last name. (The * in the <fieldList> section of the statement is special shorthand for "all fields.")

The selection criteria specified in the WHERE clause can be of arbitrary complexity. Logical expressions can be combined with AND and OR. The expression will be evaluated for each record in the recordset, and if it returns True, that record will be included in the result. If the expression returns either False or Null for the record, it will not be included.

Projection

While restriction takes a horizontal slice of a recordset, projection takes a vertical slice; it returns only a subset of the fields in the original recordset.

SQL performs this simple operation using the <fieldList> section of the SELECT statement by only including the fields that you list. For example, you could use the following statement to create an employee phone list:

```
SELECT LastName, FirstName, Extension
FROM Employees
ORDER BY LastName, FirstName;
```

Remember that the ORDER BY clause does just that, it sorts the data; in this case, the list will be sorted alphabetically by the LastName field and then by the FirstName field.

Join

Join operations are probably the most common relational operations. Certainly they are fundamental to the model—it would not be feasible to decompose data into multiple relations were it not possible to recombine it as necessary. This is precisely what a join operator does; it combines recordsets based on the comparison of one or more common fields.

Joins are implemented using the JOIN clause of the SELECT statement. They are categorized based on the type of comparison between the fields involved and the way the results of the comparison are treated. We'll look at each of these in turn.

Equi-Joins

When the join comparison is made on the basis of equality, the join is an *equi-join*. In an equi-join operation, only those records that have matching values in the specified fields will be returned.

Take, for example, the relations in Figure 5-4. This is a typical case of linked tables resulting from the normalization process. OrderID is the primary key of the Orders table and a foreign key in the Order Details table.

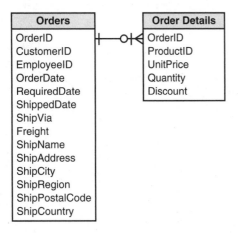

Figure 5-4. *These tables can be recombined using the JOIN Operator.*

To recombine (and consequently denormalize) the tables, you would use the following SELECT statement:

```
SELECT Orders.OrderID, Orders.CustomerID, [Order Details].ProductID
FROM Orders
INNER JOIN [Order Details] ON Orders.OrderID = [Order Details].OrderID
WHERE (((Orders.OrderID)=10248));
```

This statement would result in the recordset shown in Figure 5-5.

OrderID	CustomerID	ProductID
10248	VINET	42
10248	VINET	72
10248	VINET	11

Figure 5-5. *This recordset is the result of joining the Orders and Order Details tables.*

NOTE If you run this query in Access 2000 using the Northwind database, the result set will show the customer name rather than the CustomerID. This is because Access allows fields to display something *other* than what's actually stored in them when you declare a lookup control in the table definition. This is a real advantage when Access is used interactively, but wreaks havoc on authors trying to provide examples.

Natural joins

A special case of the equi-join is the *natural join*. To qualify as a natural join, a join operation must meet the following conditions:

- The comparison operator must be equality.

- All common fields must participate in the join.

- Only one set of common fields must be included in the resulting recordset.

There's nothing intrinsically magical about natural joins. They don't behave in a special manner, nor does the database engine provide special support for them. They are merely the most common form of join, so common that they've been given their own name.

The Jet database engine does do something particularly magical if you create a natural join that meets certain special conditions. If a one-to-many relationship has been established between the two tables, and the common fields included in the view are from the many side of the relationship, then the Jet database engine will perform something called *Row Fix-Up* or *AutoLookup*. When the cursor enters the fields used in the join criteria, the Jet database engine will automatically provide the common fields, a spectacular bit of sleight of hand that makes the programmer's life much simpler.

Theta-Joins

Technically, all joins are theta-joins, but by custom, if the comparison operator is equality, the join is always referred to as an equi-join or just as a join. A join based on any other comparison operator (<>, >, >=, <, <=) is a *theta-join*.

Theta-joins are extremely rare in practice, but they can be handy in solving certain kinds of problems. These problems mostly involve finding records that have a value greater than an average or total, or records that fall within a certain range.

Let's say, for example, that you've created two views, one containing the average number of units sold for each product category and a second containing the total units sold by product, as shown in Figure 5-6. We'll look at how to create these views later in this chapter. For now, just assume their existence.

ProductCategoryAverages

CategoryName	AverageSold
Beverages	678
Condiments	442
Confections	608
Dairy Products	915
Grains/Cereals	652
Meat/Poultry	700
Produce	598
Seafood	640

ProductTotals

ProductID	ProductName	TotalSold
1	Chai	828
2	Chang	1057
3	Aniseed Syrup	328
4	Chef Anton's Cajun Seasoning	453
5	Chef Anton's Gumbo Mix	298
6	Grandma's Boysenberry Spread	301
7	Uncle Bob's Organic Dried Pears	763
8	Northwoods Cranberry Sauce	372
9	Mishi Kobe Niku	95
10	Ikura	742
11	Queso Cabrales	706
12	Queso Manchego La Pastora	344
13	Konbu	891
14	Tofu	404

Figure 5-6. *These views can be joined using a theta-join.*

The following SELECT statement, based on the comparison operator >, will produce a list of the best-selling products within each category:

```
SELECT DISTINCTROW ProductCategoryAverages.CategoryName,
    ProductTotals.ProductName
FROM ProductCategoryAverages
INNER JOIN ProductTotals
ON ProductCategoryAverages.CategoryID = ProductTotals.CategoryID
AND ProductTotals.TotalSold > [ProductCategoryAverages].[AverageSold];
```

The results are shown in Figure 5-7.

CategoryName	ProductName
Beverages	Chai
Beverages	Chang
Beverages	Guaraná Fantástica
Beverages	Steeleye Stout
Beverages	Outback Lager
Beverages	Rhönbräu Klosterbier
Beverages	Lakkalikööri
Condiments	Chef Anton's Cajun Seasoning
Condiments	Gula Malacca
Condiments	Sirop d'érable
Condiments	Vegie-spread
Condiments	Louisiana Fiery Hot Pepper Sauce
Condiments	Original Frankfurter grüne Soße
Confections	Pavlova

Figure 5-7. *This recordset is the result of a theta-join.*

In this example, the view could also have been defined using a WHERE clause restriction. In fact, Access will rewrite the query when you leave SQL view to look like the following:

```
SELECT DISTINCTROW ProductCategoryAverages.CategoryName,
    ProductTotals.ProductName
FROM ProductCategoryAverages
INNER JOIN ProductTotals
ON ProductCategoryAverages.CategoryID = ProductTotals.CategoryID
WHERE (((ProductTotals.TotalSold)>[ProductCategoryAverages].[AverageSold]));
```

Technically, all joins, including equi-joins and natural joins, can be expressed using a restriction. (In database parlance, a theta-join is not an *atomic opera-tor*.) In the case of theta-joins, this formulation is almost always to be preferred since the database engines are better able to optimize its execution.

Outer joins

All of the joins we've examined so far have been *inner joins,* joins that return only those records where the join condition evaluates as True. Note that this isn't exactly the same as returning only the records where the specified fields match,

although this is how an inner join is usually described. "Match" implies equality, and as we know not all joins are based on equality.

Relational algebra also supports another kind of join, the *outer join*. An outer join returns all the records returned by an inner join, *plus* all the records from either or both of the other recordsets. The missing ("unmatched") values will be Null.

Outer joins are categorized as being left, right, or full, depending on which additional records are to be included. Now, when I was in grad school, a *left outer join* returned all the records from the recordset on the one side of a one-to-many relationship, while a *right outer join* returned all the records from the many side. For both the Jet database engine and SQL Server, however, the distinction is based on the order in which the recordsets are listed in the SELECT statement. Thus the following two statements both return all the records from X and only those records from Y where the <condition> evaluates to True:

```
SELECT * FROM X LEFT OUTER JOIN Y ON <condition>
SELECT * FROM Y RIGHT OUTER JOIN X ON <condition>
```

A *full outer join* returns all records from both recordsets, combining those where the condition evaluates as True. SQL Server supports full outer joins with the FULL OUTER JOIN condition:

```
SELECT * FROM X FULL OUTER JOIN Y ON <condition>
```

The Jet database engine does not directly support full outer joins, but performing a union of a left outer join and a right outer join can duplicate them. We'll discuss unions in the next section.

Divide

The final relational operation is division. The *relational divide* operator (so called to distinguish it from mathematical division) returns the records in one recordset that have values that match all the corresponding values in the second recordset. For example, given a recordset that shows the categories of products purchased from each supplier, a relational division will produce a list of the suppliers that provide products in all categories.

This is not an uncommon situation, but the solution is not straightforward since the SQL SELECT statement does not directly support relational division. There are numerous ways to achieve the same results as a relational division, however. The easiest method is to rephrase the request.

Instead of "list the suppliers who provide all product categories," which is difficult to process, try "list all suppliers where the count of their product categories is equal to the count of all product categories." This is an example of the

extension operation that we'll discuss later in this chapter. It won't always work, and in situations where it doesn't, you can implement division using correlated queries. Correlated queries are, however, outside the scope of this book. Please refer to one of the references listed in the bibliography.

Set Operators

The next four operators of relational algebra are based on traditional set theory. They have, however, been modified slightly to account for the fact that we're dealing with relations, not undifferentiated sets.

Union

Conceptually, a *relational union* is the concatenation of two recordsets. It's more or less the relational version of addition. The result of the union of recordset A with recordset B is the same as actually adding all the records in A to B.

As an example, say you need a list of all the names and addresses known to the database for a mass mailing. The Northwind database Customers and Employees recordsets both have addresses and so can easily be combined in a union operation. In this case, we'd use the UNION statement, as follows:

```
SELECT CompanyName AS Name, Address, City, PostalCode
FROM Customers
UNION SELECT [FirstName] & " " & [LastName] AS Name,
    Address, City, PostalCode
FROM Employees
ORDER BY name;
```

Note that the CompanyName field is renamed "Name" and the FirstName and LastName fields from the Employees table are concatenated. The resulting field is also "Name." The union query doesn't require that the fields in the <fieldList> of each SELECT statement have the same name, but there must be the same number of them and they must have the same (or compatible) types. The results of this statement in Access are shown in Figure 5-8.

Name	Address	City	PostalCode
Alfreds Futterkiste	Obere Str. 57	Berlin	12209
Ana Trujillo Emparedados y helad	Avda. de la Constitución 2222	México D.F.	05021
Andrew Fuller	908 W. Capital Way	Tacoma	98401
Anne Dodsworth	7 Houndstooth Rd.	London	WG2 7LT
Antonio Moreno Taquería	Mataderos 2312	México D.F.	05023
Around the Horn	120 Hanover Sq.	London	WA1 1DP
Berglunds snabbköp	Berguvsvägen 8	Luleå	S-958 22
Blauer See Delikatessen	Forsterstr. 57	Mannheim	68306
Blondel père et fils	24, place Kléber	Strasbourg	67000
Bólido Comidas preparadas	C/ Araquil, 67	Madrid	28023
Bon app'	12, rue des Bouchers	Marseille	13008
Bottom-Dollar Markets	23 Tsawassen Blvd.	Tsawassen	T2F 8M4
B's Beverages	Fauntleroy Circus	London	EC2 5NT

Figure 5-8. *The UNION statement combines the records from each table.*

Intersection

The *intersection operator* returns the records that two recordsets have in common. It is, in essence, a "find the duplicates" operation, and that's the way it's most often used. An intersection is implemented using outer joins.

As an example, suppose that you have inherited client lists from several legacy systems, as shown in Figure 5-9.

DuplicateCustomers1

CustomerID	CompanyName
ALFKI	Alfreds Futterkiste
ANATR	Ana Trujillo Emparedados y helados
ANTON	Antonio Moreno Taquería
AROUT	Around the Horn
BERGS	Berglunds snabbköp
BLAUS	Blauer See Delikatessen
BLONP	Blondel père et fils
BOLID	Bólido Comidas preparadas

DuplicateCustomers2

CustomerID	CompanyName
ALFKI	Alfreds Futterkiste
ANATR	Ana Trujillo Emparedados y helados
ANTON	Antonio Moreno Taquería
AROUT	Around the Horn
FAMIA	Familia Arquibaldo
FISSA	FISSA Fabrica Inter. Salchichas S.A.
FOLIG	Folies gourmandes
FOLKO	Folk och fä HB
FRANK	Frankenversand

Figure 5-9. *Legacy tables often have duplicate data.*

The following SELECT statement will return the duplicate records:

```
SELECT DuplicateCustomers1.*
FROM DuplicateCustomers1
LEFT JOIN DuplicateCustomers2
ON (DuplicateCustomers1.CustomerID = DuplicateCustomers2.CustomerID)
AND (DuplicateCustomers1.CompanyName = DuplicateCustomers2.CompanyName)
WHERE (((DuplicateCustomers2.CustomerID) IS NOT NULL));
```

The results of this statement are shown in Figure 5-10.

CustomerID	CompanyName
ALFKI	Alfreds Futterkiste
ANATR	Ana Trujillo Emparedados y helados
ANTON	Antonio Moreno Taquería
AROUT	Around the Horn

Figure 5-10. *An outer join combined with the IS NOT NULL operator performs an intersection.*

Difference

While the intersection of two recordsets is used to "find the duplicates," the difference operator will "find the orphans." The *relational difference* of two recordsets is the records that belong to one recordset but not the other.

As an example, given the same two recordsets shown in Figure 5-9 on the preceding page, the SELECT statement below will return the *unmatched* records:

```
SELECT DuplicateCustomers1.*
FROM DuplicateCustomers1
LEFT JOIN DuplicateCustomers2
ON (DuplicateCustomers1.CustomerID = DuplicateCustomers2.CustomerID)
AND (DuplicateCustomers1.CompanyName = DuplicateCustomers2.CompanyName)
WHERE (DuplicateCustomers2.CustomerID IS NULL);
```

The outer join operation in this statement returns all the records from the two lists. As you will recall, an outer join supplies Null for the fields that do not have a match in the other table. The WHERE clause uses the IS NULL operator to restrict the records returned to only those (unmatched) records.

If this all seems as clear as mud, try performing the operation in two discrete steps: first create the outer join as a view, and then restrict the view with the WHERE statement. This process is shown in Figure 5-11.

Step 1: Create the outer join.

CustomerID	CompanyName
ALFKI	Alfreds Futterkiste
ANATR	Ana Trujillo Emparedados y helados
ANTON	Antonio Moreno Taquería
AROUT	Around the Horn
BERGS	Berglunds snabbköp
BLAUS	Blauer See Delikatessen
BLONP	Blondel père et fils
BOLID	Bólido Comidas preparadas

```
SELECT DuplicateCustomers1.*
FROM DuplicateCustomers1
LEFT JOIN DuplicateCustomers2
ON (DuplicateCustomers1.CustomerID = DuplicateCustomers.CustomerID);
```

Step 2: Select for Null CustomerIDs.

CustomerID	CompanyName
BERGS	Berglunds snabbköp
BLAUS	Blauer See Delikatessen
BLONP	Blondel père et fils
BOLID	Bólido Comidas preparadas

```
SELECT DuplicateCustomers1.*
FROM DuplicateCustomers1
LEFT JOIN DuplicateCustomers2
ON (DuplicateCustomers1.CustomerID = DuplicateCustomers.CustomerID)
WHERE (DuplicateCustomers2.CustomerID is Null);
```

Figure 5-11. *The difference operation can be performed in two steps.*

Cartesian Product

The final set operator is the Cartesian product. Like its counterpart in traditional set theory, the *Cartesian product* of two recordsets combines every record in one set with every record in the other.

The Cartesian product (or just "product") of two recordsets is returned by a SELECT statement with no JOIN clause. The statement below will return every customer combined with every customer service representative:

```
SELECT CustomerName, CSRName FROM Customer, CSRs;
```

Cartesian products are occasionally useful either for analysis purposes or as interim results for further manipulation. Most often, though, they're produced by accident. Forget to drag the join line in the Access query designer and bingo, you've got a Cartesian product. It's amazingly easy to do, so don't be embarrassed the first (dozen) times it happens to you.

Special Relational Operators

Various extensions to relational algebra have been proposed since the relational model was first formulated. We'll look at three that have been generally accepted: summarize, extend, and rename. We'll also look at three extensions provided by Microsoft: transform, rollup, and cube.

Summarize

The summarize operator does precisely what one would expect it to do: it produces records containing summary data grouped according to the specified fields. It's an extremely useful operation in any number of situations in which you want to examine data at a higher level of abstraction than is stored in the database.

The summarize operation is implemented using the GROUP BY clause of the SELECT statement. There will be one record returned for each distinct value in the specified field or fields. If more than one field is listed, groups will be nested. For example, consider the following statement:

```
SELECT Categories.CategoryName, Products.ProductName,
    SUM([Order Details].Quantity) AS SumOfQuantity
FROM (Categories INNER JOIN Products ON Categories.CategoryID =
    Products.CategoryID)
INNER JOIN [Order Details]
ON Products.ProductID = [Order Details].ProductID
GROUP BY Categories.CategoryName, Products.ProductName;
```

This statement will return one record for each product in the Northwind database, grouped by category and containing three fields: CategoryName, ProductName,

and SumOfQuantity—the total number of each product sold—as shown in Figure 5-12.

CategoryName	ProductName	SumOfQuantity
Beverages	Chai	828
Beverages	Chang	1057
Beverages	Chartreuse verte	6
Beverages	Côte de Blaye	15
Beverages	Guaraná Fantástica	1125
Beverages	Ipoh Coffee	580
Beverages	Lakkalikööri	981
Beverages	Laughing Lumberjack Lager	184
Beverages	Outback Lager	817
Beverages	Rhönbräu Klosterbier	1155
Beverages	Sasquatch Ale	506
Beverages	Steeleye Stout	883
Condiments	Aniseed Syrup	328

Figure 5-12. *The GROUP BY clause returns summary data.*

The fields listed in <fieldList> in the SELECT statement must be either part of the <groupFieldList> or an argument to a SQL aggregate function. *SQL aggregate functions* calculate summary values for each record. The most common aggregate functions are AVERAGE, COUNT, SUM, MAXIMUM, and MINIMUM.

Aggregates are another place where nulls can bite you. Null values are included in the summarize operation—they form a group. They are, however, ignored by aggregate functions. This is usually only a problem if you're using one of the fields in the <groupFieldList> as the parameter to an aggregate function.

Extend

The extend operator allows you to define virtual fields that are calculated based on constants and values stored in the database but that are not physically stored themselves. You create virtual fields simply by defining the virtual field in the <fieldList> of the SELECT statement, as follows:

```
SELECT [UnitPrice]*[Qty] AS ExtendedPrice
FROM [Order Details];
```

The calculations defining the virtual fields can be of arbitrary complexity. This process is so simple and fast, there is rarely any justification for storing a calculated field in a table.

Rename

The final common operator is rename. The rename operation can be performed on either a recordset in <recordsetList> or on individual fields in <fieldList>. In the Jet database engine, a recordset renaming uses the following syntax:

```
SELECT <fieldName> AS <fieldAlias>
FROM <tableName> AS <tableAlias>
```

In SQL Server, the "AS" keyword is not necessary, as shown below:

```
SELECT <fieldName> <fieldAlias> FROM <recordsetName> <recordsetAlias>
```

Renaming is particularly useful when you're defining a view with a self-join, as shown in the following code:

```
SELECT Manager.Name, Employee.Name
FROM Employees AS Employee
INNER JOIN Employees AS Manager
ON Employee.EmployeeID = Manager.EmployeeID;
```

This syntax allows you to keep each usage logically distinct.

Transform

The TRANSFORM statement is the first of the Microsoft extensions to the relational algebra that we'll examine. TRANSFORM takes the results of a summarize (GROUP BY) operation and rotates them 90 degrees. More often referred to as a *crosstab query,* this incredibly useful operation is only supported by the Jet database engine; it has not (yet) been implemented in SQL Server.

The TRANSFORM statement has the following basic syntax:

```
TRANSFORM <aggregateFunction>
SELECT <fieldList>
FROM <recordsetList>
GROUP BY <groupByList>
PIVOT <columnHeading> [IN (<valueList>)]
```

The TRANSFORM <aggregateFunction> clause defines the summary data that will populate the recordset. The SELECT statement must include a GROUP BY clause and cannot include a HAVING clause. As with any GROUP BY clause, the <groupByList> can contain multiple fields. (In a TRANSFORM statement, the <fieldList> and <groupByList> expressions are almost always identical.)

The PIVOT clause identifies the field whose values will be used as column headings. By default, the Jet database engine will include the columns in the recordset alphabetically from left to right. The optional IN statement, however, allows you to specify column names, which will be listed in the order in which they're included in <valueList>.

The TRANSFORM statement on the following page provides essentially the same information as the summarize example given previously, the results of which are shown in Figure 5-12 on the preceding page.

```
TRANSFORM Count(Products.ProductID) AS CountOfProductID
SELECT Suppliers.CompanyName
FROM Suppliers
INNER JOIN (Categories INNER JOIN Products
    ON Categories.CategoryID = Products.CategoryID)
ON Suppliers.SupplierID = Products.SupplierID
GROUP BY Suppliers.CompanyName
PIVOT Categories.CategoryName;
```

The results of this TRANSFORM operation are shown in Figure 5-13.

CompanyName	Beverages	Condiments	Confections	DairyProducts	Grains/Cereals	Meat/Poultry	Produce	Seafood
Aux joyeux ecclésiastiques	2							
Bigfoot Breweries	3							
Cooperativa de Quesos 'Las Cabras'				2				
Escargots Nouveaux								1
Exotic Liquids	2	1						
Forêts d'érables		1	1					
Formaggi Fortini s.r.l.				3				
Gai pâturage				2				
G'day, Mate						1	1	1
Grandma Kelly's Homestead		2					1	
Heli Süßwaren GmbH & Co. KG			3					
Karkki Oy	1		2					
Leka Trading	1	1			1			
Lyngbysild								2
Ma Maison						2		
Mayumi's		1					1	1
New England Seafood Cannery								2

Figure 5-13. *The TRANSFORM statement rotates results by 90 degrees.*

Rollup

The summarize operator implemented using the GROUP BY clause generates records containing summary data. The ROLLUP clause provides a logical extension to this operation by providing total values.

The ROLLUP clause is only available in SQL Server. It is implemented as an extension to the GROUP BY clause:

```
SELECT Categories.CategoryName, Products.ProductName,
    SUM([Order Details].Quantity) AS SumOfQuantity
FROM (Categories INNER JOIN Products
    ON Categories.CategoryID = Products.CategoryID)
INNER JOIN [Order Details]
ON Products.ProductID = [Order Details].ProductID
GROUP BY Categories.CategoryName, Products.ProductName WITH ROLLUP;
```

This results in the recordset are shown in Figure 5-14.

This is again the same recordset shown in Figure 5-12 on page 92, with additional rows: the rows containing Null (one is shown in the figure) contain the total values for the group or subgroup. Thus, 8,137 beverages were sold in total.

CategoryName	ProductName	SumOfQuantity
Beverages	Chai	828
Beverages	Chang	1057
Beverages	Chartreuse verte	6
Beverages	Côte de Blaye	15
Beverages	Guaraná Fantástica	1125
Beverages	Ipoh Coffee	580
Beverages	Lakkalikööri	981
Beverages	Laughing Lumberjack Lager	184
Beverages	Outback Lager	817
Beverages	Rhönbräu Klosterbier	1155
Beverages	Sasquatch Ale	506
Beverages	Steeleye Stout	883
Beverages		8137
Condiments	Aniseed Syrup	328
Condiments	Chef Anton's Cajun Seasoning	453

Figure 5-14. *The ROLLUP operator adds totals.*

Cube

The CUBE operator is also available only in SQL Server and is implemented as an extension to the GROUP BY clause. Essentially, the CUBE clause summarizes every column in the <groupByList> by every other column. It is conceptually similar to the ROLLUP operator, but whereas ROLLUP produces totals for each column specified in the <groupByList>, CUBE creates summary data for additional groups.

For example, if you have three fields in the <groupByList>—A, B, and C—the CUBE operator will return the following seven aggregates:

- The total number of Cs.

- The total number of Cs, grouped by A.

- The total number of Cs, grouped by C within A.

- The total number of Cs, grouped by B within A.

- The total number of Cs, grouped by B.

- The total number of Cs, grouped by A within B.

- The total number of Cs, grouped by C within B.

SUMMARY

In this chapter, we've looked at manipulating base relations using various relational operators and seen some examples implemented in the SQL language. We've also had yet another look at the issue of nulls and three-valued logic.

Of the standard relational operators, the restriction and projection operators select subsets of a single recordset. The join, union, intersection, difference, and product operators control the way two recordsets are combined. All of these operators, with the exception of difference, can be implemented using a SQL SELECT statement. Difference can sometimes be implemented using SELECT and sometimes requires other techniques that are outside the scope of this book.

We've also looked at a few special operators. The summarize and extend operators perform calculations on the data. The rename operator controls the column headings that are displayed for the view. TRANSFORM, ROLLUP, and CUBE are special extensions to the SQL language implemented by Microsoft, each of which also provides a special way of summarizing and viewing data.

With this overview of relational algebra, we've completed Part I. Relational database theory is complex, and of course, there are issues and subtleties that I haven't been able to cover in the scope of an introductory book. But you've now seen all the major components of the theory. In the rest of the book, we'll turn to the practical aspects of designing database systems and user interfaces.

Designing Relational
Database Systems

6

The Design Process

In Part 1 of this book, we looked at the principles of relational database design. But the structure of the data is only one component of a database system—a critical component, obviously, but still only a single component. Beginning with this section, we'll look at some of the remaining aspects of designing database systems.

In this part, we'll discuss most of the activities involved in the analysis and design of database systems, including the definition of system parameters and work processes, the conceptual database model, and the database schema. The design of the user interface, because it is such a complex topic, will be discussed in Part 3.

I'll be examining only the analysis and design of database systems here; implementation lies outside the scope of this book. But analysis and design can't exist in isolation from the rest of the process, so we'll begin with a brief discussion of project life cycles.

Life Cycle Models

Once upon a time, systems analysts used a paradigm for the development process known as the "waterfall model." There are several versions of this model. A reasonably simple one is shown in Figure 6-1.

The process begins with systems analysis, sometimes called requirements analysis, since it focuses on what the organization and the users require the system to do. Once the systems analysis has been completed and approved, the entire system is designed in detail. This phase is followed by planning and budgeting, and then the entire system is built, tested, and released.

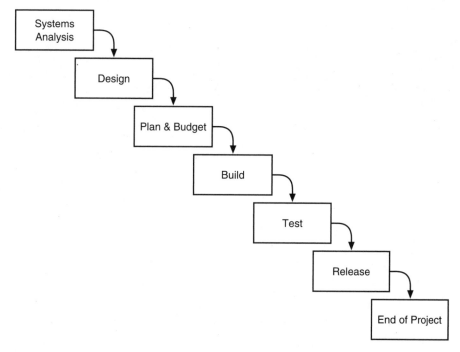

Figure 6-1. *The waterfall model.*

The waterfall model is aesthetically pleasing. Each activity is completed and approved before the next one is begun, and the model allows a fine degree of control over budgets, staffing, and time. Deliver a waterfall project on time and on budget, and your clients will probably love you.

The problem, of course, is that reality is hardly ever this neat. The model assumes that all the information required to complete a task is available during the performance of that task, and makes no allowance for new information coming to light later in the process. With the possible exception of very small systems, this situation is unlikely in the extreme.

The waterfall model also doesn't allow for changes in business requirements during the course of the project. To assume that a system that met the business's needs at the beginning of a project will still meet them at the end of a two-year or three-year development process is foolhardy. Your clients will not love you for delivering a useless system, even if it *is* on time and on budget.

Understand, however, that the activities identified in the waterfall model are perfectly sound. In fact, omitting any of them from a development project is a

recipe for disaster. The problem with the model is its linearity, its assumption that each phase need never be reexamined once it has been completed.

Several alternative life cycle models have been proposed to deal with the problems in the waterfall model. The spiral model assumes multiple iterations of the waterfall, each one expanding the scope of the previous iteration, as shown in Figure 6-2.

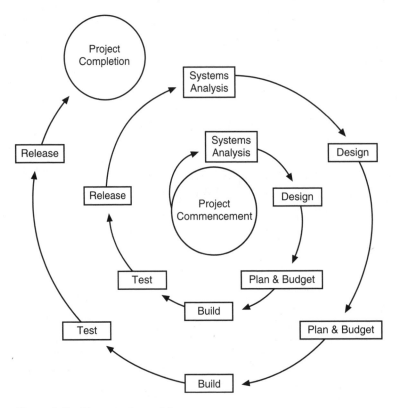

Figure 6-2. *The spiral model.*

The problem with the spiral model is that when it is strictly applied the entire scope of the project is not considered until very late in the development project, and there is a (not insignificant) chance that later iterations will invalidate earlier work. This has always seemed to me a recipe for blown budgets and frustrated developers. This situation is particularly dangerous for database projects, where expansions in scope can change the semantics of the data and a change in the database schema can require unexpected changes throughout the system.

The model that I prefer for large systems, and use in my own work, is variously described as incremental development or evolutionary development, and is shown in Figure 6-3.

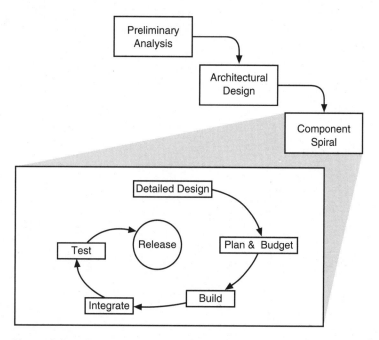

Figure 6-3. *The incremental development model.*

In this model, which is in many ways simply a variation on the spiral model, the preliminary analysis is performed for the entire system, not just a portion of it. This is followed by an architectural design, again of the whole system. The goal of the architectural design is to define individual components that can be implemented more or less independently, and to describe the interactions and interdependencies between these components. The detailed design and implementation of each component is then performed using whatever model seems most appropriate. I use the spiral model for this phase, as shown in Figure 6-3, because it allows greater flexibility in design and implementation.

Note that the spiral here includes an additional task, integration. Component integration is implicit in the spiral model as well, of course, but it's been my experience that the task is rather more complex using the incremental development approach. This is also one of the reasons I prefer to use the spiral model

during component development. Deferring the detailed design of a component until just before it is to be developed allows you to accommodate any insights gained during the integration of previous components, and hopefully avoid any of the problems you might have encountered during the integration.

The incremental development model assumes that any large system can be decomposed into distinct components, and this is not necessarily the case for all systems. It can also result in a lot of "scaffolding" code. For example, say that a data entry screen is supposed to make a call to a Microsoft ActiveX component that will perform a lookup on a customer code and take some action if a match is found, but that the ActiveX component hasn't yet been built. The development team will have to build some dummy code that allows the call to be made without error. Complex systems can include a substantial amount of scaffolding like this.

Additionally, there's always a chance that the ActiveX component will never be implemented; perhaps the budget doesn't stretch that far, or you later determine that it wasn't such a good idea after all. If you don't plan for this possibility, you could be distributing components whose only function is to keep *other* components from failing. Not an elegant situation, and certainly not one you'd like to explain to a maintenance programmer.

Because the analysis and architectural design are performed at the beginning of the project, there is the risk of them becoming obsolete, which as you will recall is one of the main disadvantages of the waterfall model. For this reason, it's important to review these two steps—particularly the requirements analysis, since it's more likely to change—before commencing the detailed design of each component. It's often a pleasant surprise how changes in requirements can be accommodated by changes to as-yet-undeveloped components, or even by changing the order in which new components are developed, without invalidating previous development work.

But the incremental development model does have several advantages. Because a "big picture" of the system is defined at the outset, the chances of wasted development work are minimized. Because large projects are decomposed into smaller components, the individual component projects become easier to manage. And by breaking the system into individual components, you have a good chance of being able to deliver some core functionality to your users early in the project. This allows the system to start paying for itself and also provides a mechanism for soliciting user input to be fed into subsequent development efforts.

The Database Design Process

Whatever overall development model you choose, you must perform certain analysis and design activities. Whether you perform them sequentially or iteratively, whether the scope of your inquiry is the entire system or only a single component, whether your techniques are formal or informal, every project should include each of these steps at least once.

Defining the System Parameters

Ideally, every project should begin with a clear definition of what you're trying to achieve, why you're trying to achieve it, and how your success will be judged. Most projects won't have this definition prior to commencement, so this is what the first phase of the design process is about. The project's goal defines the "why" of the project. Based on this, you can define the "what," the project's scope. Once you understand the goal and scope, you can begin to determine realistic design criteria, the "how." Each of these is discussed in detail in Chapter 7.

Defining the Work Processes

Although ostensibly involved in the storage and retrieval of data, the majority of database systems support one or more work processes. Your users aren't just storing data for the sake of storing data; they want to *use* it in some way. Understanding the work processes the data needs to support is crucial to understanding the semantics of the data model. Work processes are discussed in Chapter 8.

Building the Conceptual Data Model

More than simply a set of table structures, the conceptual data model defines the data usage for the entire system. This includes not only the logical data model, but also a description of how the work processes interact with the data. The conceptual data model is discussed in Chapter 9.

Preparing the Database Schema

The database schema translates the conceptual data model into physical terms. It includes a description of the tables that will be implemented in the system and also the physical architecture of the data. Physical architectures and the database schema are discussed in detail in Chapter 10.

Designing the User Interface

No matter how impressive the technical performance of your system, if the user interface is clumsy, confusing, or patronizing, the project is unlikely to be successful. To most users, after all, the interface *is* the system. User interface design is discussed in Part 3.

A Note on Design Methodologies and Standards

I'm not a great fan of checklists and step-by-step procedures for the design of computer systems. It's been my experience that they can actually get in the way of good design, as the analyst can easily become more involved in ticking the boxes than in understanding the user's requirements.

In large systems, however, with multiple analysts and several teams of programmers, it's obviously necessary to establish some common procedures for managing the process. Several methodologies are around, and most have automated tools to support them. I'm not going to make any recommendations. In the first place, this tends to be a religious issue; in the second, as with variable naming, the *existence* of a methodology is usually more important than the methodology chosen.

I do understand, however, that preparing design documents can be daunting, at least the first few times you do it. Chapter 11 contains a general discussion of the process, and if you would like a little more tangible support you can use the set of analysis checklists included in the Appendix and on the CD accompanying this book.

7

Defining the System Parameters

"A system is designed to do *something,* not *everything.*" — Robert Hall, Research Engineer, North American Aviation

The story goes that Bob Hall made this remark to a vice president who was trying to expand the scope of his project for the umpteenth time, and it almost cost Mr. Hall his job. (In system design, as in all else, it pays to know your audience.) Nevertheless, it remains one of the truest remarks I've ever heard about the system design process. If the project is going to be successful, you must be able to describe what you're trying to accomplish and draw reasonable boundaries around the project. If you can't say with reasonable certainty, "We're going to do this; we're *not* going to do that," I can promise you that what you *are* going to do is experience big trouble.

There are three steps to this process of definition:

- Determining the goal, not just of the system but of the project as a whole.

- Establishing the system's design criteria, which will be used to judge any trade-offs during design and implementation and also to evaluate the system's success or failure.

- Defining the system scope—what you will and will not attempt to do.

Determining the System Goals

Defining (or discovering) the goal and scope of a system ought to be a simple process. Sometimes, if you're really lucky, it is. Sometimes it's made part of your initial brief. More often, defining a system's scope is a complicated process combining formal analysis techniques, design trade-offs, and more than a little diplomacy.

The goal of a development project is usually the most important factor in determining both the system's scope and the design criteria by which it will be evaluated. The goal is, after all, the *reason* the system is being implemented at all. Obviously, you won't be able to make informed decisions regarding any other aspect of the project until you have a clear understanding of what you're setting out to achieve.

Do not confuse "goal" and "brief." Most projects start with a description of the system to be developed and a budget. Your brief is to "automate the current order-taking system," and you have one year and half a million dollars to do it. But "automating the current order-taking system" is a brief, not a goal. The goal is the reason, or more likely the set of reasons, the project is being undertaken.

In fact, to talk about determining the system's "goal" at all is somewhat misleading. The vast majority of systems have many goals, both tangible and intangible, and discovering them might require some detective work. *Why* is the order-taking system being automated? Is it to speed up the process? Improve accuracy? Reduce costs? Position the company in the minds of the users? Make the manager look good? The system goals probably include all these reasons and half a dozen others.

Now, I'm not suggesting that you start invading people's privacy or requesting confidential company information, and some of these goals come under the general heading of "none of your business." You don't need to know that the department head is jumping on the Internet bandwagon out of fear. You do need to know that to pay for itself the system needs to reduce the average time to process an order from 10 minutes to 2 minutes.

You might also need to understand those vague phrases sales and marketing people use, like "product positioning" and "managing user expectations." Fortunately, this doesn't require going back to school; you can simply ask your client. Everybody means something a little different by these expressions, so you'll have to ask anyway.

The problem with intangible goals like these is that they're often difficult to translate into measurable design criteria. Sometimes a little judicious digging can turn an intangible goal into a tangible one. For example, the goal "assist in managing user expectations" usually indicates a customer service problem, which will either translate easily into measurable criteria or need to be discarded.

If your client has a problem meeting delivery schedules *and* is reasonably confident that this is due to sales people agreeing to impossible delivery dates in order to make a sale, then the order-taking system has a direct bearing on the goal of managing user expectations. You could, for example, impose constraints on the length of time between the date the order is taken and the date delivery is promised. If, however, the problems are due to quality control in the

manufacturing process, an order-taking system can do nothing to help and it's incumbent on you to point this out to your client. That doesn't mean the project isn't worth undertaking; however, everyone involved needs to understand that the order-taking system can't *directly* impact the stated goal.

Not all intangible goals succumb so easily to translation, of course. "Positioning" is one of those. You might be asked to establish a Web site to "position the company on the cutting edge of technology." Most of these types of goals either don't actually mean anything or the fact of a system's existence will prove sufficient to meet them. It's easy enough to determine if this is the case; just ask the client how you'll know whether you've achieved the goal. Chances are good that if the other goals regarding performance and functionality are met, the intangible goal will be met as well.

Another kind of statement that needs to be examined carefully is a goal that is stated in general terms like "improve" and "reduce." "Increase efficiency" and "improve productivity" are very common, and very vague, goals. How are you going to know if you've achieved them? A client of mine once shared a wonderful (and almost certainly apocryphal) story about the importance of measurability in job requirements. (Design criteria and job requirements are, after all, similar in purpose.) The story goes that as a young salesman he was told that part of his job was to "promote our goods and services." So he opened the office door and yelled, "Everybody should buy our stuff because it's really neat." This is not, I'm sure, what his manager had in mind.

During the initial analysis, unless you value your sense of humor over your bank balance, you'll have to determine the degree to which some general improvement is required. Increase efficiency *by how much*? Improve productivity *from what to what*? But there's another trap to look out for here. It's all very well to say that goals should be directly measurable, and "reduce the time required to process an invoice from 10 minutes to 3 minutes" is clearly preferable to "increase efficiency." But the first statement assumes that you know how long an invoice currently takes to process, and finding that out can be an expensive exercise.

The cost of research can often exceed the risk of making a mistake. In our invoicing example, it's probably not necessary to send in a team of analysts with stopwatches to determine precisely how long it takes to process an invoice, although I've seen it done. Some years ago, I was involved in a project where a government department spent upwards of $50,000 determining whether the purchase of a piece of off-the-shelf graphing software with a recommended retail price of $2,500 was justified.

The solution to translating these general requirements into tangible design criteria lies in a sense of scale and the concept of "good enough." If you're betting the company or someone's career on the implementation of a new computer system,

you'd better be very, very sure of what you're doing. If you're building a little system that's not going to have a major effect on the company's bottom line, you can afford to be more casual. To return to our example, it's probably "good enough" to know that the average person can currently process about 25 invoices a day. There's no need to perform a detailed study because the department manager can almost certainly tell you this; it's why you were called in. I'm sure overextensive research is how the Department of Defense winds up ordering $400 screwdrivers.

Why a certain improvement needs to be made is always worth asking as well. There might be, for example, a processing backlog, and the manager is faced with either speeding up the process or hiring additional staff. If you know about the backlog and the projected increases in sales (as in our invoicing example), you can determine how much of an improvement is actually required.

The figure you arrive at might be different from the one your client initially gives you. Obviously, if your client wants to reduce the processing time by half, you should do everything you can to achieve that. But if you know the system actually only *needs* to achieve a 25 percent reduction, you have room to negotiate if you need to make trade-offs between the flat rate of processing and ease of use or system reliability.

Your clients are not going to knowingly make unreasonable demands, mislead you, or blame you for things that aren't your fault. But part of your job is to help your clients decide what the proposed database system can and cannot do to assist them. You often overhear computer people remark that their lives would be easier if their clients knew what they wanted. Your clients *do* know what they want, they just don't know how to translate that need into a computer system. That's your job.

A variation on this theme is the client who presents you with a stack of screen layouts and sample reports that might or might not be possible to implement. This is a case of being told the solution rather than the problem. It takes a certain amount of tact to examine the reasoning behind the "system design" without implying that the individual who created it is either stupid, incompetent, or simply in the wrong line of work.

All I can suggest for these situations is that you test the waters. If the client seems resistant to your questions, try saying something along the lines of "I'll be better able to help you if I understand your business environment." If this approach isn't getting you anywhere, you're going to have to either implement the system as presented or walk away from the project (which I realize is not always possible). The best you can hope for is to review the design with which you have been presented, and if you find any fundamental flaws, discuss them in terms of "I can't do this, but I could do that or that. Which would best meet your needs?"

The process of eliciting goals described earlier is not specific to database systems. The primary way in which database systems differ from other computer systems is that they have, almost as a by-product, a body of data about the organization. This body of data, whether it's a list of subscribers or a set of invoices, might have intrinsic value to the organization above and beyond the work processes that it directly supports.

Of course, I'm *not* suggesting that every project be looked at as an opportunity to create an enterprise-wide data repository. I'm suggesting that the data that forms a part of the system be examined for its value to other areas of the organization or other processes within the same area. It might be the case that the data your system will accumulate could be easily made available to some other area, although frankly, these opportunities occur far less often than some might think.

For example, if the invoicing system maintains a list of customers and the sales department needs a mailing list for sending out newsletters, it might be appropriate to make the list available to them. If nothing else, sharing the list would save some poor clerical worker from the task of typing all those names and addresses again. This is absolutely not the same as incorporating the mailing list functionality into the invoicing system.

The only reason I suggest considering the issue at all, given that it is fraught with the dangers of megalomania, is that it might be appropriate to make *minor* changes to the data structure to accommodate other uses. We'll look at this possibility in detail in Chapter 9, but let me give you a simple example here.

Remember that when I talked about atomic values I said that an address could be, within the semantics of a given system, simply a blob that gets printed on a mailing label. I recommended that in this case you consider treating the address as a single attribute. If, however, the data might be useful to another area, but only if the attributes are separated, then it is reasonable to add that small extra overhead to the current system in order to avoid duplicating the data entry elsewhere.

Be careful, however, that the extra overhead really is small and that sharing the data really is feasible. I have seen (and to my shame, even implemented) systems that require entire categories of information to be entered that have no direct bearing on the process at hand, simply because they might be useful to someone at some point in time. This is amazingly easy to do by accident, so be sure that when you talk about "planning for future growth" you don't actually mean "adding unnecessary overhead."

Once you've established your initial set of goals, you can move to the next activities in the analysis process: establishing design criteria and project scope. Do not make the mistake, however, of assuming that goals are stable. You must always be prepared to reevaluate the system goals during later stages of the project.

For any project that lasts more than a few weeks, the business requirements are subject to change. Sales can vary wildly from projections; company mergers can mean a surplus of staff rather than a shortage; any number of external events can require reevaluation of the project's goals. Checking in with the client now and again during a long project is worthwhile to ensure that nothing has radically changed.

Even with projects of relatively short duration, you might discover during later stages of the project that some of the goals were either inappropriate or unattainable. One of the major problems with the classical waterfall model, you'll remember, is that it assumes that you can know everything you need to know when you need to know it. In reality, you'll be expanding your understanding of what the system needs to do throughout the project. New understanding will often require a reevaluation of the system goals, even if that means only reviewing them and saying, "Yep, these are all still valid."

Developing the Design Criteria

After you've gained a reasonable understanding of the tangible and intangible goals of the project, you can begin developing the design criteria. Of course, things are never quite that neatly sequential, and in practice you will have been accumulating criteria during the process of goal definition. But for the sake of discussion, let's assume that you've got a list of project goals and now you need to prepare a list of criteria by which the success or failure of the system will be judged.

Design criteria are closely related to project goals. If the project goals tell you where you're going, the design criteria tell whether you've arrived. All of the design criteria for a system should directly support one or more of the system's goals. If you find yourself with important criteria that don't seem to match up with a goal, it's almost certainly an indication that your list of goals is incomplete.

Matching up each criterion to the goal it supports is not strictly necessary, but it's a useful exercise for even experienced analysts. One of the greatest dangers with any project is that you don't know what you don't know. This is particularly the case if you're an outside consultant who might not have much (or any) experience with the activities of the organization. Mismatched goals and criteria are a good indication that you haven't yet understood everything you need to understand.

Design criteria generally take one of three forms:

- Directly measurable requirements, such as "Print an aging report in less than two hours."

- Environmental criteria, such as "Operate over the existing LAN."

- General design strategies, such as "Provide context-sensitive user assistance."

The specific categories aren't dreadfully important, but the ones I've listed are a useful indication of how well you understand the system. Most criteria should fall into the first or second category. If you only have a list of design strategies, I'd be willing to bet that you don't have a clear enough understanding of the problem you're setting out to solve.

> **NOTE** Whatever forms the criteria take, when you have met them, stop. Your project is finished. Go have a party. This injunction isn't quite as trivial as it might sound. Let me give you a common example. You're optimizing a particular piece of code. To meet the design criterion, the function must calculate a certain value in less than 10 seconds. You've got it down to 9, but you're *sure* that if you try this other approach you just thought of you'll cut that time in half. Don't. Or if you must, do it on your own time. You must not continue working after all of the design criteria have been met, or the project will never be finished.
>
> The only possible exception to this rule is with research and development (R&D) projects, but then R&D projects have different goals and hence different criteria. Rather than "complete the calculation in less than 10 minutes," the design criterion for an R&D project is more likely to be "determine the optimum method for calculating whatever." Since you can never be certain that any given solution is optimum, you can never meet the criterion; so you can explore forever or until you run out of money, whichever comes first.

It's important not to commit yourself to particular designs or architectures at the stage when you're developing design criteria. You might be certain that you're going to use Microsoft Transaction Server to support system scalability, but that's an architectural decision, not a design criterion. The design criterion is that the system must be scalable to support x users.

When in doubt, remember that a design criterion is used to determine whether a project has been successfully completed. In this case, ask yourself, "If we're using Microsoft Transaction Server, is our system finished?" Maybe, but the fact that you're using Microsoft Transaction Server isn't going to tell you that. However, the answer to "If we're scalable to x users, are we done?" is yes, provided, of course, that you've met the other design criteria as well.

Directly Measurable Criteria

I've already discussed the importance of identifying objectively measurable goals. If you've been successful in this, many of your design criteria will follow as a matter of course. If the goal is to reduce processing time by 50 percent and the current processing time is 10 minutes, then the design criteria is, obviously, "Enable processing to be completed in 5 minutes or less."

It can sometimes be difficult to distinguish measurable goals from directly measurable criteria. I don't know that the issue is terribly important. The specification police will not arrest you for listing something as both a goal and a criterion. They might give you a warning, however, if you fail to support a measurable goal with one or more design criteria.

Be careful not to micromanage your design criteria. It might be the case that for a specific process to be completed in 1 minute, a given query must execute in less than 10 seconds. But that's really an implementation issue, and you don't yet know enough about the project to make implementation decisions.

Environmental Criteria

The majority of environmental constraints represent the existing operating environment and any legacy systems with which you must interact. It's relatively rare to have a clean slate on which to specify a system. In most cases, your clients will already have an existing hardware and software environment, and the new system will be expected to operate within it.

Another main source of environmental criteria is specific to database systems: the volume of data to be handled. One of my early disgraces as an independent consultant was preparing a quote for a sales-tracking system for a regional branch of a computer hardware wholesaler. After discussing their requirements, I presented them with a quote for a little system to be written in Microsoft Access 2.0, only to be told that they wanted to track sales for the entire company, with some 500 regional branches and tens of millions of dollars in sales—obviously far beyond Access's capabilities. I had assumed they only needed to track that branch's sales. Oops. (Needless to say, I didn't get the job.)

In looking at data volume, you need to examine two issues. One is the sheer volume of data, and the other is its growth pattern. A library might have millions of volumes but add only a few records a day. An ordering system might add hundreds of records daily but archive the records after the sales are complete, so the absolute number of records is never more than a few thousand. Obviously, these two patterns require different design strategies.

Supporting data volume is one situation for which you're justified in overdesigning the system. As a general rule, I'd say plan for at *least* 10 percent more capacity than the largest figure provided by your client. For smaller systems, I'd increase that to between 20 percent and 25 percent extra capacity. Data volume is less an issue with larger volumes of data. A well-designed client/server system can support 100,000 records as easily as it can support 10,000. A LAN-based Access system originally designed to support a few thousand records will probably not scale well to a few million, no matter how well it is designed.

The other primary source of environmental criteria is the number of users the system needs to support. Most systems have more than one category of user,

and you'll need to define the requirements for each. For example, the order-processing system will have users entering orders, obviously. It will probably have a second group of users inquiring about the status of orders and perhaps updating the data, and a third group producing reports from the entire database. Each of these groups needs different support from the system, so each should be specified in separate design criteria.

You must also distinguish between users who are connected to the system and those who are actually using the system. The Jet database engine, for example, has a limit of 255 users connected to the database at any one time. This means that 255 people can have the database open simultaneously. It *doesn't* mean that 255 people can update the database simultaneously.

General Design Strategies

Some project goals don't translate easily to simple numeric measurements. A goal such as "improve data entry accuracy," for example, is extremely difficult to quantify. This is a situation in which the cost of determining how many errors are made will probably exceed the benefit of having a number by which to measure your success.

You shouldn't ignore these kinds of goals, but you can state them in terms of design strategies rather than measurable criteria. In this case, the design criterion might be "improve data entry accuracy by allowing users to select from lists wherever feasible" or "reduce the incidence of credit exceptions by implementing appropriate credit checks prior to accepting the invoice."

Just as with the measurable design criteria, you should not be too specific here. You're not designing the system; you're only establishing criteria by which its success will be judged. The examples above talk about doing things "wherever feasible" and performing "appropriate credit checks"; the specifics are deferred to later stages in design when the system requirements are better understood.

But you should also avoid "motherhood" statements. "The system must be user-friendly" sounds admirable—after all, nobody wants to work with a user-*antagonistic* system. But it's not useful. Determining whether a system conforms with the criterion "The system will comply with the *Windows Interface Guidelines for Software Design*" is possible. Whether a system is user-friendly, however, is too often a matter of debate. You want your design criteria to reduce contention, not increase it.

Determining the System Scope

Once you know why you are implementing a system, you have a basis for deciding what functionality reasonably falls within the scope of the system and what does not. As with design criteria, the functions within a system's scope should directly support a specified goal.

Say, for example, that improving the efficiency of the sales order process is a project goal. The printing of invoices directly supports that goal and clearly falls within the scope of the proposed system. The production of a product catalog, on the other hand, does not, and therefore lies outside the scope of the system. This remains the case even when the catalog is produced by the same people and shares a certain amount of data with the order-taking system.

Sometimes in these situations it makes sense to redefine the goals of the system. In the preceding example, the system might become a "Sales Support" system rather than an "Order Taking" system, and "Produce Product Catalogs" would become one of the project's goals. Redefining goals can be a useful mechanism for checking how complete your definition of goals has been.

But this can also be a dangerous process. You don't want to be using the desired scope of the system to define the goals. That's very much a case of putting the cart before the horse. I know from experience how tempting it can be to expand a system's scope to include easy or interesting functions. I also know from experience how embarrassing it is when you don't have a good answer for a user who asks, "Why would I want to do that?"

Two situations exist in which it's sensible to break the rule that if a given function doesn't directly support a goal, it's outside the scope of the system. The first situation is when the function has clear value to the users and that value clearly outweighs the cost of implementation. The product catalog goal described above might be a good example of this.

In this instance, while you might expand the goals of the system, it's probably safer to include these functions under the general scope category "Added Value Functionality." This makes it clear that the functionality is not strictly necessary and it can easily be dropped from the system at a later date if you discover that its implementation is going to cost more than expected, or if you simply run out of time and money.

The second situation in which you might need to include functionality that doesn't directly support a system goal is when the client insists on including it. It might seem perfectly obvious to you that producing an employee phone list has nothing whatsoever to do with processing orders, but if the client wants it, they want it. You can point out that the functionality doesn't support any of the specified goals, but your job is to satisfy your client's requirements, not define them.

Cost-Benefit Analysis

You might find it worthwhile to perform a cost-benefit analysis on the scoped functionality. This is particularly true if the proposed system has several components. The relative cost-benefit ratios of the various components will help you determine the order in which the components should be implemented.

If you're considering expanding the scope to include "Added Value" function-ality, a cost-benefit analysis can serve as a reality check on the system.

All else being equal, components with the highest benefit per cost should be implemented first. This strategy provides the best "bang for the buck" and allows the system to start paying for itself as early as possible. This is particularly true for projects that will take considerable time to complete. If you can deliver the core functionality quickly, you have a sound basis for evaluating future development, and you reduce the risk of changes in the business environment making the system unusable later.

If the system can start paying for itself relatively early in the development process, you might also find it possible to fund some of those "fun and interesting but not strictly necessary" functions that you had to weed out while defining the system's scope. Of course, the reverse occasionally happens as well. Clients might find that the initial functionality adequately meets their goals and delay the devel-opment of future components indefinitely.

Performing a formal cost-benefit analysis is, of course, subject to the rule about the cost of making a mistake outweighing the cost of researching the answer. Cost-benefit analyses aren't difficult, but they can be time-consuming, and it's obviously not sensible to spend two days analyzing a system that will take one day to write. In many situations, an informal analysis (otherwise known as gut feel) is more than sufficient.

There are many ways of performing cost-benefit analyses, although the principle is simple. The estimated benefit of a function divided by the estimated cost of the function will give you a numeric value. The higher this value, the higher the relative value of the component when compared to other components.

NOTE	We're talking, always, about *estimated* costs and *estimated* benefits. The only time you'll know for certain how much a function costs is after it's been implemented, and you won't know for certain how much benefit has been gained until after the system has been in use for some time.

Where cost-benefit analysis gets tricky is in determining common units of measurement. All costs must be measured in the same units, and all benefits must be measured in the same units, although the costs and benefits units need not be the same. You can, for example, compare costs in time against value in dollars. The resulting ratio is used for comparison with other values calculated using the same units, so the result is perfectly valid.

Estimated cost can usually be measured in either hours or dollars, and it's normally straightforward to convert between these two in a business environ-ment. Because both of these terms are somewhat loaded, however, it might be

better to express costs in some derived value, like "units of work." This avoids the possibility of confusing a cost-benefit analysis with either a price quotation or an implementation schedule.

Assigning common units of measurement to benefits can be more problematic. You might estimate, for example, that automating a given work process will increase efficiency by 20 percent and reduce errors by 50 percent. The 20 percent improvement in efficiency can be translated into hours saved, and from there, into dollars if necessary. But it might not be so easy to assign a value to the improved accuracy. It might be possible to estimate the cost (in either time or dollars) of finding and fixing mistakes. But that doesn't allow for other intangible, but very real, benefits, such as the good will gained by getting a customer's order correct.

In these situations, you can use multiple benefit estimates. For example, you might estimate benefits in terms of "Dollars Saved," "Dollars Earned," and "Intangible Benefits." You then calculate three ratios, one for each value. This can make comparison a little complex—you and your client might find it difficult to determine whether a function with the values 3/6/2 should have higher priority than one with values of 6/2/3. In this case, you can normalize the values in some way to derive a single cost-benefit estimate.

You might decide to add the values for each benefit category together if they're all of relatively equal importance. Admittedly, you're adding apples and oranges, but at this point it's acceptable to think of them simply as fruit. Sometimes an average value seems more appropriate. I generally do both.

If, as is most often the case, the categories are not of equal importance to the organization, you can assign a relative value to each category, and multiply each category by that importance factor. For example, given the benefit categories cited above, you might decide that "Dollars Saved" is not terribly important but "Intangible Benefits" is and that "Dollars Earned" is twice as important as "Intangible Benefits." So you would assign a modifier of 1 to "Dollars Saved," 2 to "Intangible Benefits," and 4 to "Dollars Earned." The resulting figures are shown in the following table.

	Dollars Earned (mod: 4)	Dollars Saved (mod: 1)	Intangible Benefits (mod: 2)	Total	Weighted Total	Average	Weighted Average
Function 1	3	6	2	11	22	3.6	7.3
Function 2	6	2	3	11	32	3.6	10.6

Just as it's often better to assign benefit category modifiers on a relative basis, it's better to assign benefit estimates in relative, rather than absolute, terms. For example, it's often difficult to assign Function X intangible benefits of 3. But it's usually possible to say that Function X is likely to have twice the intangible benefits of Function Y and that Function Y and Function Z are likely to have the same intangible benefits.

Cost-benefit analyses can be useful tools for capturing the proposed benefits of a system. They provide a simple way to compare the relative values of various components. But they are only tools, based on best-guess estimates, and you must not mistake these estimates for absolute values. Even though Function X has a benefit ratio of 12 and Function Y has a ratio of 2, it might still be appropriate (or necessary) to implement Function Y first.

The results of a cost-benefit analysis have to be reviewed in conjunction with other factors, such as system dependencies. They must also be reviewed as your understanding of the system improves. Reevaluate your estimates prior to commencing work on each component. You might find that your experience with the *actual* costs and benefits of the previous components will alter your estimates for future components.

SUMMARY

In this chapter, we've looked at the activities involved in gaining an understanding of a system at the beginning of a project. You must first determine the system's goals and then translate those goals into tangible design criteria that can be used to determine the success or failure of the project. You must also determine the system's scope—the boundaries of what will and will not be undertaken as part of the project.

These activities are a kind of step zero; they're the things you must do *before* you begin designing the system in earnest. In the next chapter, we'll examine the first step of the design process proper: the definition of the work processes the system will support.

8

Defining the Work Processes

Although many database systems are designed simply to store and retrieve some set of data, the majority are intended to assist in performing one or more activities. These activities are the *work processes* that the system will support. A work process is simply a set of one or more discrete tasks that together represent some activity meaningful to the organization. "Process a sales order" and "Find a customer's phone number" are both examples of work processes, although they are of very different complexity.

A *task* is a discrete action, a step in the performance of a work process. The sales order process, for example, might consist of the tasks "Record sales order," "Check customer credit," "Check stock availability," and "Ship order." The process of finding a customer's phone number, however, probably consists of only the single task "Find customer record."

Distinguishing between a task and an activity can sometimes be difficult; the distinction is fairly arbitrary. Drawing the distinction is rather like determining what represents a scalar value in a data model, in which a single attribute in one model might be decomposed into multiple attributes in another. An activity that is treated as a task in one system might be treated as a process in another and then decomposed into separate tasks at a lower level of detail. As it is with the data modeling process, the decision must be based on the semantics of the problem space.

Some systems don't lend themselves to work process analysis. Ad hoc reporting tools, for example, don't support a specific process as much as they support certain *kinds* of activities. In these instances, it's more appropriate to build user scenarios. These are discussed at the end of this chapter.

Determining Current Work Processes

Defining the system scope is actually the first step in analyzing business processes, since the definition will tell you the processes you need to analyze. The order in which you examine the various processes within the system's scope is usually unimportant. Even if you're planning on implementing some system components prior to others (incremental development), you should perform at least a cursory analysis of all the work processes the system is going to support before you begin implementation. Doing this allows you to find any dependencies between processes that might affect the order in which components must be implemented.

Speaking to Users

Having identified the work processes that are within the scope of the system, your next task is to capture everything that is currently done in order to carry them out. You needn't worry overmuch at this point about what represents a task and what is, perhaps, a separate work process that requires further analysis. Just find someone who can tell you, "Well, we get this document from the sales person, and first we just look through it to see if they've completed it correctly; if they have, well, then we pull the customer file, and…" Ask lots of questions, and write it all down. You should also get copies of any forms or reports that are either used as input during the process or produced during it. Your goal is to understand what happens; you're not yet analyzing the process.

By the way, many people refer to this phase of the analysis as "user interviews." I prefer "discussions" or some other neutral term. It's easy to underestimate how intimidating computers can be, even to people who currently use them. Lots of people still worry that they're going to be replaced by a computer, and "user interview" can easily be mistaken to mean, "We're going to decide who gets the sack." This is particularly true in large organizations in which it's not usually possible to speak to everyone, and many people might be unsure exactly who you are or what you're supposed to be doing.

Whenever possible (and it isn't always), you should try speak to the individuals who actually perform the process rather than to a manager or supervisor. My experience has been that managers tend to have a rather ideal view of the work processes under their jurisdiction. The person who performs an activity on a daily basis is in the best position to tell you the problems and interruptions he or she faces. Of course, you should speak to supervisors as well, since they often have the best understanding of *why* specific tasks are performed and the ramifications of not performing them or performing them incorrectly.

During your discussions, be sure to look for any possible exceptions to the process. If the user says, "We check the order for completeness," for example,

be sure that you know what happens if it *isn't* complete. Chances are that they just bounce it, but you need to know whether they try to find the information themselves; perhaps your system can make the process easier. In fact, for every activity that a user performs, you should ask what can go wrong and what happens when it does.

Since we're specifically interested in database systems here, you should also pay particular attention to how data is getting used during the process. What bits of information are being used? Where do they come from? What form do they take? What happens if they're not present or not in the correct form? The answers will form raw material for the conceptual data model we'll discuss in the next chapter.

Many work processes consist of tasks that are performed by different individuals. Obviously, you should speak to all the people involved whenever that's possible. This recommendation also applies to people whose tasks are ostensibly outside the scope of the system. Take, for example, the sales order process described earlier. The "Ship order" task might in fact be "Send order to the Shipping department," and what happens to it in the Shipping department might be outside the scope of your system. It's still a good idea to talk to people from Shipping to confirm that they're getting all the information they need and getting it in a form that's useful to them.

Similarly, if a report gets printed at any point in the process, you should find the person who receives the report and learn what he or she does with it. You'll be amazed at how many pieces of paper on average get passed around an organization for no apparent reason. (Then again, maybe you won't.) Or, as is more often the case, there *is* a reason for the report but it contains the wrong information, or it contains the right information but in the wrong format, so it's being neatly filed somewhere and is not being put to the use for which it was designed.

Identifying Tasks

After you've talked to the people who are currently performing the work your system is going to support, you should have a reasonable understanding of the activities involved. Your next step is to organize this information into a set of tasks. The key is identifying the business rules that apply to the process.

At the beginning of the chapter, I defined the term "task" as a discrete action. It's now possible to define more precisely what "discrete" means in this context. It means two things: that the action has an identifiable beginning and ending, and that all the pertinent business rules are valid before the task has begun and after it is completed. The rules might be temporarily broken, however, while performing the task.

A *business rule* is nothing more than a constraint that originates in the problem domain, as opposed to constraints that derive from, for example, a data type. Thus "No orders can have a ship date of April 36" is not a business rule, since it's dependent on the domain of dates. (And it's a pretty silly rule, anyway.) But "No orders can have a ship date prior to the order date" is dependent on the problem domain; it is a function of the way the organization does business. Thus it is, or at least could be, a valid business rule. The term "business rule" is used, by the way, even when the organization isn't technically a business. The database you're building to track your collection of antique thimbles is still subject to business rules.

The vast majority of business rules relate to the way data is handled. "Customer zip code cannot be empty" and "Invoice date must be on or after ship date" are examples of data-related business rules. Other rules, such as "Sales manager authorization is required when orders will cause customers to exceed their credit limit," do not directly constrain a data value, although they might be triggered by a data value as this one is.

Don't worry; finding the business rules that pertain to a work process isn't as difficult as it might sound. This is what all those "How can this go wrong, and what happens if something does?" questions were about. You don't need to worry too much at this point about what the details of the rules are. The details are part of building the conceptual data model, which you'll do later. All you need to do here is group the various activities you've identified in such a way that you're reasonably confident the business rules *can* be valid on either side of the action.

Let's look at an example. Say your list of actions for processing a sales order includes the following tasks:

1. Check sales order for completeness.

2. Retrieve customer file if existing customer.

3. Record shipping information.

4. Enter order details.

5. Assign customer number for new customer.

6. Check item availability.

7. Check customer credit limit.

8. Pick order.

9. Pack items.

10. Prepare shipping documents.

The first thing to notice about the list is that things seem to be done in a somewhat random order. That's OK. You're only trying to understand how things are currently done. Cleaning up the process happens later. Some of the items also seem to contain a different level of detail. We'll look at that in a minute. For now, let's just identify the tasks.

Item 1, "Check sales order for completeness," has a discrete beginning and ending. The action takes place when a new order is received, and it is completed when the entire document has been checked. We can assume that all the business rules are valid at the beginning of a process, so there's no problem there. If the initial sales order document doesn't comply with the business rules, it will be rejected. So we know that if the process continues to the next step, the rules will be valid. So item 1 qualifies as a task.

The only business rule that pertains to item 2, "Retrieve customer file," is that the individual retrieving the file must have access to it. We'll assume that anyone performing this process has access to the files, so that task criterion doesn't apply. The action begins when the sales order has been checked, but since the file is used during later actions, it doesn't have a discrete end point. So it's not a task; it's one of the steps within a task.

In fact, the customer file is used in item 3 ("Record shipping information") and item 5 ("Assign customer number"), which is the first clue that these items belong to the same task. Indeed, it's clear that items 2 through 5 can be grouped together into a single task, called perhaps "Record order." In this case, item 4, "Enter order details," is clearly a part of recording the order. Don't be surprised, however, to find that some tasks are performed simultaneously. In a manual system, it's easy for someone to be filling out two forms at the same time. The fact that the forms logically belong to separate tasks doesn't matter.

We now have a new task consisting of four discrete steps. It begins when the original document has been checked for completeness, and it ends when the entire order has been recorded. But there's a problem. Your client doesn't allow customers to place orders that exceed their credit limit, but the credit limit isn't checked until item 7, "Check customer credit limit," *after* the user has checked that the ordered items are available. Until the order is confirmed to be within the customer's credit limit, however, you can't be certain that the business rules are valid on either side of the task. So item 7 is part of the "Record order" task.

Item 6, "Check item availability," isn't logically part of recording the order, however. In fact, item 6 represents a discrete task that begins once the "Record order" task has been completed and ends upon confirmation that there is sufficient stock to ship. So item 6 is a task on its own. Don't say I didn't warn you.

In situations like this, be sure to find out *why* the tasks appear to be done out of order. It's most often simply a matter of convenience, but occasionally these

inconsistencies result from some operational constraints that can have an impact on your system processes.

In this instance, if the item availability is checked first simply because that's logistically an easier check to make, you can rearrange the activities. But you might discover some interaction between the order entry process and the production process that requires stock levels to be checked immediately, and this interaction would have to be accommodated in your system.

Notice that it's not necessary to specify in detail the business rules that apply to a task. You do need to be reasonably sure that the rules, whatever they might be, will be valid. In this case, we can assume the order will be rejected if it doesn't comply with all the relevant rules, so we needn't examine them in greater detail at this point.

If we were to discover later that an order shouldn't be accepted unless there is sufficient stock to fill it, the "Check item availability" task would become a step in the "Record order" task. As we'll see in the next section, moving activities around between tasks and between logical levels is a fairly simple process. The crucial issue here is to identify the activities.

Analyzing the next three items on the list—8, 9, and 10—depends on the scope of the system. If shipping of products is part of the system to be developed, these items need to be looked at carefully. If, as is more likely the case, the scope of the system ends when the completed order is passed to the Shipping department, these items can simply be lumped under a single task, "Submit order."

We happen to know, of course, that several things will occur after this point, and there's no reason to throw that information away. From inspection, it's clear that each of these remaining items are tasks themselves. In fact, the final item on the list, "Prepare shipping documents," might even be an entire work process. But all of those tasks lie outside the scope of the project, so we'll list them as steps to preserve what we know but we won't otherwise concern ourselves with them. Our revised task list is shown below:

Task 1: Check sales order for completeness

Task 2: Record order

    Step 1: Retrieve customer file

    Step 2: Record shipping information

    Step 3: Enter order details

    Step 4: Assign customer number

    Step 5: Check customer credit limit

Task 3: Check item availability

Task 4: Submit order to Shipping department

    Step 1: Pick order

    Step 2: Pack items

    Step 3: Prepare shipping documents

During the process of organizing activities into tasks and processes, you will almost certainly discover things that you don't understand as well as you thought, in which case you should go back to the users for clarification. In any case, you should review the processes with the users. Often, seeing the process written down will prompt them to provide additional information—steps they've missed or exceptions that you forgot to ask about.

Analyzing Work Processes

Now that you have a clear idea of how things are currently done, it's appropriate to examine the work processes for possible improvements. As I said earlier, most organizations have a great deal of inertia. This applies equally well to processes as to working with documents. The deployment of a new computer system provides an excellent opportunity to clean up some of the dead wood.

There's an old efficiency rule that says you should never handle a piece of paper more than once. Like many rules, this one isn't always practical, but it's not unusual to discover that a work process can be simplified by reordering the tasks so that bits of work aren't traded back and forth between individuals or processes. For some reason, this sort of "I do A and give it to you, then you do B and give it back to me, then I do C" process is difficult to see when you're involved in the actual work but is immediately apparent when the activities are written down.

To do this kind of analysis, you must be very clear about the task dependencies. Within any given process, some tasks are dependent on others and must be completed in a specific order. You couldn't, for example, transmit the order to Shipping before you record it. The order of other tasks can be reasonably independent. It doesn't matter greatly, for example, if you assign the customer number before or after recording the shipping details.

It's particularly important to look at data dependencies. Some tasks are responsible for creating information, such as customer numbers, that is used by other tasks. One client of mine, for example, used a sales order process similar to the one outlined in the previous section, except that the Accounting department established the customer number and initial credit limit rather than the Sales department, which was responsible for order processing.

The client's initial work process looked like this:

Task 1: Check sales order for completeness

Task 2: Record order

    Step 1: Retrieve customer file

    Step 2: Record shipping information

    Step 3: Enter order details

Task 3: Perform customer credit check

    Step 1: Check customer references

    Step 2: Check customer credit limit

    Step 3: Assign customer number

Task 4: Complete order

    Step 1: Check item availability

    Step 2: Submit order to Shipping department

Task 3 was performed by the Accounting department, which returned the order to the Sales department only if the results of the credit check were acceptable. The problem with this, of course, was that the initial data entry had already been performed. Not only did this mean the work was wasted if the customer wasn't approved, it also meant extra work, since the dead orders had to be periodically removed. It also involved the data entry personnel in arguments between the Accounting department and the sales people, who wanted their orders filled (and their commissions paid). Changing the order of the tasks so that the credit check was performed *before* the order was given to the data entry people eliminated the inefficiency and hassle.

In addition to confirming the dependencies between tasks, you should check for tasks that no longer need to be performed. These are rarely obvious, but sometimes if you trace the data through the process you find items that are being created for use in another task or process that no longer needs them. It is less likely that whole tasks, or even steps within tasks, are unnecessary. Most people are pretty smart about avoiding busy work, but the situation can be masked by the interaction between processes. The production of unnecessary reports is the most common example of this.

This is not, of course, a justification for making wholesale changes to your client's business practices. Nor would I recommend telling your great aunt Gertrude that she should change the way she organizes the knitting patterns she's asked you to computerize. And, in fact, it is rare to find major inefficiencies in work processes. But your job is to help your clients do their job better where you can, and reviewing the work processes is a part of that.

Documenting Work Processes

As with all other areas of the design process, the amount of time you spend analyzing the work processes and the formality of your documentation should be in proportion to the complexity of the system. A simple system for tracking names and phone numbers might require nothing more than an hour's conversation and some quick notes for your own use.

Unless you're the client as well as the designer, however, I'd recommend at least two meetings for even the simplest projects. The purpose of the second meeting is to review your understanding of the client's needs and confirm that what you've understood and plan to do is, in fact, correct.

More complex projects might require weeks of discussion with dozens of people and correspondingly complex and formal documentation. A structured list of tasks and steps like those used in this chapter might still be sufficient to document simple processes. For more complex processes, I prefer to use a picture.

Although the Entity Relationship (E/R) diagrams used to document data relationships are reasonably standardized across the industry, there is less consistency in work process diagrams. The diagramming methodologies in use tend to be closely related to specific analysis techniques. If you know one of these methodologies and are comfortable with it, there's no reason to change. The purpose here is to understand and convey information. Data flow diagrams and process quality diagrams are all useful tools. Specific diagramming techniques have always seemed to me a rather silly thing to get religious about, although people certainly do often enough.

In the absence of a formal technique, you can easily derive your own. You need five symbols, representing the task, the document, the data item, the decision point, and events such as the start-point and end-point of a task. The symbols I use in my own work are shown in Figure 8-1.

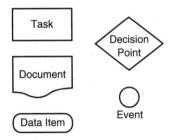

Figure 8-1. *The work process symbols.*

If there are relatively few steps required to complete a task, I list them within the Task box. If there are too many steps for this to be convenient, I expand

each task as a separate diagram and use the Task box to represent each step. Sometimes, for clarity, I will use shading or a bold outline to indicate that a task is done by an external group, such as when the Accounting department performs the credit check for new customers.

The data item symbol can represent either a single attribute, such as a customer number, or an entire entity, such as the customer as a whole. When the item is actually created by the task, you can use either shading or a bold outline to indicate this. Some analysts also like to indicate when a data item is "consumed" by a task, that is, when the item is used by the task but never shared with any other tasks later in the process. Frankly, I have rarely found this to be useful information and prefer to keep my diagrams uncluttered.

Having determined the symbols you will use (and I strongly suggest you choose symbols that are easy to draw rather than those that have any intrinsic meaning), you then need a way of organizing them. I use an arrow to indicate dependency and a branching line to indicate that tasks can be performed in any order. An open circle on a line indicates that the task is optional, just as it does in an E/R diagram. These connections are shown in Figure 8-2.

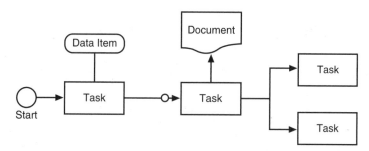

Figure 8-2. *The work process connections.*

If you find that your work processes are too complex to capture using this simple technique, I suggest you look into one of the more developed methodologies described in any good textbook on systems design and analysis. Several are listed in the bibliography.

User Scenarios

An alternative to formal work process analysis is the identification of *user scenarios*. A user scenario consists of two components: a set of one or more *user profiles*, which identify the various types of users of the proposed system, and *usage scenarios* for each user profile, which are narrative descriptions of the way the user is expected to interact with the proposed system—the activities he or she is expected to perform.

Although user scenarios can be used to capture the same information as a work process analysis, user scenarios tend to focus more on the ways users interact with the proposed system rather than on the specific steps of a transaction. Because of this focus on user interaction, it can sometimes be difficult to prepare a user scenario that doesn't anticipate the user interface of the system.

The intention, however, is to focus on users' goals and expectations, and as such, the user scenario is particularly useful for systems that must support a variety of ad hoc activities. It allows the analyst to focus on the *kinds* of tasks users need to perform without getting bogged down in the mechanics of processes that have not yet been defined.

For example, even the rather simple scenario "Sales representatives will use the system to track the status of their customers' orders through each of the phases of the process, from initial entry through shipping, invoicing, and eventual payment" adequately explains how this user group will interact with the system. But it does so without forcing any decisions to be made regarding the detailed functionality of the user interface.

The development of user scenarios and work process analyses are not, of course, mutually exclusive. Work process analyses are a useful tool for thinking about the processes themselves, while user scenarios allow the designer to focus on how each type of user will interact with the system. For most systems, these are equally important issues. When the project is large enough to warrant the effort, it is certainly worthwhile to perform both types of analysis, particularly since user scenarios can generally be based on the information gained during the work process analysis without additional interviewing or analysis.

SUMMARY

In this chapter, we've looked at how to gain an understanding of the activities a proposed system is intended to support. This can be done by performing work process analysis of various degrees of formality, by the creation of user scenarios, or by a combination of both. In Chapter 9, we'll look at the design of the conceptual data model: the logical description of how data will be created, structured, and utilized by the system.

9

The Conceptual Data Model

At this point in the design process, you should have a clear understanding of what you're setting out to achieve. You've defined the scope, compiled a set of design criteria, and analyzed the work processes. Now it's time to start building the data model.

Remember that a conceptual data model contains a description of the entities, their attributes, and the relationships between them. It isn't a database schema, which describes the physical layout of the tables. You don't yet know enough to create this. You need to understand the user interface and the architecture that you'll use to implement the system before you can create the schema.

Identifying the Data Objects

In the earlier phases of the analysis, you will have gathered or created a set of source documents. These include both the documents provided by the client—sample input forms, reports, and so forth—and the work process documentation you prepared. The first step in creating the data model is to review these sources and make a list of all the bits of data the system needs to deal with.

Start with a work process. It doesn't really matter which one, but I usually choose one of the central ones for the project, since the core processes usually involve the majority of the entities. Most work processes are triggered by some piece of paper, like when a salesperson hands the order entry clerk a sales order. Sometimes they're triggered by some other kind of an event, in which case one of the first tasks is usually filling out a form. Continuing our order-processing example from Chapter 8, a sample Sales Order form might look like the one shown in Figure 9-1.

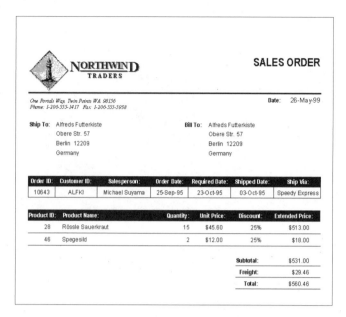

Figure 9-1. *Most work processes are triggered by a piece of paper such as this sales order.*

Find a sample of this first chunk of data, and write down all the bits of information it contains. Don't worry about classifying these bits as entities or attributes yet, just write them down. Do make a note of any repeating groups, and you'll also want to include any data items that your work process analysis has identified as missing. Your initial list of data items might look like the one in Figure 9-2.

Figure 9-2. *The initial list of the Sales Order form's data items.*

Now that you've compiled the list, you can start to extract the entities, attributes, and relationships. For each item on the list, you identify whether the item is an object or some fact about an object. Objects become entities, and the facts become attributes of the entity. The results of this analysis will probably look something like Figure 9-3.

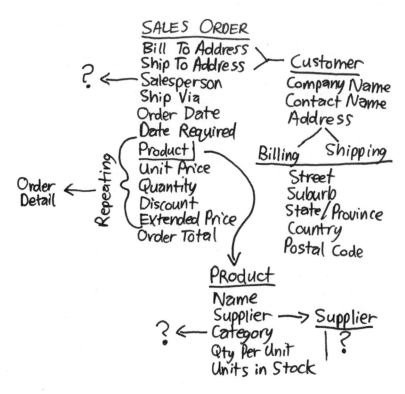

Figure 9-3. *The initial definition of the entities and attributes on the Sales Order form.*

As you can see, the Bill To and Ship To items have been identified as facts belonging to the added Customer entity. It's not, however, immediately apparent whether the two addresses belong only in the Customer entity, only in the Sales Order entity, or in both. The principle at work is the same as that for including the Unit Price in an Order Detail item. Just as the current selling price for a product is logically different from the price at which a specific product was sold, the current billing and shipping addresses for a client are logically different from the addresses to which *this* invoice and order were sent.

Whether the shipping and billing addresses are also attributes of the Customer entity is something of a judgment call, based on the nature of the system and

its users. Including these attributes in the Customer entity allows defaults to be set during the order entry process, which reduces the time required to enter the order and the opportunities for making data entry mistakes. It does, however, add the overhead of maintaining these values in the Customer entity. If the organization's customers typically have many shipping addresses (retail chains, for example), this overhead might be onerous, and a better solution is simply to enter the shipping address as part of the order entry process.

Sometimes it makes sense to walk a middle ground. You can add multiple shipping address attributes to the Customer entity, for example, but not require that users fill them out. If there is a single address, the system can use that as a default. If there are multiple addresses, the system could present users with a list and allow them to choose. Or you might implement some conditional processing that uses the most recent address entered as a default but allows users to choose another from the list as required.

You might also consider having the Customer entity updated by the order entry process. If there is no address, or if a user enters a new address, the system could ask whether it should be added to the customer record. These are user interface issues, not really data model issues, but the two are so closely tied that it's impossible to separate them entirely.

The Salesperson data item also seems to indicate that an Employee entity exists somewhere, but we don't yet know what that needs to look like, hence the question mark. Chances are that other documents or processes will use this entity. If so, we can add the required attributes. If not, you might decide to leave Salesperson as an attribute of a Sales Order entity. Remember, these decisions must always be based on the semantics of the system. There's absolutely no value to be gained from creating an Employee input screen with managers, departments, and phone extensions if the data is only going to be used to list a name on a Sales Order.

The Product item has been identified as an entity, and the group of items identified as repeating in the first diagram (Product, Unit Price, Quantity, and Discount) is identified as an Order Details entity. An initial set of attributes has been identified for the Product entity, presumably from another source document, and from this list the Supplier and (Product) Category entities have been identified, although again no details are yet available.

Because we're defining the entities on a conceptual level, we don't care at this point whether attributes such as the Extended Price of an Order Detail entity or the Units In Stock of a Product entity are stored as values or calculated when required. We don't yet know whether they can in fact be calculated. That will come later.

One interesting bit of data is the Ship Via attribute. Many order forms have a couple of check boxes for the shipping method, listing the values "Parcel Post,"

"FedEx," and "2nd Day Air," perhaps. Are these entities or attributes? It depends. (You guessed, didn't you?) How many options are there? If there are more than two, you won't be able to conveniently model this as a single attribute.

How stable are the options? The chances are that you're dealing with external service providers here. Is the organization likely to change providers or add additional ones? How responsive does the organization need to be to special delivery methods? Will they turn down a sale that requires sending the goods by Sherpa to the top of Mount Everest? If not, your model needs to be able to account for all these options.

Modeling the shipping method as a separate entity allows the items to be changed or added at any time, but at the cost of more complexity in both the data model and the user interface. The difference might be only a matter of a few keystrokes, selecting an item from a combo box rather than clicking in a check box with the mouse. But those extra keystrokes can, if you're not careful, add up to a clunky, slow interface.

If the company must allow for special delivery methods, you'll need to consider carefully how to account for this. You must walk a fine line between allowing sufficient flexibility to handle all reasonable cases and imposing unnecessary overhead on users. In this example, the best solution would probably be the addition of an optional Special Instructions attribute, but this must also be accounted for in the data model and in any system processes.

These decisions can affect the system constraints in unexpected ways. In this instance, although the organization clearly needs to know how to send the goods to the customer, it's no longer simply a question of requiring that a shipping method be specified. The system must specify that the Shipping Method and Special Instructions attributes cannot *both* be empty, a slightly more complex rule that must be implemented at a different level in the model.

If the actual shipping of goods is within the scope of the system, treating the Shipping Method as a distinct entity might be a good idea and might in fact be required, but allowing for exceptional methods can add significant overhead to the system. How does one capture the shipping details for a shipping method one can't know about in advance? You can either create a generic shipping entity containing the attributes most methods provide, such as a docket number and pickup time, or you can specify the known methods and leave special handling as just that—an exceptional case to be dealt with outside the system.

The danger here is in overcomplicating the system and placing unnecessary overhead on users. It's far too easy to get excited about the functionality the system is capable of providing and lose track of the overhead involved. Yes, providing default values is a good thing, *provided* they can be easily maintained and the maintenance is done regularly (preferably as a by-product of some other task). Making it possible for the receptionist to handle delivery inquiries is good,

but is it worth the effort to enter shipping details for a thousand orders just so that they're available for the five customers who inquire?

These decisions only require thinking through the implications of the design decisions you make. But this is easy to overlook when you're in the first flush of thinking, "Isn't this cool? It will save us *so* much time." When you capture a piece of data anywhere in the system, consider whether it can be used elsewhere in the system, either to provide a default or as a constraint. If you're entering the shipping details *anyway,* why not make them available to the receptionist?

Conversely, whenever you use a piece of data, consider where it will be created and how it will be maintained. As a general rule, it's better to present users with a list of choices than with a text box. But there's a cost in creating and maintaining the list, and in building the maintenance interface. All of these things must be balanced when you're making decisions about the structure of your data model.

Certainly, your goal is never to require that a piece of data be entered twice. But by the same token, you don't want to force users to go somewhere out of their way to enter a piece of data just so that it can be used for the task they want to do. We'll talk about this issue a great deal in Part 3, but identifying where bits of data are created and where they're used is the crucial first step in the process.

Defining Relationships

After you've been through all your source documents, you'll have a draft description of the entities and attributes in the problem space. Two tasks remain: establishing the relationships between these entities, and reviewing each entity's attributes and constraints.

Although theoretically you could review the attributes first, I find it easiest to start with the relationships, since some of these will become additional entities and some will require that attributes be added to entities you've already identified.

If you're like me, what you have after your first pass through the source documents is a bunch of handwritten notes with arrows and scribbles and "see page 12"s that nobody else could possibly decipher. So the first step in defining relationships is to get these organized neatly. You can start by building the first draft of the Entity Relationship (E/R) diagram of your data model. (If your notes are really messy and you're worried that even *you* might not be able to read them in three weeks, you might also list the attributes you've identified for each entity.)

Start by choosing an entity, usually one of the core entities in the system, and then add the entities that have some relationship with it. You can define the

nature of the relationships (one-to-one, one-to-many, many-to-many) as you go, or you can simply draw a straight line to remind yourself that there *is* a relationship, and then come back and analyze it later. I usually analyze as I go, but you might find it easier to get all the entities down first and then review them.

The first draft of the E/R diagram for the order-processing example is shown in Figure 9-4. This is a simple example, and the diagram is quite easy to read. (Assume we've decided that Salesperson is an attribute only of the Sales Order entity and not an entity in its own right.) If you're working on a complex example, you might want to create multiple diagrams, each one describing only a subset of the data. In this case, it's a good idea to use some sort of automated support for the diagrams. Otherwise, making sure they're synchronized can get tedious.

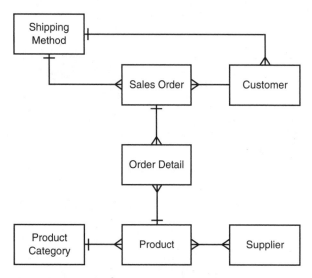

Figure 9-4. *The first draft of the Order Processing E/R diagram.*

Once you have your draft E/R diagram prepared, you can begin to analyze the relationships in more detail. For each relationship, you want to determine the following:

- The cardinality of the relationship

- The optionality of each participant

- Any attributes of the relationship

- Any constraints on the relationship

Figure 9-5 shows the Order Processing E/R diagram after review.

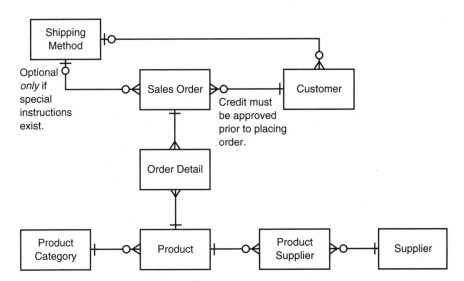

Figure 9-5. *The Order Processing E/R diagram after reviewing the relationships.*

The Cardinality of the Relationship

You might already have indicated the relationships between entities in your first draft, as I did in Figure 9-4. If not, now is the time to do so. Even if you did, it's a good idea to review your decisions now that you have a more complete picture of the whole model.

Where you discover a many-to-many relationship, you should add the junction entity to the model, with a one-to-many relationship on each side. The relationship between Supplier and Product in our model is many-to-many, and so we need to add the entity Product Supplier to resolve it. Note that the relationship between Sales Order and Product is also many-to-many, but in this case the Order Detail entity functions as the junction.

The Optionality of the Relationship

Having established the kind of the relationship between any two entities, you should now consider whether the relationship is optional for either or both participants. In our example, the relationship between Customer and Shipping Method is optional in both directions—that is, customers are not required to have a default shipping method, and shipping methods can exist without being used by a customer.

The relationship between Product Category and Product, on the other hand, is only optional in one direction. A Product Category need not have products assigned to it, but all products must be assigned to a Product Category.

The relationship between Sales Order and Shipping Method is even more complex. A shipping method can exist independently of a sales order, so the Sales Order side of the relationship is optional. The Shipping Method side of the relationship, however, is optional only if the sales order has special instructions. This is an important constraint and should be noted on the diagram.

The Attributes of the Relationship

In most situations, all that you need to record about the relationship between two entities is the fact of its existence. We need to know, for example, that a specific Customer placed a given Sales Order, and that's *all* we need to know. Sometimes, however, we need to know additional facts about the relationship—when it began or how long it lasted, for example. These facts are attributes of the relationship itself, not of either of the participants.

Where the relationship itself has attributes, it must be modeled as an entity. In the order-processing example, we might decide to designate one Supplier as having "Preferred Supplier" status. Since we already have a junction entity between Product and Supplier, the Preferred Supplier attribute can simply be added to that entity. If that were not the case, we would have needed to add an entity to represent the attributes of the relationship.

Additional Constraints on the Relationship

Finally, we want to consider whether any additional constraints pertain to the relationship. What are the minimum and maximum number of records that can exist on the many side of a one-to-many relationship? Are there any conditions that must be met before the relationship is allowed to exist? Are there any conditions under which the relationship *must* exist?

In our example, the requirement that the relationship between a Sales Order and a Shipping Method is optional only if Special Instructions have been indicated is one such constraint. The rule that customers cannot place an order until after their credit has been approved is another. Again, this rule has been indicated by an annotation on the diagram. If there are many constraints or the constraints are too complex for a simple annotation, you might need to document them elsewhere. You should, however, at least indicate on the diagram that such constraints exist.

Reviewing Entities

Now that you've begun to get a picture of the entities in the system and how they're related, it's time to start analyzing each entity in detail. For each entity, you'll want to identify the following information:

- The relationship between the entity and the problem space

- The work processes that create, modify, use, and delete the entity

- Any other entities it might interact with or depend on

- The business rules and constraints pertaining to the entity

- The attributes of the entity

The Relationship Between the Entity and the Problem Space

Identifying the relationship between the entity and the problem space is usually straightforward. "The Customer entity models the individuals and organizations who buy our products." The biggest problem here, I've found, is thinking up a sentence that isn't hopelessly tautological. "The Employees entity models the organization's employees" seems hardly worth saying.

If a relationship is modeled as an entity, things can be trickier since the entity won't map directly to the problem space. "A supplier can provide multiple products, and any given product might be provided by any number of suppliers. The Product Supplier entity models this relation, as well as the Preferred Supplier status of any given Supplier for a specific Product."

Some things in the problem space—a Sales Order is probably the best example—are modeled using one or more logical entities in the data model. I refer to these as *composite entities*. The sales order document is represented by *both* the Sales Order and Order Detail entities.

I have generally found it cleaner to handle composite entities as a single object for documentation purposes. For example, "The Sales Order and Order Detail entities represent a single order placed by a Customer. The Sales Order entity models the order itself, while the Order Detail items represent each product being ordered."

Work Processes That Affect the Entity

Although you might have already identified where data items are used in the work process analysis you performed earlier, it's useful to include that information in the entity documentation as well. That way, if it's necessary at some point to make a change to the structure of the entity, such as adding an attribute, there's a single place to identify all the processes that can be affected.

Identifying the processes that operate directly on an entity is also usually a straightforward process. Identifying those that *indirectly* interact with the entity might require more work. It might not be immediately obvious, for example, that the order entry process can modify a customer's default shipping method, or that a "Special Bonus" identified for a product category can affect the discount and thus the total value of a sales order. And yet these are exactly the kinds of interactions that are a maintenance programmer's nightmare if they're not carefully documented.

Most analysts document these interactions in the work processes analysis, which is obviously useful if your changes are to the processes themselves. Sometimes, however, the changes are to the model itself, either directly because of a change in the business environment or indirectly because a change to an existing process requires alterations in the model. In this case, it's far easier to scan the entity documentation for the specific entity you're changing than to sift through *all* the work processes to determine which might be affected by the change.

Think of including work process information in your entity documentation as cross-referencing, which it is. Like all cross-referencing, it can be tedious to implement and maintain, but it will make your life a lot easier in the long run.

Interactions Between Entities

E/R diagrams are wonderful tools, but they're capable of showing only so much information. If the entities in your system have complex interactions that can't easily be represented on the diagram, it's important to document them in the entity descriptions. Even if you've added annotations to the diagram, you should expand on any interactions that aren't immediately apparent in the notation.

If the model is complex enough to warrant multiple entity diagrams and a given entity appears in multiple diagrams, it might be useful to list all of the entities to which it is related in the entity description. This tends to be the case with entities that provide look-up values in multiple places. A Courtesy Title entity, for example, that contains entries such as "Mr.", "Mrs.", "Dr.", and "Ms." might be referenced in a dozen places. If you need to make changes to the entity, it's useful to be able to find all the referencing entities in a single spot.

As a general rule, however, the E/R diagram provides adequate documentation for the interaction between entities. Only exceptional cases like those cited above warrant additional information.

Business Rules and Constraints

The next bit of documentation required for an entity is to note any entity-level constraints that pertain to it. All entities are subject to the constraint that they must be uniquely identifiable, of course, and I generally find it useful to identify the attributes that will serve as the primary key for the table in the entity description.

Any constraints that reference multiple attributes, such as the "Shipping Method and Special Instructions attributes cannot both be empty" rule in our example, should also be documented, and this is the time to do so.

Attributes

The final bit of documentation required for the entities is a list of attributes and their domains. In compiling the list, you'll want to start with the list of attributes you identified when going through the source documents, and then be sure to add any foreign keys that are required for referential integrity.

You'll also want to check that each entity has at least one candidate key that can be used to uniquely identify each instance. This will become the primary key for the table in the database schema. Remember that primary keys cannot contain null values. Because of this, it might not always be possible to use an existing attribute or combination of attributes as a key. If this is the case, you'll need to add an arbitrary system-generated identifier.

In our example, the Customer entity probably needs an artificial identifier like this. If we assume that a customer might be either a company or an individual, you might have an initial attribute list like that shown in Figure 9-6.

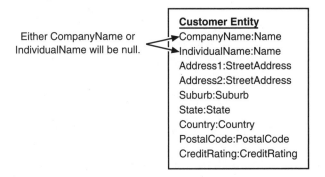

Either CompanyName or IndividualName will be null.

Customer Entity
CompanyName:Name
IndividualName:Name
Address1:StreetAddress
Address2:StreetAddress
Suburb:Suburb
State:State
Country:Country
PostalCode:PostalCode
CreditRating:CreditRating

Figure 9-6. *The Customer entity attribute list.*

Even if we set aside for the moment the issue that names are not unique, we still have a problem. If the customer is an individual, the Company Name will be null. If the customer is a company, the Individual Name will be null. Something is *always* going to be null. So these fields cannot be used as the candidate key even if we could assume that they uniquely identify the record, which we can't.

This leads me to the next problem with the Customer entity. Names are not unique. In our example, the entire list of attributes doesn't even guarantee uniqueness, since it's possible for two individuals with the same name to live at the same

address. John Smith is not guaranteed to tell you that he's actually John Smith Jr. and not to be confused with his papa, who lives in the same house.

There is certainly no question that John Smith Sr. and John Smith Jr. are different people and should be represented by different records. However, the attributes that uniquely identify them are none of our business. Can you imagine being asked about your living arrangements when you place an order for groceries? "Pardon me, sir, but do you happen to have a relative of the same name residing with you? Just checking for our computer system." Not in the best tradition of customer service, really.

Fortunately, there's a simple answer: the Customer Number. And if the organization doesn't already have a method of assigning these numbers, both Microsoft Jet and Microsoft SQL Server provide a mechanism for assigning them automatically (the AutoNumber and Identity data types, respectively).

If you do use an arbitrary identifier, though, be sure to provide an alternate form of identification. You don't want to put a user in the situation of having to refuse an order because the customer has forgotten his or her customer number. Asking a customer, "Are you the John Smith who lives in Oakridge or the one who lives in Cincinnati?" is one thing, asking him to call back after he's found an old invoice is quite another.

The Customer entity is also an example of the second reason to use an arbitrary system identifier. Even if we could assume that the combination of name and address were sufficiently unique for our purposes, that still leaves way too many fields to copy everywhere. Remember that every primary key of an entity will be used as a foreign key in any entities that reference it. It's obviously much more efficient to duplicate a single attribute than five or six.

Domain Analysis

In Figure 9-6, the attribute listing takes the form Name:Domain. Many analysts ignore the existence of domains and specify the attributes directly in terms of their data types and constraints. So if you ignore this step of the process, you'll be in good company. You won't be *correct*, but it's unlikely that anyone will fault you for it.

The reason I perform domain analysis in my own work, and recommend that you do so as well, is that it saves work and provides additional information. As far as I'm concerned, anything that's easier and better is a good idea. And this task has the added advantage of being technically correct, as well.

Let's take just one example: the CompanyName and IndividualName attributes in Figure 9-6 all specify that they derive their values from the domain of Name.

We can now define the Name domain as follows:

"A string of one or more words in proper case, with a maximum length of 75 characters. Only characters and the punctuation marks period (.) and comma (,) are allowed."

We have to define the domain only once, and we can reference it any number of times throughout the system. We could have defined these constraints for each applicable attribute, but why bother? Furthermore, because these attributes are defined on the same domain, we know that they can be logically compared. This wouldn't necessarily be clear if we had defined the attributes directly.

Finding the customer with the same value in the CompanyName field as in the IndividualName field might not be the most useful thing to do, but it is at least a possible thing. The same could not be said of comparing company names to customer numbers that might, coincidentally, have the same structure and constraints.

The technical definition of a domain is "the set of values from which an attribute can draw its values." This is conceptually straightforward, but how does one define a domain? Essentially, you need to identify three things:

- The data type of the domain

- Any restrictions to the range of values accepted by the data type

- Optionally, any formatting that pertains to the domain

Choosing a Data Type

The first step in defining a domain is to choose the core data type that will be used in the database schema to represent it. This is one instance where it's practical to break the rule about separating the database schema from the conceptual data model.

The data type serves as a shorthand description of a range of values. While "Integer" is not a domain unless you're modeling mathematics, values of the domain "Quantity" are almost certainly integers. I wouldn't recommend getting too involved with the specifics of database engine types, however. At this point, the choice of database engine is still subject to change.

The "data type" of a domain can also be another domain. You might have already defined a generic Date domain, which specifies, for example, that all dates in the system must be on or after 1 January 1900 and formatted using a four-digit year. It's perfectly acceptable to define the Event Date as "A Date after 23 October 1982 (the date on which trading commenced)."

Restricting the Range of Values

Having identified the base data type for your domain, the next step is to specify the values within that data type's range that are valid for the domain. Sometimes the easiest way to do this is by specifying a rule: "Quantities must be positive whole numbers."

Sometimes it's simpler to list the valid values for a domain. "Region must be one of: Northwest, Northeast, Central, Southern." In this instance, you will almost certainly want to include the domain as an entity in the data model. This is far easier than typing the values everywhere they're referenced, and also allows them to be easily changed after the system has been implemented.

The only possible exception to this rule is when the domain values are few in number and cannot possibly change. Say, for example, that you're modeling a questionnaire or an exam, and you have an Answer domain that consists of the values "True" and "False." There is no point in modeling these two options as an entity. There are no other possible values, and referencing a table during implementation will almost certainly be more trouble than typing in the rule directly.

You will also use an entity to model domains that must be defined using more than one attribute. The best example of this is the domain of State. If you must account for multiple countries, you cannot determine whether a given state value is valid without reference to the country specified.

If a customer is located in Australia, for example, "New South Wales" is a valid state, but "Alabama" is not. In this case, the domain look-up entity would consist of both the Country and State attributes. This example is not strictly a domain definition, and it's modeled using required relationships in the E/R model. It is, however, easy to think of this sort of situation as a kind of composite domain, and treat it as such.

After all, the point here is to simplify the task of identifying the constraints that pertain to the system, and bending the domain definition for domains that appear repeatedly in the data model saves time and reduces the chance of error.

Your domain specification must also indicate whether nulls or zero-length strings, or both, are acceptable values for attributes defined on the domain. It's useful to explicitly declare this in your definition even if you're modeling the range using a system entity, in which case the nullability can be determined by the relationship between the two entities.

Performing the domain analysis and identifying the list of attributes for any given entity are closely related, iterative processes. In actual practice, you'll probably find it most effective to define the domains at the same time that you're listing the attributes. If the domain of an attribute is already defined, you can simply list it. If not, you can define the domain while you have an example in front of you.

During this process, you might find that certain attributes have restrictions in addition to those defined for the domain. This is perfectly proper and not at all unusual. You might have defined an Event Date domain, for example, which represents the date on which any event can occur. This date is restricted to dates after the company began trading. In the Sales Order example, both the Order Date and the Shipping Date would be defined on the Event Date domain. The Shipping Date attribute, however, must *also* be after the Order Date. This is an entity-level constraint and should be listed as such in the entity description.

In defining domain constraints (and additional attribute constraints, for that matter), you should try to be as specific as possible *without compromising usability*. We'll discuss this in greater detail in Part 3, but at this point you should be aware that the more precisely you define a domain, the more assistance you can provide users. If you accidentally eliminate values, however, you will get in the users' way and can ultimately make the system unusable.

Defining the Format

It's not strictly necessary, but it's often a good idea to specify the appropriate format for a domain. If you specify once that all dates must be displayed as DD-MMM-YYYY, you need never do it again.

Normalization

It might have come as a surprise that nowhere in this discussion of data modeling have I discussed normalizing the data model. It's been my experience that if you start with the data bits and then organize them into entities, reconciling repeating groups and many-to-many relationships as you go, you're likely to have a data model that is in third normal form.

But it certainly does no harm, particularly when all of this is fairly new to you, to review the model for compliancy. Remember, every entity in the model should be dependent on "the key, the whole key, and nothing but the key."

SUMMARY

In this chapter, we've looked at building the conceptual data model of the system. The process begins with a review of all source materials to identify the data items used by the system, which are then organized into a set of entities. The relationships between the entities are reviewed, and then each individual entity and its attributes are analyzed.

In the next chapter, we'll look at translating the conceptual model into the physical database schema that will be implemented against the chosen database engine.

10

The Database Schema

In the last chapter, we examined the conceptual data model, which defines the logical structure of the data. In this chapter, we turn to the database schema, which describes the physical structure of the data. Remember that the database schema is still a logical construct. In building the database schema, you will describe the physical structure of the data in fairly abstract terms. The actual physical representation is the responsibility of the database engine and need not concern you.

Systems Architectures

Before describing the database schema, you must make some decisions about the architecture your system requires. Unfortunately, the literature uses the term "architecture" to describe two distinct (although interrelated) models. To clarify things, I'll call one of these models the *code architecture* and the other the *data architecture*. But be aware that these are my names; you're unlikely to find them elsewhere.

Code Architectures

What I call the "code architecture" is variously called the "application model," the "layered paradigm," and the "services model" in the literature. The code architecture describes the way code is logically structured. Code structure is largely an implementation issue, and as such it lies outside the scope of this book. However, the code architecture can affect whether data integrity constraints are implemented in the database schema, and so we will discuss it here, albeit somewhat superficially.

In the bad old days, system architectures were monolithic: huge blobs of code with minimal structure. Anyone who's had the misfortune of trying to modify (or even understand) a monolithic system of any complexity will never look at a plate of spaghetti in the same way again. To impose some order on this mess, programmers began to structure their code into discrete components in various ways: subroutines, modules, or objects, depending on language capabilities. The

problem with this approach is that instead of creating spaghetti, you can easily create tortellini—independent chunks of code that interact in *some* way, but it's anybody's guess how.

To manage this modern pasta, many developers are organizing components into services, sometimes called layers, that perform tasks at a discrete logical level. There are innumerable ways of organizing the layers. We'll look at two of the most common types: the three-tiered and four-layer models. (Please don't ask me why when you have three of them, they're "tiers," and when you have four, they're "layers." Just to confuse us, I suspect.)

Three-tiered model

The three-tiered model organizes components into User Services, Business Services, and Data Services. Microsoft Visual Modeler—the graphic modeling tool integrated with Microsoft Visual Studio 6.0—supports this model, as shown in Figure 10-1.

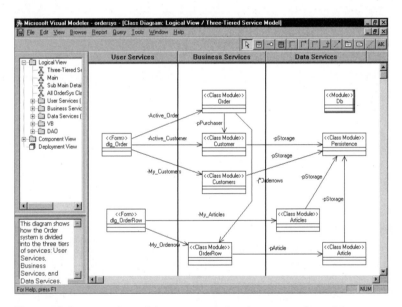

Figure 10-1. *Visual Modeler supports the three-tiered model.*

Within the three-tiered model, code components that present information to users and respond to user actions are assigned to the User Services tier. The entire user interface is encapsulated within this tier. The Business Services tier is responsible for enforcing business rules and validating user input. Business Services components interact with both the User Services and Data Services tiers. Code components in the Data Services tier, which interact only with the Business Services tier, are responsible for maintaining data.

The three-tiered model is clean, and Visual Modeler is certainly handy, but I've found its use in actual development problematic. There always seem to be certain types of functionality that don't clearly belong to any specific tier. For example, say a given piece of data needs to be formatted before it's displayed to users. A social security number might be stored as a string of 9 digits but displayed as 999-99-9999. Does the formatting belong to the User Services or the Data Services tier? You could make a case for putting it in either tier. Similarly, is transaction management part of Business Services or Data Services? When you begin to design complex systems using hierarchical data and data shaping, these types of decisions can get hairy.

Provided that you're consistent, it doesn't really matter where you put these types of functions, but this is precisely where the model fails. If you must refer to a set of external conventions—such as "formatting belongs to the User Services tier, and building hierarchical data sets is a part of the Business Services tier"—then the overhead of the model begins to outweigh its benefits.

Four-layer model

Dividing the code architecture into four layers instead of three eliminates many of the problems associated with the three-tiered model. The four-layered model, often called the "layered paradigm," organizes code components into a User Interface layer, a Data Interface layer, a Transaction Interface layer, and an External Access Interface layer, as shown in Figure 10-2 on the following page.

The User Interface layer corresponds to the User Services tier of the three-tiered model. The User Interface layer is responsible for user interaction, including presenting information to users by means of window objects; responding to changes in the state of window objects, such as a form resize; and initiating user requests.

The Data Interface layer is responsible for maintaining data in memory (as opposed to maintaining it permanently, which is handled by the External Access Interface layer and the database engine, as we'll see). It explicitly includes most of the functionality that can be contentious in the three-tiered model, such as being able to format data and create virtual recordsets. (A *virtual recordset* exists only in memory; it's not permanently stored anywhere.)

In most cases, a component in the Data Interface layer is tightly coupled with a specific component in the User Interface layer. Theoretically, however, a Data Interface component can support multiple User Interface components, as Figure 10-2 shows. A system might include, for example, a Customer Maintenance form showing information for a single customer and a Customer Summary form showing information for multiple customers. Since both of these forms represent a Customer entity, they might share the code for formatting and validating the CustomerNumber, which is a function of the Data Interface layer.

In physical terms, a User Interface component usually corresponds to a form in Microsoft Visual Basic or Microsoft Access, while the associated Data Interface component is typically implemented in the form module. Certain procedures might be shared by multiple forms, however, in which case the procedures would be implemented in a shared module.

The Data Interface layer is responsible for validating data but is not responsible for business processes. The code that ensures that the CustomerNumber value specified in an order is known to the system, for example, is part of the Data Interface layer. The code that enforces a specific sequence of events, such as preventing an order from being shipped until the customer's credit is approved, belongs to the Transaction Interface layer.

The Transaction Interface layer coordinates the use of data by the application. Components at this level are responsible for building and initiating queries, receiving information from the External Access Interface layer, enforcing business processes, and handling errors and violations reported by the External Access Interface layer.

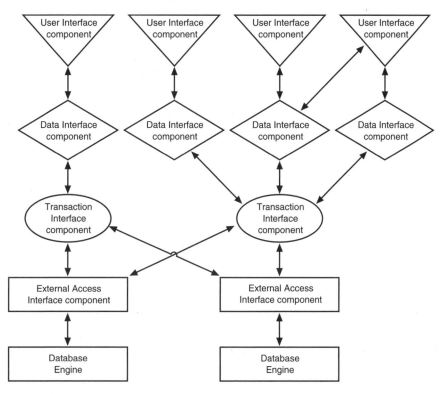

Figure 10-2. *The four-layer model.*

The components in the Transaction Interface layer are more likely to be reused than Data Interface components. Transaction Interface layer components are good candidates for implementation as objects in both Visual Basic and Access. A Customer object, for example, might expose an *Update* method that is called by multiple components in the Data Interface layer. Note that because the Data Interface layer should (at least ideally) be independent from components at the User Interface layer, the values to be updated must be listed explicitly. In other words, the call would take the following form:

```
MyCustomer.Update CustomerNumber, CustomerName...
```

The *Update* method would then create the UPDATE query statement, hand it to the External Access Interface layer for execution, and handle any error conditions that might result, either by resolving them directly or by handing them back up the chain for display by the User Interface layer.

The External Access Interface layer is responsible for communication between the application and external data sources. In database systems, the code components at this level handle the communication with the database engine. They execute queries and hand the results (including any error messages) back up the component chain.

Ideally, you should design the procedures at this level to isolate the transaction from the specifics of the database engine you choose. Theoretically, it should be possible to upsize an application originally designed to use the Microsoft Jet database engine to SQL Server simply by replacing the External Access Interface layer. In reality, this can be a little difficult to pull off.

Remember that the Transaction Interface layer is responsible for building queries; the External Access Interface layer only executes them. Given the syntactic differences between various implementations of the SQL language, implementation is rarely so straightforward. A recordset created by a single TRANSFORM query against a Microsoft Jet database requires multiple statements to be created using SQL Server.

If you can predict all the queries executed by the application in advance, you can avoid syntax problems by including the queries in the database schema. Parameter queries can be enormously helpful here. You don't need to create the SQL statement to select the customer named Jones on the fly—you can pass "Jones" in as a parameter to a preexisting query.

Unfortunately, it isn't always possible to predict all the necessary queries in advance, particularly if you're providing an ad hoc query capability to users. In this case it's almost impossible to insulate the Transaction Interface layer entirely. (At any rate, I've never found a complete solution to the problem; if you figure it out, I'll be grateful if you'd share it with me.) In the meantime, you might have

to write some conditional code in the Data Interface layer components, such as the following:

```
theEngine = myData.EngineName
Select Case theEngine
    Case "SQLServer"
        ' build a SQL Server flavored query
    Case "Jet"
        ' build a Microsoft Jet query
    Case Else
        ' return an "unknown engine" error to the Data Interface layer
End Select
```

If your application is intended to support a single database engine, it's tempting to roll the Transaction Interface layer and the External Access Interface layer together. I don't recommend it. Although it does take a certain amount of time to design the External Access Interface layer, the process isn't difficult, and once written it will save you hundreds of lines of code elsewhere in the system. Furthermore, once you've written a component that communicates to, say, SQL Server 7.0 using ADO 2.0, you need never write it again. You can use it in any other systems you write, without modification. The only time you need a new External Access Interface layer component is when either the underlying database engine or the object model changes.

Code architectures and the database schema

The code architecture you choose impacts the database schema in two areas: insulation of the External Access Interface layer (or the Data Services layer, if you're using the three-tiered model) and data validation. We've already talked about insulating the External Access Interface layer from a change in database engines by predicting necessary queries and including them in the database schema. This approach has the added advantage of improving performance, sometimes significantly. Data validation is a somewhat trickier issue. We'll look at the "what" and "how" of data validation in detail in Chapter 16. What we'll consider here is the "when" and "where."

Some designers advocate embedding all data validation functionality in the database engine itself. This approach isn't without merit: all of the data integrity constraints and business rules are implemented in a single place, where they can be easily updated. Unfortunately, the approach is not without problems, either.

In the first place, certain rules *can't* be implemented at the database-engine level. For example, without triggers in the Jet database engine, it's impossible to enforce a rule that prevents a primary key value from being changed once the record is created. Even in SQL Server, which is generally more powerful in this area, you can't implement every rule directly in the database engine.

Secondly, waiting until the data has been submitted to the database engine before validating it can reduce the usability of the system. As a general rule, you should validate data as soon as it's entered. In some cases, this means validating the data as soon as a key is pressed, such as when you prevent the entry of alphabetical characters in a numeric field. In other cases, you should validate the data when a field is exited or when the last of a sequence of fields is entered, such as when you're enforcing the rule that the DesiredDeliveryDate value must be equal to or later than the OrderDate value.

Even in a stand-alone application running on a single machine, submitting a data set to the database engine after each keystroke, or even after each field is exited, results in deplorable performance. If you're making a round-trip across a network or, heaven forbid, across a wide area network or the Internet to a database engine at a remote site, performance will be so poor your users will be better off using index cards (and they might).

The only solution is to submit the data to the database engine for validation after the entire record has been completed. But by this point, a user's attention will have turned to the next task. To report a problem that resulted from an entry made 10 minutes ago is disruptive and confusing.

To make the system as responsive and usable as possible, you must implement data validation in the application. If the database is used by only a single application and the validation requirements are relatively stable, you might decide to implement data validation *only* at the application level and entirely forego any validation by the database engine. This eliminates duplicate effort, but it's a fairly dangerous approach.

If another application is implemented against the same database in the future, nothing but good intentions prevent the new application from inadvertently undermining the integrity of the database, and we all know what road is paved with good intentions. Even if the database is never shared with another application, it's vulnerable to users using ad hoc tools such as Access or the SQL Server Enterprise Manager to manipulate the data. A strict security model that prohibits data changes except by the application itself can help prevent this, but at a cost of restricted access to the data.

For these reasons, I believe that best practice is to implement data validation in both the application and the database schema. Access implements this automatically. When you define a validation rule for a field at the table level and then drag that field onto a bound form, the form inherits the validation rule.

In versions of Access prior to 2000, this feature is unfortunately also a good example of the problem with duplicate validation. If, after including the field on a bound form, you then change the validation rule at the table level, the changes are not reflected in the form. Microsoft Access 2000 does update the

rule, but the problem remains in Visual Basic. If you reference the field on multiple forms (in the same or multiple applications), you must manually change the validation rules in each of the forms (or rather, in the Data Interface layer components supporting each of the forms).

To overcome this problem, some designers query the database engine for validation rules at run time. This technique has a certain amount of overhead, but if your validation rules change frequently, the overhead might be offset by the ease of updating the rules in a single place.

Retrieving the validation rules from the database engine can be done when the application first starts, when a form is loaded, or before each record is updated. I recommend doing it when the form is loaded. If you do it on application start-up, you might download unnecessary information pertaining to forms a user never loads. If you do it before each record is updated, you can be absolutely sure that the rules you're working with are as current as possible, but it means requerying the schema for each record and, realistically, how many systems are *that* volatile?

In the extremely unlikely event that a rule changes while a user has a form open *and* the user enters data that complied with the old rule but violates the new rule, the problem will be caught by the database engine anyway, so no major harm will be done. Besides, the very thought of tinkering with the database schema while the system is being *used* is enough to give me nightmares.

Data Architectures

In addition to making decisions about how the code for your system should be structured, you must also decide on a data architecture. You will recall from Chapter 1 that a database system consists of a number of discrete components: the application itself, the database engine, and the database. (See Figure 1-1 on page 5.) Based on the four-layer code model, we can now refine this structure somewhat, as shown in Figure 10-3.

In determining the data architecture for the application, you decide where each of the layers will live. Theoretically, each layer (or even each individual component) can exist on a different computer, communicating across a network of some kind. At the other end of the scale, all the components can exist on a single, stand-alone computer. In reality, a few more-or-less standard configurations have been shown to be effective in various situations, and we'll examine each of these in turn.

Single-tier architectures

Each logical grouping of components in the data architecture is referred to as a "tier." The simplest architecture, of course, is a single-tier system, in which all the components exist in a single logical tier, and the simplest version of a single-tier data architecture is a stand-alone system.

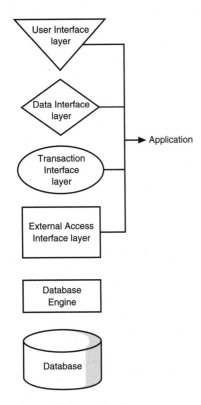

Figure 10-3. *A database system consists of six discrete layers.*

In a stand-alone system, all the components exist on a single machine and are available only to the user physically working at that machine. Although the machine might incidentally be connected to a network or the Internet, the database system is not available to other users. Because all processing occurs on the local machine and the data is stored locally, the only performance constraints are the capabilities of the machine—its processor speed and memory. Stand-alone systems tend to be very memory-hungry; that's one of the reasons other configurations are sought.

The majority of stand-alone systems use the Jet database engine. It's certainly possible to implement a SQL Server system on a single machine, but for reasons that will become clear later, it's debatable whether such a system qualifies as single-tier. An exception is the Microsoft Data Engine (MSDE) distributed with Access 2000. MSDE is a kind of "SQL Server Light" that runs in a single-tier architecture.

A common variation in the single-tier architecture is the networked database. In this model, you physically locate the database (or at least parts of it) on a computer across a network, but all processing is performed locally.

> **NOTE** Don't be tempted to put the application itself on the network drive. This is theoretically possible but definitely *not* recommended because of the load it puts on the network. Instead, you should put the application on the local computer and use linked tables to access the networked data.

A networked database—which is possible only using the Jet database engine, not SQL Server—allows multiple users to access the data simultaneously. The maximum number of simultaneous users of a Jet database is theoretically 255. In reality, the practical maximum depends on what they're doing and, ultimately, on how efficient the system is. Clearly, 20 people entering data as fast as their little fingers can type are going to put more strain on a system than 50 people reviewing sales and pondering product strategy.

Reducing the network load has the most direct effect on the database schema. Remember that all processing occurs on the local machine; in a sense, you treat the computer on which the database resides as nothing more than a remote hard disk. But response time across a network is typically much slower than accessing a local hard drive. Furthermore, the network has a limited capacity, and all users on the system must compete for it. So you want to reduce the amount of information you're shuffling back and forth. Again, this is largely an implementation issue; if you're directly involved with implementation, I suggest you consult the sources listed in the Bibliography and contained on the CD that accompanies this book for more information.

However, two aspects of the database schema can directly impact network performance: the location of database objects and the appropriate use of indices. I've already mentioned the importance of having the user interface objects stored locally. In addition, you might want to consider placing copies of data that doesn't change very often on users' machines.

For example, product lists tend to be fairly stable, and they're typically referenced frequently. Provided the Products table isn't too big (a few megabytes is fine; a gigabyte is pushing it), you might want to consider storing a copy of it on each user's machine. In most situations, this will reduce network traffic and improve performance. Of course, you'll need to provide some mechanism for updating the data when necessary, but this doesn't present too much of a problem.

Lists of postal codes, states, countries, and an organization's regions or branches are also good candidates for local storage, since these lists tend to be small and stable. They also tend to be referenced frequently. (There's no point in storing a copy of a table that's used only by the system administrator once a year on every user's workstation.) Sales orders or lists of customers or students, on the other hand, are usually *not* appropriate for local storage. Information in these sorts of recordsets changes frequently, and sharing the most current recordset version is the whole point of a networked database.

The second way the database schema can affect network performance is in the use of appropriate indices. You can think of an index as a sort of minitable that is maintained in a specific order. It contains only the fields required to order the records and a "pointer" to the record in the real table, as shown in Figure 10-4.

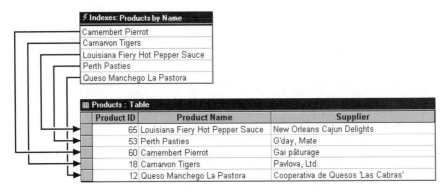

Figure 10-4. *An index is a kind of minitable, with the records stored in a specific order.*

Note that I'm using the word "pointer" rather loosely here. This pointer isn't the same as a memory pointer or an object pointer as those terms are used in programming. In fact, the physical implementation of indices doesn't match the model presented here very closely at all, but the model will work. If you *really* want to know the ugly details, the *Microsoft Jet Database Engine Programmer's Guide* is a good place to start.

Instead of physically rearranging the records in the base table, a task that would be prohibitively time-consuming in most situations, Microsoft Jet sorts only the index file. This is (usually) substantially faster and also allows the base table to be quickly and easily accessed in multiple orders, since more than one index can be maintained for any given table.

SQL Server provides a special kind of index, called a *clustered index,* that does control the physical ordering of data. There can be only one clustered index per table.

The importance of indices from a performance point of view is that in many cases Microsoft Jet can perform an operation using only an index, without reading the base table itself. This often provides a noticeable performance improvement even for stand-alone systems (even reading data from a local drive takes time), and in networked situations the improvement can be critical.

To take just one example, say you have a Customers table containing 100,000 records, each 1500 bytes long. The application needs to find a specific record,

say the one for Jones Construction, whose CustomerID is JONSCON. You execute a statement like the following:

```
SELECT * FROM Customers WHERE CustomerID = "JONSCON"
```

Without an index or a primary key declared for the table, the Jet database engine must read each of those 100,000 records to determine which ones match the specified condition. That's at least 150 megabytes of data being sent across the network. If the CustomerID is indexed, either explicitly or by declaring it a primary key, the Jet database engine needs to read only the index, which is probably just a few kilobytes, and can then quickly locate the correct record in the base table.

The performance improvement from using indices can be amazing, but of course you don't get it for free. There's a certain amount of overhead involved in using indices: every time you add or update a record, Microsoft Jet must update the indices on the table. Usually this overhead is negligible, but if you are using too many indices on any one table, it can start to impact performance. Taken to extremes, the time required to maintain the indices will exceed the time saved by using them.

Two-tiered architectures

In a two-tiered architecture, the database and the database engine are both located on a remote computer. They can be on the same computer or on different ones. In fact, the database can be spread across several physical computers; logically, the system will still be two-tiered. This architecture is possible only using SQL Server or another database server such as Oracle; it is not possible with Microsoft Jet.

At first glance, the difference between a networked database and a two-tiered system might not seem great. Use Microsoft Jet locally or SQL Server on a remote computer—what's the big deal? The big deal is that in a networked database all the processing is performed on the local workstation, but in a two-tiered system the processing is spread across two processors. The workstation is responsible for handling user interaction, and the remote computer handles the data access. SQL Server performs all the data manipulation, including query execution, and "serves" the results to the client workstation. For this reason, two-tiered database systems are better known as *client/server* systems.

To make the difference between a networked database and a two-tiered system clearer, take the following SQL statement, which we used when we talked about the importance of indices:

```
SELECT * FROM Customers WHERE CustomerID = "JONSCON"
```

In a networked database, the Jet database engine will read the index (assuming one is present), determine the correct record, and then fetch the record. In

a client/server system, the application will submit the statement to SQL Server and get the correct record in return. (Of course, what actually happens in each situation is rather more complicated, but this simple model will serve.)

With a request like this, the performance of either architecture will be good enough that you might not see much difference between a networked database and a client/server database. In fact, client/server performance can be slower under some circumstances. But with complex queries and scores of users, using a client/server system significantly improves performance and responsiveness.

System responsiveness can improve in a client/server system because while the server is busy calculating the results of a command, the workstation can be doing something else, like responding to additional user requests. The reverse is also true. While the workstation is busy responding to a user (or waiting around for the user to do something), the database server is free to process other requests. SQL Server is more sophisticated than Microsoft Jet in many ways, but this system responsiveness is essentially why client/server systems can support more users than a networked database. Yet another case of the whole being greater than the sum of its parts.

To make a client/server system work, you must push as much data processing onto the server as possible. Whereas in a networked database it often makes sense to store queries locally, in a two-tiered client/server system they should remain on the server.

If you're linking to SQL Server through Access, you need to be careful about issuing commands that will execute locally. For example, a SELECT statement that contains a user-defined function will be executed by Access rather than being passed to SQL Server, because SQL Server doesn't support functions in SELECT statements (neither does Microsoft Jet, which is why a query containing a user-defined function can't be executed from Visual Basic, even if the query is stored in an .mdb file).

From an implementation standpoint, there are many more issues to consider in building client/server databases. Again, I refer you to one of the many excellent books available on the subject, some of which are listed in the Bibliography.

N-tiered architectures

Spreading the processing load between two systems in a two-tiered system can, if implemented correctly, significantly improve application performance and responsiveness. Spreading the load across additional systems can provide similar benefits. Referring back to the four-layer code architecture shown in Figure 10-3 (on page 157), it's usually the Transaction Interface layer and External Access Interface layer components that are distributed to additional intermediate systems.

Unfortunately, the implementation complexity seems to increase exponentially, as well. Connectivity, security, process management, all these issues become

infinitely more complex when you move to three or more logical tiers. Since the complexity of these systems often requires additional servers of various descriptions, such as the Microsoft Transaction Server, these systems are usually referred to as "n-tiered." (Apparently, with physical tiers, as with husbands, one stops counting after the third.)

Fortunately, this implementation complexity is just that—an implementation issue. Your development team might decide to explore a new career in basket weaving, but an n-tiered architecture hardly affects the *design* of the database. You must be especially rigorous in keeping the logical levels of the code architecture distinct, but a database schema that performs correctly in a two-tiered environment should scale to n-tiers without alteration.

Internet and intranet architectures

Deploying a database across the Internet or an intranet is essentially a special form of n-tiered architecture. The specifics of the technologies are different—you'll use HTTP as a transfer protocol, and the user interface is more likely to be Internet Explorer than Access—but logically the architectures are very similar.

The most important difference between a database system deployed on the Internet and one deployed in a more traditional environment is that the Internet is stateless. In a typical client/server environment, the application will request a user name and password when it first starts up and then use this information to connect to SQL Server. Once the connection is established (assuming the user name and password are accepted), the server usually maintains the connection for the duration of the session. As long as the connection is maintained, the server knows who the client is, and when the client makes a request, it can respond appropriately. All this "I know who you are" business is called a *state* and is maintained by the database server.

When the database system is deployed across the Internet, however, the database server will no longer maintain state information. Each time the application makes a request from the database server, it must reestablish the connection and reidentify itself. Once the database server has complied with the request, it forgets all about the application that made it.

Under most circumstances, the slight overhead involved in making a new connection for each request has very little impact on the database system, and it certainly doesn't affect the database schema. But the stateless nature of the Internet has another implication that *does* affect the application and might also require changes to the database schema.

Most Internet applications aim for a *thin client*. This means that applications do as little processing as possible on the client, usually just the user interface. But consider the case of a query that returns a lot of records, more than can be reasonably displayed on a single screen. In a traditional application, the result set is cached, either on the client or the server.

But in an Internet application, the results can't be cached on the server side because the server wouldn't know where to send the next batch. If they're cached on the client side, the data-handling components (the Transaction Interface and External Access Interface layers) must reside on the client as well, and these components are certainly not "thin." They're decidedly pudgy, in fact.

ActiveX Data Objects (ADO) provides a mechanism called *paging* for handling these situations. Before submitting the query, the application can establish the number of rows to be returned at one time using the PageSize property of the *Recordset* object. You might set this to 15, for example, to return the records in lots of 15. The AbsolutePage property specifies which particular page you want, while the PageCount property returns the total number of pages. This is like the TOP N clause of a standard SQL SELECT statement, except that you have a "middle N" capability as well.

On the server side, paging results in the reexecution of the query each time a user requests a new page. For queries having a reasonably fast response time this represents no problem. For complex queries that are relatively slow to calculate, you've got big problems. An application that makes a single user wait a couple of minutes for a response is marginally acceptable. An application that makes several thousand users wait minutes every time they want to see the next five records is going to be pitched in the rubbish bin where it belongs.

If you're faced with a complex query in an Internet application, you have a couple of options. The first, and in most cases preferable option, is to optimize the query to within an inch of its life. Create temporary tables, denormalize the data, do whatever you need to get the response time down to an acceptable level.

If this isn't possible, you might have no choice but to create a fat client by moving the data-handling components out to the client side. This architecture allows you to cache the query results on the client side, effectively reproducing an environment similar to a networked database (with a few complications, just to keep you on your toes).

However, as a general rule, fat clients are more appropriate on an intranet than the Internet, Microsoft's Distributed Networked Architecture notwithstanding. Many people have a perfectly reasonable aversion to downloading code components, but this situation is less likely to arise in an application that's publicly available. If it does arise, you can only hope that your content is sufficiently valuable to overcome their resistance.

Database Schema Components

Once you've completed the conceptual data model and decided on the system architecture, you have most of the information you need to build the database schema. The database schema is a description of the data objects you will include in the database. If you've chosen anything other than a stand-alone

data architecture, the database schema will also define where each object is to be deployed.

If you're implementing your system in Access, your database schema will include the definition of each table, query, and relationship. It will not include a description of the system's forms, reports, and code components, even though these are also stored in an .mdb file. If you're implementing the system in SQL Server, your database schema will include the definition of each table, view, stored procedure, and trigger in the database.

Defining Tables and Relationships

The definition of the physical tables in the database schema is derived directly from the conceptual data model. Entities become tables, and the table's fields are the entity's attributes. For the most part, this is a simple process of direct translation. The only areas that require special attention are constraints, relationships, and indices.

Constraints

As part of defining the conceptual data model, you defined constraints for entities, attributes and domains. Whether or not you implement these constraints in the database schema depends, as we've seen, on the choices you made about the system architecture. As I've said, some designers prefer to implement all constraints only at the Data Interface and Transaction Interface layers of the four-layer model, or the Business Services layer of the three-tiered model.

In most circumstances, I recommend that you implement the appropriate constraints at both levels. Assuming that you agree with me and have decided to include constraints in the database itself, you will define them as part of the database schema. We discussed implementing data integrity in detail in Chapter 4, but it's worthwhile to review it here.

Most domain and attribute constraints will become field-level constraints in the database schema, usually as validation rules in Access. Access also supports the CHECK constraint clause used by SQL Server if you chose to create the database using SQL statements rather than DAO or the Access user interface.

Entity-level constraints usually become table constraints, again, either as validation rules or through the SQL CHECK constraint. You implement the entity integrity constraint, which specifies that each instance of an entity be uniquely identifiable, by defining a primary key for each table.

Whether you're implementing the database using SQL Server or the Jet database engine, you might find that some of the constraints defined in the conceptual data model can't be implemented as part of the table definition. In SQL Server, you might be able to enforce the constraint using a trigger. Since the Jet database engine doesn't support triggers, you'll need to implement these constraints as part of the application.

Relationships

We discussed the ways relationships between entities are modeled in a relational database in Chapter 3 and again in Chapter 9. The first step is always to include a unique identifier from the primary relation in the foreign relation. At the level of the database schema, this means that the primary key fields from the primary table will be included in the foreign table.

Some designers stop there, preferring to handle referential integrity only in the application rather than allow the database engine to do so. As with all database validation, in my own work I do both: I validate referential integrity in the application for usability and in the database engine for safety. I suppose if I were a man, I'd wear both a belt and suspenders.

Indices

We discussed previously the importance of indices for system performance. Every table should have at least one index, which the database engine will create automatically when you declare the primary key. In addition, you should create an index on any field or combination of fields that you will use to join tables. This usually isn't a problem for the table that represents the primary relation since the fields used for the join are the primary key. However, you might need to declare additional indices in the table representing the foreign relation if the field or fields used for the join don't make up the entire primary key in the foreign relation.

If the foreign key field or fields participate in the primary key but aren't the *whole* key, I define a separate index on the foreign key. For example, an OrderItems table usually has a primary key of {OrderID, ItemID}. Even though the primary key index could be used to join the table with the master Orders table in most circumstances (well, every circumstance I can think of), I would probably still create a separate index on OrderID just to be certain.

Any fields that will be used to sort the data should also be indexed. For example, customer lists are usually sorted by customer name and orders by date, even though neither of these fields usually participates in the primary key or forms part of a join. Indexing the fields will make the sorting process easier and more efficient.

It's possible to go overboard in creating indices, so be careful here. Remember that a small, but cumulative, amount of overhead is involved in maintaining each index. Any field that will be used for sorting the table frequently should be indexed, but you can always use the SQL ORDER BY clause to sort records without using an index.

The practical maximum number of indices per table really depends on how often the table is updated. (The overhead is incurred only when a record is added or the indexed field is updated.) For a table such as Orders that the system will update more or less constantly, I'd be careful about maintaining more than

10 or 15 indices, including those used to support joins and the primary key. You might be justified in using more indices on a Products table, on the other hand, which is typically updated infrequently but used in many ways throughout a system. As always, you must base the decision on how the data is to be used.

Views and Queries

Both Access and SQL Server provide a mechanism for storing SQL SELECT statements. These stored statements are called *views* in SQL Server and *queries* in Access. (I'll call them queries here, as that's the more common term.) In most cases, using a stored query will be faster than executing a SELECT statement on the fly; this isn't always the case, but the situations in which it isn't are so quirky that you can take this as a general rule.

You can begin deciding what queries to include in the database schema by examining the conceptual data model for complex entities. Remember that a complex entity is a single logical entity that is modeled by two or more tables for efficiency. You should include a query that denormalizes any complex entities in your model. Most of these will be tables in a one-to-many relationship such as Orders and OrderItems, but you might also have complex entities that have been subclassed with one-to-one relationships, and you should include queries to support them as well.

Users will frequently need to find particular records in the primary entities in the system—a specific customer or order, for example—and this is the second place to look for queries to be included in the database schema. All these common searches should be supported by a parameter query allowing users to specify the particular record to be found at run time.

Sometimes you'll need to provide more than one "find" query for an entity. A user might need to find an Order by looking up the OrderDate, CustomerID, or OrderID, for example. Each of these should be supported by a separate parameter query.

On the other hand, users won't search through all tables. You might have a table in the database schema that contains a list of US States. These lookup tables are extremely useful, but it's extremely unlikely that users will ever need to search for a specific state record.

You should also look for queries in the forms and reports implemented by the application. You'll need queries to link the fields and also to support lookups such as those used for combo boxes. If the system has form dependencies, you'll need a parameter query to support them as well. An example of this might be a dialog box that's called from an order entry form to display Customer details.

Based on the system's work processes, you will also want to include in your database schema queries (and perhaps stored procedures in SQL Server) that perform actions. If you know that the system will regularly archive orders or

update product prices, it will be more efficient to support these activities with queries or stored procedures than to issue the commands on the fly.

Additional action queries will probably be added to the database schema during implementation. Unlike indices, essentially no overhead is involved in queries and stored procedures once they're implemented, so you need not hesitate about adding them to the database schema.

Remember that systems development is not a strictly linear process. While changes to the tables themselves during implementation can cause problems (and the further in the development process, the greater the problems), adding queries to the schema is trivial and to be expected.

Security

After you understand the system work processes and build the conceptual data model, you must consider the administrative requirements for the system. Administrative requirements don't necessarily impact the database schema directly, but they are nonetheless business rules that must be accommodated in the release system.

Administrative requirements are, in a sense, "meta-requirements," in that they concern the system *itself* rather than the problem space the system is modeling. They fall into two categories: security requirements, which determine who can access the system; and availability requirements, which determine such things as how often the system must be online (24 hours a day seven days a week, or normal working hours, for example) and how users will back up data. Since availability is almost exclusively an implementation issue, we'll discuss only security here.

The implementation of a security scheme can be a complex business. Fortunately, the processes are well documented for Access and the Jet database engine and for SQL Server. Even more fortunately, database design is distinct from implementation, so you need only consider the logical security arrangements during this phase of the process, and at a logical level the principles are simple.

Security Levels

You must first decide the level of security required. Note that we're talking about securing the data here, not the system code, which is an implementation issue. Access and Visual Basic both provide mechanisms for protecting your code from accidental or malicious damage. At the lowest level of security is a completely unsecured system that allows everyone access to the database at any time. This is obviously easy to implement and administer, as you don't need to do anything in particular.

If your data has any value, however, implementing a completely unsecured system is reckless. It might make sense, however, if the client has implemented

a network security scheme by which access can be restricted. There's no need to duplicate security precautions.

The next level is *share-level security*. At this level, you assign the whole database a password and anyone knowing the password has full access to the system. This is also easy to implement and administer, requiring only that the password be changed periodically. Share-level security is adequate in many situations.

User-level security, although it requires more effort to implement and administer, provides the most discrete control over the database. User-level security allows the system administrator to assign specific privileges for each object to individual users: "Joe can add and edit information in the Customers entity but can only view Orders. Mary can add and edit information in the Customers and Orders entities. Neither Joe nor Mary can delete records of either type."

Actually, to call this "user-level" security is somewhat misleading. Security privileges *can* be assigned to individual users, but they can also be assigned to generic user roles to which individuals are assigned. This is a more effective mechanism for implementing security, as it requires far less administration.

Using this model, you first identify the types of users—system administrators, order-entry clerks, salespeople, and so forth—and then determine the security privileges each role has for each object in the system. It's not necessary to assign privileges for the data objects; in fact, it's not a good idea to do so. You might decide that salespeople need to be able to add, edit, and delete records in the Customers table, but you don't want them messing about with the table itself. You can assign them privileges to a Customer maintenance form, but not to the table. This ensures that they can't inadvertently bypass the special processing provided by the maintenance form.

Often you need to allow people to view only a portion of the data. For example, you might allow everyone to view the Name and Extension fields of the Employee table but allow only managers to view the Salary field. Or you might allow salespeople to see the Orders placed by their own clients but not anyone else's. To accommodate both these situations, you can assign privileges to queries and deny access to the underlying tables.

Auditing

In addition to controlling who has access to the data, perhaps you also need to know what users have done. These requirements can vary widely. Some organizations want to track who logged on to the system and when. Others require a detailed audit trail of who made what changes. Others require something in between.

How you model your auditing requirements depends on the exact requirements. If you simply need to track who used the system, a single entity with the attributes UserName, LogOn, and LogOff will probably suffice. Simply create a record when a user logs on, and update it when he or she logs off.

Sometimes you also need to know who added a record. This can be accommodated in the primary entity with one or two additional attributes: CreatedBy and perhaps CreatedOn.

Tracking deletions can be more complex. You have a couple of options here. You can prevent users from actually deleting records at all and set a Deleted flag instead, perhaps adding DeletedBy and DeletedOn attributes as well. This is a useful technique if you want to copy the records to an archive file before removing them from the database.

Alternatively, you can allow the deletions but write the necessary information to a log file, in the same way that you would if you needed to track the users who logged on. Of course, you'll probably have to create additional attributes. There's not much point, after all, in knowing that someone deleted a record unless you have some way of reconstructing what the record *was*.

If you need to know in detail what changes were made, you'll need to add an additional audit table to the model for each entity. This could track the user making the change, the date on which it was changed, the record changed, and the old and new values.

If you're going to implement any of these auditing features using a Jet database, you'll have to prohibit users from direct access to the tables, since that would allow them to bypass your security measures. SQL Server doesn't require this, since it supports database triggers, which cannot be overridden.

However you model the auditing requirements, you must also consider how this information will be used, by whom, and under what circumstances. Obviously, you need to restrict access to the audit tables. You might also need to add work processes to your system design to accommodate the auditing. Do the system administrators need to be able to reverse changes made? Are usage reports necessary?

In my experience, most auditing requirements are simply a form of insurance, and the information is intended to be used only in exceptional circumstances. If this is the case, you might not need to expand the work processes at all. The system administrators can easily use Access interactively or use the SQL Server Enterprise Manager to manually interrogate the data and perform any actions required.

SUMMARY

In this chapter, we've looked at translating the conceptual data model into a physical database schema. We began by examining two architectures for structuring the code in your system—the three-tiered model and the four-layer model—primarily from the perspective of how the choice of code architecture can impact the database schema.

We've also examined several possible data architectures. A single-tier system locates both the application and the data on the same logical machine. A single-tier application can run as a stand-alone application, or the data can reside on a network but be accessible only to a single user. Networked applications implemented using the Jet database engine are also logically single-tier, but the data may be accessed by multiple concurrent users.

You can implement two-tiered, or client/server, applications using SQL Server. In this logical architecture, the server machine performs the data manipulation, while the client is responsible for responding to the user. The basic principles of two-tier applications can be elaborated to three or more machines in what is known as an n-tiered application.

We then turned to the translation of the conceptual data model into a database schema. This is usually a straightforward process, as the only new information is the definition of indices and queries to be implemented in the database. Finally, we looked at the impact that security requirements can have on the database schema, and we briefly reviewed the design of a security scheme at the logical level.

In the next chapter, we'll take a quick look at some of the issues involved in communicating your system design to the client and the development team.

11

Communicating the Design

Unless you're building a database system for your own use, you need to be able to communicate the results to other people. Please note that I've said "communicate," not "document." All the documentation in the world isn't going to accomplish anything if it's obscure and unreadable. You can't learn a language by reading a dictionary, and you can't understand a project by reading tables of data.

Basic written communication skills are critical to this task, so if you have any doubts about your abilities, get a good book or sign up for a course at a local community college. I *promise* it will be time well spent. If your grasp of English grammar is faulty, your clients are bound to wonder what else you haven't understood quite as well as you should have. (And here endeth the sermon.)

Audience and Purpose

Understanding your audience is important in any writing, but particularly so in communicating a system design, since you're likely to have several types of readers with different requirements.

To understand who's going to be reading the document, and therefore what you should include, you need to consider what you and your readers are trying to achieve. Your clients need to confirm that you've understood their requirements and gain some assurance that the system will achieve their goals. They don't need (or want) to understand the details of how the system is to be implemented. If the document is going to be used as the basis for development, however, the development team needs exactly those details that will make the client's eyes cross.

Sometimes the best solution is to prepare several documents: one for the client and a different one for the development team. This is a particularly good approach if you're using an iterative development model, since it closely matches the model.

In these situations, I usually write multiple documents:

- A Requirements Specification, aimed primarily at the client, that documents my understanding of the system in (relatively) nontechnical terms.

- An Architectural Specification, read by both the client and the development team but aimed primarily at the latter, that details the interactions and dependencies between components.

- A separate Technical Specification for each component, for use by the development team.

For simpler systems, a single document will usually suffice. Just be sure that you've considered the needs of each of your audiences and provided the information required by each in a format they can easily understand.

Document Structure

Unless you're working in an organization that has specific documentation standards with which you must comply, the ultimate structure of your document depends on its scope and your own taste. It can be as simple or as complex as you think is appropriate; there is no standard format. I'll give you some guidelines in this chapter, but I'm doing so on the assumption that you'll adapt them to your specific needs.

If you've followed the recommendations I've made regarding the system analysis, you'll find that the document easily falls into several well-defined sections that (not accidentally) coincide with the previous chapters in Part 2. You'll probably also want to include an Introduction or Executive Summary aimed at management.

Executive Summary

In large organizations, a steering committee often oversees development projects. Even with small projects, usually someone in a management position who isn't directly involved in the project has oversight or budget responsibilities. If someone is overseeing your project, it's a good idea to include an Executive Summary aimed directly at that person.

These individuals are generally not terribly interested in the details of the system. They have a few specific questions they want answered, and the more efficiently you answer them, the better. Management is usually looking for answers to questions like the following:

- What problems does the proposed system address?

- Is this the best and most cost-effective solution?

- What other solutions have been considered?

- How long will it take to implement the system?

- How much will it cost?

- What are the risks?

Answering the first question should be simple if you've defined the system's goals and scope. You only need to restate them here. I like to be as explicit as possible about listing anything that might have been considered for inclusion in the system but was rejected. I find it's good insurance against finger-pointing later.

If you're an outside consultant, you might not be able to address the second and third questions regarding other solutions. If you do have access to this information, however, it's useful to include a brief description of other solutions that might have been considered and the reasons for their rejection. Management finds it reassuring to think that due consideration has been given to alternatives.

But do keep your answers to the second and third questions brief. If you've done an extensive evaluation of off-the-shelf applications and rejected them in favor of a custom solution, you'll probably have detailed information comparing cost, functionality, support, and so on. This isn't the place for it; put it in an appendix. As a matter of fact, the entire Executive Summary shouldn't be more than a few pages long.

Answering questions about time and cost can be tricky, and it's almost always scary. But answering questions becomes more manageable if you consider what you're asking management to buy into. If you're developing a simple system, you probably have a good idea of the answers, based on the defined scope. With large, complex systems, you won't yet know how long or how much, but that's OK. You'll know what the next step is, and that's all you need approval for at this point.

If you can realistically say something like, "It is not yet possible to estimate the actual time or cost for full implementation, but we expect it to be in the range of x to y. The next phase, however, will require only z to complete, and will result in....", then you should be fine. Just be sure that whatever follows the "result in..." is tangible and intrinsically valuable to the organization. In my experience, people are very hesitant to commit funds to "additional research."

I've also found that adequately addressing the final question, regarding risks, is one of the most effective ways of establishing your credibility. Spend time thinking about what could go wrong. Are there technical issues that haven't been resolved? Are things likely to take longer than expected? Where? Why? Be paranoid.

Now go back and be realistic. How likely are these things to happen? Yes, it's *possible* that your entire development team will be incapacitated by the plague or that the office will be destroyed by an airplane crash. But it's not very likely. What *is* likely is that sometime during the project *something* will go wrong, and management will want to know that you've thought about likely issues and have

contingency plans. You needn't list everything, perhaps only the top two or three concerns in a few paragraphs, but it is important that the risk issues be addressed.

If you're an outside consultant, I recommend that you not skirt the issue of your competence. Obviously, the first question anybody considering hiring you will ask is whether you can do the job. The Executive Summary probably isn't the best place to talk about your credentials, but you should address the risk of nonperformance. The details of risk negotiation are up to you; I won't presume to make recommendations. It's just been my experience that directly addressing the issue helps establish your credibility as a businessperson.

System Overview

Whether you have included a formal Executive Summary or a less structured Introduction, the first section of the document proper is the System Overview. This is one section of the document where the needs of all sections of your audience are similar. Both the development team and the client need to understand the overall scope of the project. The difference is only one of detail.

If you haven't prepared a formal Executive Summary, some of the information that might otherwise have been in that section should be included in the System Overview. Even if you have prepared an Executive Summary, you might want to discuss some of the issues in greater detail. Alternatively, some issues—such as the comparison of alternative solutions or risk management—can be extensive enough to warrant separate sections.

Your main goal in this section, however, is to establish the "big picture" of the system, which you should be able to accomplish by explaining the system parameters: the system's goal and scope, and the design criteria.

There isn't a great deal to say about communicating the system goal and scope. If you've understood them, you simply write them up in terms your audience can understand. If you haven't understood them, you better go back and find out now.

Again, I recommend being as explicit as possible about areas that are *excluded* from the scope of the system, including those that might be implemented later. Anything considered for inclusion in the system should be listed here, even if you've decided to exclude the area from the system's scope. Spend some time identifying areas that you think *might* have been considered for inclusion but were never explicitly discussed. This is the time and place to make sure you and your client are operating under the same assumptions.

If you have prepared a cost-benefit analysis for the system, it should be included in this document but not necessarily in this section. It's a question of style, but I prefer not to embed pages and pages of tables in the main document. It makes for a much more readable document if you include only summary information—perhaps one or two tables—in the main document and put the rest in an appendix.

The same holds true for documenting goals and scope. You might have prepared a detailed analysis of functionality, cross-referenced by the goal it supports, and normalized by the importance of the goals. This is a wonderful tool and will be useful throughout the project. But if the table is more than one page long, it belongs in an appendix rather than in the main text. Just include a summary table with a textual description and refer the reader to the appropriate appendix for more details.

Work Processes

The best way to communicate system work processes depends on how you've captured them. If you've used an outline format, you can include that in the text. If you've prepared work process diagrams, you'll want to include them in the document as well. Just be sure to include an explanation of the symbols you're using. In either case, be sure to explain what you mean by the terms "process," "task," and "activity," or whatever terms you're using.

No matter what form your work process description takes, include a narrative description of the work process. In the first place, preparing a narrative is a good double-check on the formal description. It's amazing how often you'll find minor errors this way.

In the second place, it's critical that people evaluate the work processes, and in my experience outlines and diagrams tend to be glanced at rather than understood. By providing a graphic and a narrative version, you're encouraging people to understand, and the two forms of information will help clarify each other.

If you're proposing changes to the work processes, include both the current and the new versions and highlight any changes in the narrative. Obviously, you'll want to explain why the proposed changes will improve workflow or resolve problems. You'll often find that the client will point out something that was overlooked in your initial analysis if you include an explicit discussion of the changes you're proposing.

Documentation of work processes is one area in which the needs of your various audiences can conflict. The development team will be expecting a discussion couched in technical terms: transactions being committed and data items being updated. Clients, on the other hand, need the process described using whatever terms they use. These can, coincidentally, be the same as computer terms, but they probably won't be.

When in doubt, err on the side of the client. On practical grounds, it's likely to be far less a stretch for the development team to understand the client's terms than the other way around. If you must use technical terms, make sure that you've adequately defined them in the document.

Unfortunately, this is much easier to say than to do. When you work full-time with computers, it's easy to forget that some of these terms aren't really in common usage.

I keep a checklist of words like "transaction" and even "file" and do a final review before submitting a document to a client. It's not difficult to do using the Find functionality of your word processor. Confused clients are rarely happy clients.

Conceptual Data Model

After completing the initial analysis of the system, you'll probably have a set of Entity Relationship (E/R) diagrams, a listing of domains used in the system, and some notes regarding data constraints. It's simple to get these organized into a presentable format. The entity analysis, perhaps illustrated by an appropriate E/R diagram for complex entities, is adequate documentation of the model. I usually treat the domain analysis as a kind of glossary in a separate section, referenced within the model proper.

This is one place where page after page of tables is probably inevitable. And there is no avoiding the fact that this is a fairly technical discussion, but it's one your clients can't avoid. All you can hope to do is make the process as painless as possible.

First, use the least technical terms you can, and use no more of them than you need to. "Table," "field," and "record" are probably inevitable, for example, but "entity," "relation," and "attribute" are best avoided. I know that less technical terms are imprecise. But they are close enough. Also make sure to define any terms you use (preferably without giving your users a short course in database design).

In practice, this isn't much of a problem. Once you've explained that each table represents a "thing" and that the fields are the "bits of information" about that thing, your clients are usually ready to go. You might have an occasional query about zip codes being handled as character fields or some such, but I prefer to deal with such issues informally as they arise.

If the document is doing double duty as a technical specification, you'll need to include any technical details the development team requires. I try to keep these details separate from the main tables, usually as a subheading under each entity. It doesn't take long for the clients to realize that they don't need to understand "this stuff." In these situations, I usually tell my clients that they need to review the attribute list for completeness and the domain analysis for accuracy, but they can ignore the rest.

In theory, the client should review the relationships among entities as well, but in practice I've rarely had clients catch any errors or misunderstandings in this area, and then only when I reviewed the model with them face-to-face. It's all just a little too foreign.

You'll have better luck asking users to review field sizes and data types. But even here, if you have serious concerns, it's safer to schedule a review meeting with the appropriate people. I find this tedious, but it's critical that these things be correct, so it might be unavoidable.

Alternatively, you might highlight the items you're concerned about. People's attention tends to wander when they're presented with 50 pages of tables to review, so if you highlight the items you need confirmed, you're likely to get better results.

Database Schema

Just as the database schema itself is largely a direct translation of the conceptual data model, the documentation of the schema generally looks like the documentation of the data model.

The information in the database schema is critical to the development team, but since it contains little additional information, it's largely irrelevant to the client. If you're not preparing separate documents, consider putting the table and query specifications in an appendix. The data architecture and security specifications, however, need to be confirmed by the client.

I usually document the data architecture using a combination of diagrams and a narrative description. This is another case of the two forms of communication reinforcing each other. The security requirements can be documented by a simple narrative description, but sometimes an outline or graphic can be useful if the security structure is complex.

User Interface

It's a good idea to prepare a draft user interface document to discuss with the client before you go too far into the user interface designs discussed in the remainder of this book. For small systems, however, a draft might unnecessarily delay the design process.

Even when you don't intend to perform a formal user interface design, it's often useful to dummy up some sample screens marked "DRAFT" or "SAMPLE." Sample screen layouts such as these can help users visualize the proposed system. You need to be careful, though. No matter how often you indicate that screen shots are only samples and subject to change in the release system, they inevitably *do* set user expectations. If the released system looks too different, all your good intentions might have only muddied the waters.

Setting user expectations is usually a problem only if the functionality for which you've provided a sample screen gets dropped from the scope of the project later. I have had users expect all the screens shown in the initial requirements, even though they'd seen and approved a later interface specification that excluded them. In these situations, I've learned to include the dropped screens in a section called Functionality No Longer Included or words to that effect. A brief description of the functionality being excluded and the reasoning behind the decision are extra insurance that everyone knows where they are.

Once you have defined the user interface, you need to communicate it to the users. There are two primary mechanisms for doing this: a prototype and an interface specification. I almost always prepare both, if for no other reason than building a nonfunctional prototype is the easiest way for me to prepare the illustrations, around which I structure the specification.

Interface Prototyping

The best tool I've found for communicating the interface for a new system is the interface prototype. Many users, particularly those without a lot of experience with computers, have trouble making the leap from seeing a set of screens on paper to imagining what the system will look like and how it will operate. Giving them an interface prototype means they won't have to make the leap.

Prototypes come in all shapes and sizes, and they can be used for any number of purposes. One of the simplest is just dummy screens and menus tied together to model the flow of the release system. The only code in an interface prototype is that required to link the screens together. All the controls are in place, but they are not tied to data or otherwise functional. Likewise, the only menu commands that do anything are those that display a dialog box. (Well, that's not quite true. I usually give the other menus secondary menu items that say, "This command will do such and so. This functionality has not been implemented in the prototype.")

The only exception to the "no-code zone" rule is when the physical display is determined by the data. For example, say you've designed a screen for entering and editing customer details, but the screen details depend on whether the customer is an individual or a company. You might decide to have the visibility of controls dependent on the choice a user makes in an option box. You'll need to implement this in the prototype.

I usually build the interface prototype using whatever front-end tool I expect to use in the final system. This is fast and efficient, but dangerous. You're building a prototype here, not a system, and so it's appropriate to take all kinds of shortcuts that would never be acceptable in production code. But it's hard to resist the temptation to use the prototype as the basis for the release system.

After all, all those screens and menus are already built, and it's a waste of time not to use them, right? Wrong. Those screens and menus are *prototyped,* not built. If you use the interface prototype as the basis for the release system, you run the risk of perpetuating the shortcuts you took, and they *will* come back to haunt you.

Because of this danger, some designers recommend that your interface design be done using a drawing tool rather than using a programming tool such as Microsoft Access or Microsoft Visual Basic. You should use whatever tool suits you best. For me, that means the programming tools I use every day. For you, it might be a drawing tool or even a presentation tool such as Microsoft PowerPoint. (I have one client who religiously takes screen shots of my prototypes and transfers them

to PowerPoint for his internal presentations.) The important thing is to be clear about what you're doing—you're documenting a design, *not* building a system.

Interface Specification

Although an interface prototype is a wonderful tool for giving users a sense of how the system will operate, it has intentionally limited functionality. For this reason, it cannot replace an interface specification. (The reverse of this is not true, however. A careful interface specification *can* eliminate the need for a prototype.)

Like the documentation of the data model, the user interface specification must include technical information that can't be entirely avoided by the client. The same recommendations apply—keep the technical terminology to a minimum, and wherever possible separate the really technical stuff that can be conveniently ignored by the client from the main body of the document.

If you've built an interface prototype, preparing the interface specification is straightforward. I include a bitmap of each screen; a narrative description of its purpose; and a table listing each control, its data source (if any), and any processing that the form implements. If you haven't built a prototype, you'll want to describe the layout in some other way, but the remaining information is the same.

In most systems, it's useful to include an overview of the system flow. If the system will support a number of distinct work processes, you might want to provide a model of the screen flow for each process. It's simple enough to do this by annotating the work process diagrams.

Change Management

Your design documentation will probably go through a couple of revisions before it stabilizes. Once it's reasonably stable, and certainly before you go to the next phase of the project, you'll want to place the document (or document set) under change control.

Note that "change control" is not the same as "freezing the specification," which I don't believe is realistic for even the smallest systems. If you plan for the inevitable changes, you'll make your life easier in the long run.

There are several ways to implement change control. I generally resist editing the documents; I've found it much easier to issue change sheets that function as additions to them instead. If the changes are extensive it might be easier to rewrite and replace either the whole document or sections of it, but this is an unusual occurrence.

If it's possible to establish a central location for the master specification, it might make sense to change or annotate the document. You can do this, for example, using the revision tools provided by a word processor such as Microsoft Word. The document could then be placed on a network share or perhaps published on an intranet.

The only problem I've found with putting the document in a central location is ensuring that people are working from the current version of the document and not from hard copies they've printed to scribble on. But the existence of a change management plan is generally more important than the details of the plan itself.

Special Tools

Two utilities that are part of Microsoft's suite of programming tools can be useful for publishing and maintaining design documentation: Microsoft Visual SourceSafe and Microsoft Visual Component Manager. Visual SourceSafe is designed primarily as a tool for controlling changes to source code during a development project, but the same tool can be used to manage the documents associated with the project.

I find Visual SourceSafe particularly useful for managing documentation when multiple designers are working on a project. The process of checking out documents before editing them eliminates the possibility of people overwriting one another's work, and it ensures that the most recent version of all documents is always available for review.

Visual Component Manager is a front end to the Microsoft Repository. It's bundled with the Enterprise edition of Microsoft Visual Studio. It's intended as a tool for administering documents and code components once they have been published, rather than for use during development. Visual Component Manager allows individual databases to be set up for each project, and I find it convenient for maintaining all the related documents in a single location.

If the project is developed using Visual Studio, the same project database can be used to administer all the code components as well, neatly keeping all the bits together. Unfortunately, Visual Component Manager is not integrated with Microsoft Access, although the Repository on which it is based is extensible and could theoretically be modified to do so.

SUMMARY

In this chapter I've given you some guidelines for communicating the system design to the client and the development team. You can consider them one designer's opinion. The strategies outlined here work for me, but more than in any other area I've discussed, you should adapt them to suit your own working methods and the needs of your clients.

Although this is the end of Part 2, we have not yet finished our examination of the database design process. In Part 3 we'll turn to the most critical component of your application: the user interface.

Designing the
User Interface

12

The Interface as Mediator

After you've completed the analysis tasks described in the previous section, you should have a good understanding of what the system you're designing needs to do. In Part 3, we'll look at some issues you need to consider when building the interface to the system.

We'll begin in Chapter 12 by looking at general approaches to designing interfaces and the different models you'll want to think about. The amount of information I can provide here is, of necessity, limited. To refine your user interface design skills, you'll need to turn to other sources. Several excellent books are listed in the bibliography, and a visit to your local technical bookstore will undoubtedly reveal others.

Effective Interfaces

In the minds of users, a system's user interface *is* the system; everything else is just stuff they're happy to ignore. The design of the user interface is therefore critical to the success or failure of a project. Get it right, and your users will forgive the occasional infelicity in implementation. Get it wrong, and it won't really matter how efficient your code is.

The irony here is that if you *do* get it right, hardly anyone will notice. Really elegant interfaces are invisible. Even if you get it wrong, no one might notice. The interfaces of many computer systems, particularly database systems, are so awkward that your system will be just one more of the mediocre, mildly abusive computer systems people have come to expect.

So if no one's going to notice, why bother? Well, why not? It is, after all, your job. At the risk of sounding like your mother, if you're going to design computer systems at all, doesn't it make sense to do it as well as you can? Designing effective interfaces *does* require more work than simply slapping a front end on

a database. Effective interfaces can also require more work to implement, although this isn't necessarily the case. In addition, the payoffs can be huge, and they're not all of the "virtue is its own reward" variety. An effective user interface minimizes the time users require to learn and implement the system. Once the system is implemented, productivity gains are higher if users don't have to struggle to bend it to their will. Chances are good that both of these issues were addressed in the project goals. They certainly impact the infamous bottom line.

Effective interfaces that closely match the users' expectations and work processes also minimize the need for external documentation, which is always expensive. And while users might not consciously notice how wonderful your user interface is, they'll certainly notice that your system seems to just work better than the one designed by UsersAreScum, Incorporated. That can effect *your* bottom line the next time a project or promotion comes up.

So, what constitutes an effective interface? To my mind, it's one that helps users accomplish their tasks and otherwise gets out of the way. An effective interface doesn't impose its requirements on users. It *never* forces users to play by its rules; it plays by the users' rules. An effective interface doesn't force users to learn a bunch of uninteresting stuff just to use it. And finally, it doesn't behave in unexpected ways.

We'll look at these three principles in this chapter, but first we'll take a brief look at a few models that are useful to consider when thinking about the design of user interfaces.

Interface Models

Alan Cooper, in his superb book *About Face: The Essentials of User Interface Design*, describes the way users think about systems (and the way systems think about users) in terms of three models: the mental model, the manifest model, and the implementation model. These three different ways of thinking about systems are useful tools for making decisions about the design of your application's user interface.

A user's *mental model* describes what the user *thinks* is happening. This doesn't often match what's really happening, but that's OK. I have a vague notion that my body "burns" food to provide me energy in the same way that an automobile engine burns gasoline. I do know that the processes are really quite different, but I don't care. I have to put gasoline in my car to keep it running and food in my body to keep *it* running. My mental model is perfectly adequate to get on with things.

The same is true of computer systems. Whether I'm using a typewriter or a word processor, if I hit a character key, a character appears. The mental model is the same. What's actually happening, of course, is quite different. What *actually* happens is the *implementation model*. All that behind-the-scenes stuff about

pulling levers or running code is part of the implementation. Users don't care, and shouldn't be forced to.

The user interface is the *manifest model* that sits between a user's mental model and the developer's implementation model. It is, if you will, the model of the process that the system *reveals* (manifests) to the user. Your goal in designing an interface is to hide as many details of the implementation model as possible. The ideal system exactly matches the users' mental model. It won't often be possible to match the mental model of the process *exactly*. But the closer you can get, the better.

If you're interested enough in computers to be reading this book, your mental model won't match the users' mental model. My mental model of using a word processor is that I hit a character key and an ASCII code is stored in RAM somewhere. This isn't very close to the implementation model, but it doesn't resemble what the average clerical worker thinks is happening either.

This is the great danger of designing interfaces: even if you aren't directly involved in the implementation, you almost certainly will know something about it. You have to either develop a knack for temporarily forgetting the implementation details or ask a user guinea pig to provide you with his mental model.

The best practice is to conduct formal usability tests using a prototype of the system. Although this is rarely possible, any kind of usability research is worthwhile. If you've built a prototype, find a few users and have them play with it. Ask them what they think is going on. You'll get some surprises. If you haven't built a prototype, you can ask about a similar system or even use a paper mockup. I haven't had a lot of success with this last technique, however. I've found that users get confused between an interactive screen and a report when both are presented on paper.

When you've gathered as much information as you can, think about where the implementation model (what's really going on) is intruding on the users' mental model, and then resolve those areas. Are you using the wrong terminology? *Always* use the words the users use. Are you forcing users to think about "editing records" when what they want to think about is "changing addresses?" This could be a terminology problem, or it could be a problem in the system structure, which we'll look at in the next chapter.

User Levels

I can't imagine that anyone ever intentionally set out to build a system that isn't "user-friendly." Perhaps usability wasn't a high priority, but no one would set out to build a system that's user-antagonistic. The problem is that "user-friendly" is one of those nice, well-intentioned expressions that doesn't mean much, so you're left scrambling around to find ad hoc definitions.

Two definitions of user-friendly that are often mooted are "easy to learn" and "easy to use." If we put aside for the moment the question of what, exactly, "easy" means, we still have to ask ourselves, "Easy for whom?" The system that's easy for a beginner to learn is not necessarily easy for an expert to use. Your best approach is to consider the needs of each level of user and accommodate each with different facets of the interface.

Beginner

Everyone is a beginner at some point. Very few people remain that way—they will either pass through the "newbie" stage to intermediacy, or they'll discard your system entirely in favor of someone else's. For this reason, you must be careful not to build in support for beginners that will get in the way of more advanced users.

Beginners need to know *what* your system does before they start to learn *how* to use it. The best way to present this information is outside the main system itself. For simple systems, an introductory dialog box that describes the system can be sufficient. (Just be sure you always include a means of dismissing the dialog box permanently.) For more complex systems, a guided tour might be more appropriate.

Online help isn't a good option for beginners. They might not know it exists or, if they do, how to use it. I have had some success using an online user's guide, however, by including a link to it from the introductory dialog box and from the Help menu. To be successful with beginners, these guides must be task-oriented. Beginners don't want to know what "menu item" means; they want to know how to create an invoice.

Intermediate

For most systems, the majority of users fall into the intermediate category. Intermediate users know *what* the system does, but they often forget the details of *how*. This is the group you must support directly in the user interface. Fortunately, the Microsoft Windows interface provides a lot of tools for helping these users.

A well-designed menu system is one of the best tools for reminding intermediate users of the system capabilities. A quick scan of the available menu items will immediately remind them of the functions available and at the same time allow them to initiate the appropriate task.

An excellent second level of support for intermediate users is online help. Writing online help is outside the scope of this book. In this context, however, I will mention that most intermediate users will use the index as their primary access mechanism. The index should therefore be as complete as you can possibly make it.

Expert

Expert users know what to do and how to do it. They're primarily interested in doing things *quickly*. The more shortcuts you can build into your system, the happier you will make this group of users. In my experience, expert users tend to be keyboard-oriented, so make sure that you provide a way to move around the system using the keyboard if you're catering to this group.

Expert users also appreciate the ability to customize their working environment. Providing this functionality can be an expensive exercise, however, so you will want to carefully evaluate the benefit before including it. If you *do* decide to include some level of interface customization, even if it's only a matter of arranging windows on the screen, be certain to maintain the changes between sessions. Nothing is as irritating as having to rearrange everything every time you load a program.

Putting Users in Charge

Just behind "user-friendly" in the nice-but-useless terminology stakes is the expression "user-centered." What does that mean? Well, unlike "user-friendly," it does have a meaning, albeit a rather vague one. A system is user-centered if it *always* responds to the users' requests and *never* imposes a specific method of working.

This principle is perhaps easiest to understand by way of an example. An acquaintance of mine, a developer for whom I have a great deal of respect, described his method to ensure that users enter data in the order most convenient for the system. He locks all the controls on the form except for the first one; once data is entered in that control, he unlocks the second, and then the third, and so forth.

Not only is this technique as far from user-centered as one can get, it's not going to work. Users often have good reasons for not entering data in a specific order—it might be unavailable or inconvenient to enter at the moment. If you force them to enter something, they will. They'll enter any old garbage that the system will accept. So you've offended them, imposed on them, and ultimately accomplished nothing.

We'll look at this issue in some detail in Chapter 16, when we discuss data integrity. Artificially enforcing data integrity is the primary way database systems try to wrestle control from users. The second way is by being obsessively modal. A *mode* is a system condition that limits users' interactions. The classic modes in database systems are add, edit, and view. A system that requires users to return to a main menu before editing the record they've just been looking at is ridiculously inefficient. Requiring them to choose a menu item or click a button before editing is not much better.

Unfortunately, many designers use this kind of modality as a matter of course. Perhaps in a mistaken attempt to protect users from accidental changes or because the use of Add, Edit, and View menu items was conventional 20 years ago, they perpetuate the paradigm in the Windows environment, where it is inappropriate. I strongly recommend that you assume the users know what they're doing. If they want to change a record, let them. They shouldn't be forced to ask permission to do so.

If you're going to allow users this much freedom, you must give them safety nets. Multiple levels of undo are easy to implement in both Microsoft Access and Microsoft Visual Basic. You might even want to include a Revert To Last Saved menu option to allow a user to discard all changes to the current record.

I don't like asking users to confirm changes before saving a record, although in some situations it might be justified. The whole idea of "saving" is foreign to most users. Remember the users' mental model. They've just made a change, and now you're asking them if they want to make the change, which is very confusing. Once they sort out what it means, most people just get in the habit of choosing "OK" every time the confirmation dialog box appears anyway, so the dialog box doesn't do much good.

Confirmation messages of this type are another instance of imposing on users without accomplishing much. In the few instances when I have implemented confirmation messages (usually at the insistence of the client), I've provided a mechanism for turning them off (generally in the Properties dialog box).

However, some extensive changes can't be undone, or at least not easily. Accidentally changing a field on a record can be easily fixed. Accidentally deleting all the records in a table can't. If you allow users to do things that you consider really dangerous, the best option is to provide a method for undoing the action. If that's not feasible, then by all means get them to confirm the action.

Just be sensible about how you define "really dangerous" and give your users useful information about the implications of their actions. The message box shown in Figure 12-1 will only scare them.

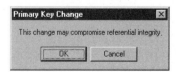

Figure 12-1. *This is a spectacularly unhelpful message box.*

The message box shown in Figure 12-2 is much better. Not only does it explain the situation in the users' terms, it also provides them with options besides OK and Cancel (which the average user interprets as "I am an idiot" and "I am an idiot. I offer my most humble apologies.")

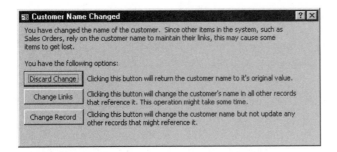

Figure 12-2. *This message box explains the implications of a user's action and gives her several options.*

Minimizing the Memory Load

People aren't particularly good at remembering things, which is one of the reasons we use computers. It follows that a good user interface doesn't make users remember any more than is absolutely necessary. Obviously they're going to have to learn (and remember) what your system does. And they'll need to remember some things about how to use it. But you should minimize the amount of information users need to remember wherever possible.

One approach is to comply with Windows interface standards and conventions. The *Windows Interface Guidelines for Software Design* gives one a set of conventions. You will rarely have a reason to change them and shouldn't do so arbitrarily. The Microsoft Office products—in particular, Access—set other de facto standards. If you vary from the standards, make sure you have a good reason. Otherwise, you probably aren't doing your users any favors.

You might think that your navigation widgets are *much* cooler than the default video buttons provided in Access. But pity the poor users. They've learned to press the ▶✱ button to move to a new record. Now you're making them remember that in *your* program they must click on that incredibly cute photograph of your cat having kittens.

Of course, the Windows interface guidelines only go so far, and they don't cover all situations. In most cases, you'll be able to extend the general guidelines to cover the specific situation you address. Where you do have to make decisions, stick to them. We'll talk about the importance of consistency in the next section.

It should be obvious that if you're trying to reduce the amount of information a user has to remember, you should never make them enter the same information twice. We've talked about the use of default values in this situation. You'll also want to make sure that you carry forward any relevant information if users must work through a series of forms.

Furthermore, users should never be asked to enter information that could reasonably be selected from a list. Computers are notoriously picky, and users

shouldn't have to worry about whether John Doe's Customer record was entered as "John Doe", "J. Doe", or "J.C. Doe". But note that I said "reasonably." Asking a user to wait while the system fills a combo box with 65,000 records is not reasonable. What is reasonable is providing them with a means of filtering the list and then picking from a manageable subset.

When you do present lists to users, include as much additional information as possible, particularly if the list items are not necessarily unique. Users shouldn't have to remember that "John Smith" is the one who lives in Madrid, while "Johnny Smith" lives in Milan. Microsoft Access list boxes and combo boxes allow you to show multiple columns of data. In Visual Basic, you can concatenate the relevant fields.

In both environments, consider displaying subsidiary information by means of a context menu. Technically, the display should be by way of a command, such as "Details", on the context menu. (Note that there is no ellipsis following the menu item, even though it displays a dialog box. Including an ellipsis is a common error.) However, if the details are short, you might want to display them directly in the context menu. This saves users a little time.

Finally, users should never be forced to remember obscure coding schemes. You might be using a system-generated number to ensure uniqueness of a record, but in most cases users should be unaware of its existence. Unless the number has some objective use like an invoice number, don't even display it.

Many organizations have developed lists of abbreviations representing things like product categories or sales regions. The rule I use to decide whether or not to use these abbreviations in the system is whether they're used in casual conversation. You want to avoid a situation where people *talk* about "the Southwest region" but have to enter "SWR". Only if they use "SWR" in conversation should it be used by the system. Even then, I would probably allow entry of both "SWR" and "Southwest" in the region field.

Being Consistent

Consistency in a user interface means more than just getting the File and Edit menus in the right place. The way your system interacts with users should also be consistent. When designing database systems, you need to pay attention to three areas: how users move through records in a table, how complex entities are represented, and how users initiate editing and adding records.

Most systems have a series of forms that represent each of the major entities in the system. You might, for instance, have a Customers form, a Products form, and a Sales Orders form. You must decide how users will move through the underlying recordsets. Unless you have a strong reason for using different mechanisms, you should choose one method and use it in every form.

By default, bound forms in both Access and Visual Basic display the first record in the underlying recordset and contain navigation buttons that allow users to move through the recordset. For various reasons, you might want to change this default interface. You might, for example, want to display only a single record and provide some other mechanism for choosing records to be displayed—perhaps a separate search form or a combo box control from which users can choose a record. Figure 12-3 shows an example of the latter technique, taken from the Access Developer Solutions sample database.

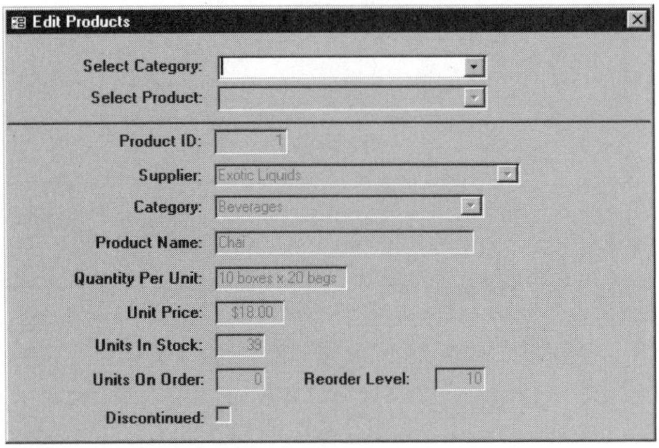

Figure 12-3. *A combo box can sometimes be a useful mechanism for users to choose a client, but you must use it consistently.*

Changing the default navigation mechanism is fine—in fact, there are often good reasons for doing so—but having chosen one, you should use it for all the forms in your system. It's unnecessary and confusing for users to have standard navigation buttons on the Customers form, a Find Order button on the Sales Order form, and a Products form presented in datasheet view.

The exception to this rule is if you have several categories of forms. You might decide to handle the forms used to maintain lookup tables differently than those used for entering primary entities. In this case, as long as the interface is consistent within the category, you're not placing an undue burden on users.

The second area where you need to be consistent is in representing complex entities. If you have entities that are modeled using more than one table in a one-to-many relationship (Sales Order entities are the classic example), you should be consistent in how you present them to users. You wouldn't want to present the line items of a sales order in a datasheet and the multiple contacts for a customer in a list box.

Unfortunately, consistency in this area is more difficult to maintain, particularly if there are more than two recordsets involved. A single form that has one datasheet for customer contacts, a second for addresses, and a third for products ordered can get ugly. You need to be inventive in these situations. Perhaps you can embed each datasheet in a tab control or use pop-up forms containing the datasheets. You might have to decide on *two* display methods and keep them as consistent as possible.

The final area to watch for consistency is the mechanism for creating and editing records, which must be absolutely consistent throughout the system. If one form allows editing in place but another requires users to explicitly enter edit mode by clicking on an Edit button or choosing a menu item, you've got a real user-confuser on your hands. Of course, edit modes aren't a good idea in general, as we've seen.

Sometimes, there are good reasons for locking records—that is, for not allowing editing in place—once they're saved. For example, you might allow users to change orders only prior to their shipment, after which time they become historical records that shouldn't change. Some designers implement a mechanism to check whether the order has been shipped when a user asks to edit it. Doing this is acceptable only if *all* forms behave this way.

A better solution is to allow editing in place but to lock all the fields on the form when a shipped order is displayed. This requires more work to implement, but it's work done by the system, not by the users, so it doesn't count. And it allows editing in place to be implemented in the rest of the system, where the locking of historical records doesn't apply.

SUMMARY

In this chapter, we've looked at some of the underlying principles in designing user interfaces. We began with a look at three interface models: the users' mental model of the system (what they *think* is going on), the system's implementation model (what's *really* going on), and the manifest model (what the system *shows* users about what's going on).

We then looked at three categories of users: beginner, intermediate, and expert. We briefly discussed the special requirements of each category and how those requirements might be best met by the system's user interface. Finally, we examined the three cardinal rules for user interface design: putting users in charge, minimizing the memory load, and being consistent.

In the next chapter, we'll turn to the overall system architecture and look at more tangible issues in user interface design.

13

User Interface Architectures

When you set out to design the user interface for your system, the first decision you must make is how to structure the overall system interface—the *user interface architecture*. In this chapter, we'll discuss several more-or-less standard architectures that are described in *The Windows Interface Guidelines for Software Design* and implemented in popular software.

You can invent your own user interface architecture, but as always when you're wandering away from existing standards, you should have a good reason for doing so. Remember that consistency, not just within applications but also between them, makes life easier for users.

Supporting the Work Processes

The most important principle in deciding how to structure the interface is that the choice must be based on the work processes your system supports, *not* on the structure of the data. Pay attention to what your users are trying to accomplish, and structure the system to support those activities.

It's an easy mistake to make: you look at the entity-relationship (E/R) diagram for the system and see an entity called "Customers," so you build a Customers form for creating and editing customer records. Then you build an Orders form that has a read-only reference to the Customers table. In an effort to make the system "user-friendly," you allow users to choose the customer name from a list, and you fill in the rest of the fields for them based on the information in the Customers table. Your form might look like the one shown in Figure 13-1, taken from the Northwind sample database.

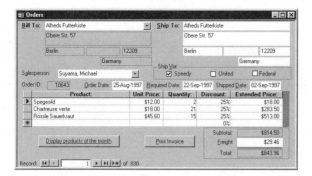

Figure 13-1. *The Orders form from the Northwind sample database.*

This isn't a bad form, as forms go, but think about the users' task: they're entering a sales order. They open the Orders form only to discover that the customer isn't yet known to the system. So they have to leave the form, go someplace else in the system and enter the new customer, and then *finally* they get to enter the order. If the Orders form hasn't been closed, they'll probably need to remember to press Shift+F9 (or something equally self-evident) to refresh the Customers list. Painful.

Some designers address this problem by using the NotInList event of a combo box to allow users to enter a new name. When the event is triggered, these designers display a message box asking whether to add a new customer, and if a user confirms the addition, the Customers form opens.

This solution saves a few keystrokes, but it still forces users to stop what they're doing (entering a sales order) and do something else (maintain the customer list). It would be far better to allow users to complete the task at hand without interruption. If a user enters a customer name that's not in the list, the fields that would otherwise have been filled in will be blank. (This is sufficient notice that the customer is new, by the way; there's no reason to scare people by beeping at them and displaying unnecessary message boxes.) After a user has filled in the fields, the system can quietly add the new customer record in the background.

If all the fields in the customer record can be obtained from the Orders form, you're done. If additional fields exist (as is often the case), you *might* decide to ask users whether they'd like to add that information after they finish filling in the sales order. (But be sure not to ask until the order is finished—it's rude to interrupt.) You should base your decision on the circumstances under which the order is being entered—in other words, on the work processes.

If the order is being entered by a sales clerk with the new customer standing in front of her, after the order is taken is an excellent time to capture that information. "Since you're a new customer, would you mind providing some additional information…" In the same way, if the additional customer information

(or at least some of it) is on the Orders form being used for data input, allowing users to easily enter the information while it's in front of them will save them from digging the papers out later.

But if users have a stack of sales orders to enter and the additional customer information *isn't* immediately available to them, they're going to dismiss the dialog 99 percent of the time without entering the additional information. Constantly prompting users to enter information they don't have isn't helpful, it's harassment. A better approach would be to flag the incomplete records to allow users to easily find them later when the information *is* available.

You might want to ask users whether they want to go directly to Customers maintenance (or whatever it's called in your system) when they exit the Orders form. But do this *only* if finding and entering this information is a sensible next step for the individuals who enter the sales orders.

Document Architectures

User interface architectures can be divided into two groups based on whether the application displays only a single window—a single document interface (SDI)—or displays a primary window inside of which additional windows can be opened—a multiple document interface (MDI).

Neither style of interface is intrinsically better or more user-friendly than the other. They both have advantages and disadvantages that we'll discuss in this section. Your choice of user interface architecture should be based on the work processes the system will support.

Single Document Interfaces

The SDI, as you might expect, presents users with only a single primary window. It can display additional dialog boxes for supplementary information. The SDI approach is suited to systems that are intended to maintain a single logical entity (which might be represented by any number of physical tables in the database). For example, a simple system for maintaining employee information might best be presented using an SDI.

The SDI has much to recommend it, since a single window is so easy for users to manipulate and keep track of. It conforms to the document-centered approach to user interface design recommended by the user interface wizards at Microsoft.

SDI systems are simple to build in Microsoft Visual Basic. It isn't possible to directly implement them with Microsoft Access, since all forms are contained in the Access window. You can, however, achieve the effect of an SDI by maximizing the system's primary form on application startup and eliminating its minimize button. In Access 2000, you can also specify that the form window be shown in the task bar. So with careful management, your Access system can be, for all intents and purposes, an SDI application.

Workbook applications

A workbook interface architecture is a special kind of SDI. In a workbook, different views of data are shown on tabs of a single window rather than in separate windows. Microsoft Excel is a good example of a workbook.

This interface architecture has the advantage of providing a secure context for users without restricting them to a single form. However, it can be mildly tricky to implement with acceptable response times. But provided performance concerns are adequately addressed during implementation, the workbook is an extremely useful paradigm for presenting different views of an object or for presenting views of a closely related set of objects when users don't need to compare them.

For example, you might want to use a workbook to display a summary report of the month's sales on one tab, a pie chart showing sales by category on another tab, and a bar chart displaying year-to-date sales on a third tab. These are related bits of information, and it's reasonable to expect that users would want to view the reports as a group. They probably don't need to see all the reports simultaneously, since the different reports are related but not directly comparable.

The tabs in a workbook have an implicit order that can be useful. Say that you're supporting a work process that consists of a number of discrete tasks and these tasks are often, but not always, performed in a specific order. You might use a workbook tab for each task. The order of the tabs supports the order in which the tasks are performed without forcing users to comply with that order.

On the other hand, a workbook isn't generally a good method for separating work processes—which tend to be quite distinct activities—or for presenting information that needs to be directly compared. Remember that only a single tab is visible at any given time, and you don't want to place an unfair burden on your users' short-term memories.

The Outlook-style interface

Another special kind of user interface architecture is what I think of as the "Outlook-style interface," since Microsoft Outlook is where I first saw it. This style of interface divides the application window into two panes, one containing a set of icons and the other containing documents, as shown in Figure 13-2.

I like this style of interface for applications that support multiple work processes. The icon bar on the left provides an immediate context for users, and dividing the bar into panels allows icons to be grouped into functional areas.

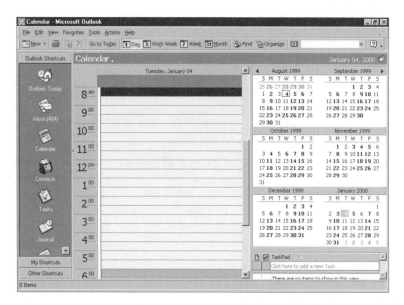

Figure 13-2. *The Outlook interface divides the application window into two panes.*

Unfortunately, neither Access nor Visual Basic provides intrinsic controls for implementing this style of interface, despite the fact that it's implemented in the Microsoft Access 2000 Database window, as shown in Figure 13-3. However, Outlook-style ActiveX controls, which you can integrate into either environment, are available from third parties.

Figure 13-3. *The Database window in Microsoft Access 2000 uses an Outlook-style interface.*

If you do adopt this architecture, it's a good idea to allow users to hide the icon bar, as Outlook does. The icon bar is a good navigation mechanism, but once users have loaded the document they want to work with, they tend to stay there awhile, and the icon bar takes up scarce screen real estate.

Multiple Document Interfaces

The majority of database systems use some version of an MDI. An MDI allows multiple child windows to be opened within the primary window.

Child windows can each contain different kinds of information, such as a form showing customers and a form showing orders. They can also show different views of the same information, such as a form with information about a customer and a report showing sales for that customer. Alternatively, they might show multiple instances of the same kind of information, such as one customer form showing details for Jones and another instance of the same form showing details for Smith.

As with SDIs, there are several ways of structuring MDI applications, each of which is suited to different requirements. We'll discuss the primary structures, but these configurations are not exhaustive, nor are they necessarily mutually exclusive.

The "classic" MDI architecture

The classic structure for an MDI application is for a primary window to contain multiple child windows of either the same or differing types. Microsoft Word is a good example—the Word window can contain multiple open documents at one time. The number of child windows open is (to the best of my knowledge) limited only by available memory.

MDI applications are useful in many situations where users need to compare several different bits of data or the same data in different formats. But MDI applications can be scary for new users: choosing "New Whatever" from the File menu doesn't occur to a lot of people when they're presented with an apparently empty window.

Word allows a command line startup switch (/n) to automatically open a new document window on application startup, and you might consider doing something similar in your own application if you adopt this interface architecture. You might, for example, provide a switch that causes the Orders form to open for data entry.

Be sure to provide a mechanism for turning this functionality off, however, as it can be irritating to users for whom it's inappropriate. You also need to be careful during implementation that you aren't inadvertently displaying error messages to users who immediately close the window or, worse yet, adding empty records to the database.

The major problem with the MDI interface is the inconsistency in the containment model. The parent window visually contains the child windows opened within it, but the application it represents doesn't necessarily contain the objects represented in those windows. This tends to be a more acute problem in applications such as Word, where the documents are actually distinct objects in the file system. Database applications usually do a far better job of isolating users from file system complexities. But even simple database applications are not completely effective in accomplishing this.

For example, look at Figure 13-4. Assume that a user has been switching back and forth between the windows and that uncommitted changes are pending in all of them.

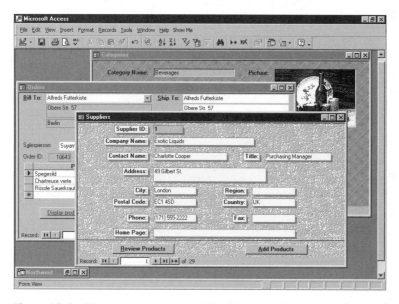

Figure 13-4. *The containment model in MDI applications can confuse users.*

If the user selects Save from the File menu, what's going to happen? Only the changes in the Suppliers window will be committed. *You* know that, because you know that menu options only apply to the current window. But does the user know that? Isn't it reasonable to expect that when you tell "Northwind" to save, "Northwind" will save all the changes you've made regardless of where you've made them?

The Windows Interface Guidelines for Software Design specifies that the item "Save All" can be added to the File menu to save all uncommitted changes in all open windows. This is undoubtedly a solution, but it's at best a compromise. It still requires that users understand that there's a difference between the MDI application and the objects on which it operates.

This difference is part of the implementation model, not the users' mental model, and it's one of the most difficult concepts for users to understand. Even relatively sophisticated users can get confused about what's stored where. I still get confused about what formatting is stored with the document and what's stored with the style sheet in Word, and I've been using the product extensively for many years.

All this having been said, however, classical MDI applications do have their place. They remain the best available solution for the majority of applications that require multiple windows to be open simultaneously.

Switchboard interfaces

A switchboard application displays a central form on application startup, as shown in Figure 13-5. Most of the buttons on the form are tied to either forms or reports.

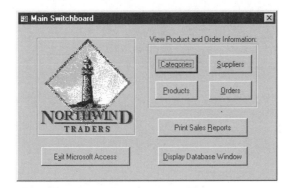

Figure 13-5. *A switchboard is displayed when the application starts up.*

The databases generated by the Access New Database Wizard use the switchboard structure, and so this structure has become quite common for database applications developed in that environment. It would be easy to implement similar behavior using Visual Basic.

I must admit to a prejudice against switchboards. Something about them feels DOS-like and clunky. I also worry that they encourage the "Find a Record/Edit a Record/Print a Record" menu structure that is so incredibly tedious for users.

Switchboard applications can be useful, however, if you have several distinct work processes that are being supported within the same application, and you either don't want to buy into the implementation complexity of the Outlook-style interface or your application requires multiple windows open simultaneously. A top-level switchboard that contains a button for each work process is an elegant mechanism for guiding users into the application.

The important thing to remember in designing switchboard applications, as with any other interface architecture, is to structure the switchboard choices around the work processes, not around the data. You should have a button for every activity users will want to perform, *not* for every form and report in the system.

Project interfaces

I think of a project interface as a switchboard application without a containing window. Instead, a "Project" window (which need not be called that, of course) provides a mechanism for opening windows independently on the desktop. The Visual Basic SDI interface is a good example of a project interface, as shown in Figure 13-6.

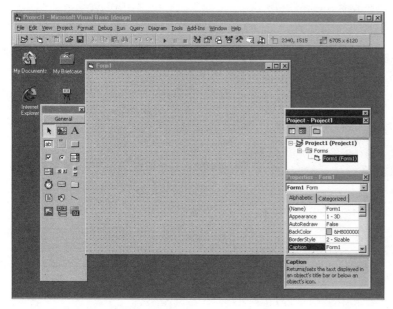

Figure 13-6. *Visual Basic in SDI mode is a project interface.*

Once open, these independent windows are displayed in the taskbar and users can manage them independently. They are also controlled by the Project window. When the Project window is minimized or closed, the secondary windows are also affected.

The project interface, by eliminating containment, avoids the model inconsistency inherent in classic MDI applications, but it substitutes another inconsistency: the relationship between the Project window and the (apparently) independent secondary windows.

Consider this scenario: A user opens a secondary window by double-clicking in the Project window, and then to free up space on the desktop, minimizes the Project window. Poof, the window the user just opened has disappeared. Yes, it can always be restored from the taskbar, but what a user-confuser.

If you like the idea of a project window, I think that the model of the Database window in Access is preferable to a conventional project interface. The Database window provides the navigation advantages of a project window without the potentially frightening side effects, since it's part of a classic MDI application.

Wizards

The final form of interface architecture that has a role in database applications is the wizard. Wizards are made up of a series of pages displayed in a dialog box, as shown in Figure 13-7.

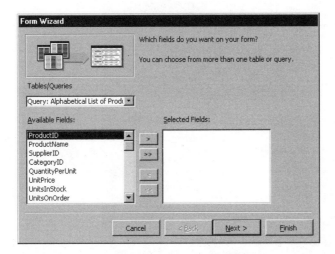

Figure 13-7. *Microsoft Access 2000 uses wizards extensively.*

Wizards are most often used to support tasks that are performed infrequently, such as installation or hardware configuration. But it's certainly appropriate to use them to support infrequent work processes in database applications.

Wizards can also be useful to support complex work processes. If a work process consists of many distinct tasks that must (or at least can) be performed in a specific order, a wizard might be a good interface choice. Wizards are particularly useful if the work process has a lot of conditional tasks: "If condition a, perform task 3 and then task 4; if condition b, skip to task 6."

Using wizards for complex work processes is feasible, however, only if the individual tasks can be completed in the order in which the wizard presents them. This occurs less often than one might expect. If the tasks needn't be

entered in a specific order, a wizard isn't the best interface, or at least shouldn't be the *only* interface for completing the task.

When using a wizard in a database application, you need to give careful consideration to how and when data entered by users should be stored. The usual model is that if a user presses Cancel at any point during the process, the system is returned to the state it was in before the wizard was initiated—that is, any data the user might have entered is thrown away.

Depending on the application, you could consider either saving the data as each wizard page is completed or giving users the option of saving previously entered data when they cancel. I don't recommend either of these as a general rule, but if the wizard has a lot of data entry, it might be justified.

Alternatively, you might consider allowing users to temporarily halt a wizard and continue it later. This is a very usable solution, but it does add quite a bit of implementation complexity, since it requires a temporary data store, some mechanism for determining where a user stopped, and the ability to resume from that point.

SUMMARY

In this chapter, we've looked at various ways you can structure the forms in your system. At the highest level, you have a choice between an SDI system that displays all its data in a single window and an MDI system that uses multiple windows.

SDI systems have two variations: workbooks and the Outlook-style interface, each of which has advantages in certain situations. More variety exists in MDI applications, from the classic MDI through the switchboard architecture supported by the Access Database Wizard applications, and including the project architecture exemplified by Visual Basic. Finally, wizards can be a useful architecture for supporting infrequent tasks and complex work processes.

In the next chapter, we'll turn from the organization of forms to the structure of the forms themselves, when we look at determining form layout based on the structure of the entities in the data model.

14

Representing Entities in Form Design

In this chapter, we'll look at how to structure individual forms based on the way the entities displayed on them are represented in the data model. (We've been concentrating so hard on work processes in the last few chapters that you might be wondering why you did all that data modeling.) Your decisions about what data to include on any given form are based on work processes, but having made those decisions, the form layout and choice of controls will be determined by the actual data structures the forms represent.

The first decision you must make is how a form maps to the Entity Relationship (E/R) model. Does this form represent a single entity, two entities in a one-to-one relationship, two entities in a one-to-many relationship, or more than two entities? Each of these entity structures lends itself to certain kinds of form layouts, which we'll look at in this chapter. Of course, just like the architectures we explored in Chapter 13, these layouts are only general guidelines, not rules. These are the layouts that, in my experience, most naturally fit certain types of data structures.

Simple Entities

The easiest kind of entity to represent on a form is a simple entity that is represented by a single table in the database. If such an entity participates in any relationships, it is either on the many side or the other participant will not be included on the form.

For example, look at the E/R diagram in Figure 14-1, representing the Customers entity and its relationships.

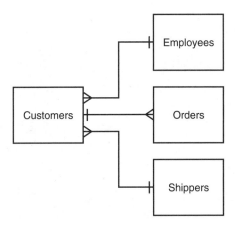

Figure 14-1. *This E/R diagram shows the entities that are related to Customers.*

The Customers entity is on the many side of all the relationships shown in the diagram except for the relationship with the Orders entity. Somewhere in the application, you will probably have a form for maintaining customer information. (This is true even if all the data is initially captured as a by-product of other activities.) You probably won't include the Orders entity on this Customers form. Orders are logically distinct, and users would maintain them elsewhere in the system.

The Customers entity is therefore on the many side of all the entities that are included on the customer maintenance form and so can be treated as a simple entity. This makes for a straightforward form layout. You don't need subforms or grid controls. Simply choose the control that best represents each field (as discussed in the next chapter), slap it down on the form, and you're finished.

Well, you won't *slap* it down, you'll arrange all the controls neatly, with a seven-unit margin and four units between each control, and with the most important items placed in the upper left corner, as described in *The Windows Interface Guidelines for Software Design,* right? But you get the idea. There's nothing tricky required unless you run out of space on the form.

But you might very well run out of space. Technically, you can add 754 controls during the lifetime of a Microsoft Access form or report (with controls deleted later still counting toward the total) and have a maximum of 254 controls on a form in Microsoft Visual Basic (with control arrays counting as a single control).

Practically, you won't want users to have to deal with more than about 25 to 30 controls or control groups at one time. (Note that I said "controls or control groups"; a group box containing three or four radio buttons counts only as one logical control.) So what do you do if you have a simple entity with 75 attributes? You must show only part of the data at any one time.

The easiest way to structure a form that represents an entity with too many attributes to display comfortably is to break the fields down into groups or categories. I usually start by picking out the attributes that are used to firmly identify the entity. By this, I mean not just the candidate key attributes, but also whatever descriptive attributes users will need to be certain they're working with the correct instance.

For a Customers entity, for example, this group of identifying attributes probably includes the name and address details, and perhaps the Sales Representative attribute. For a Products entity, it might include the ProductCategory, Name, and Description attributes. This group of attributes should be on the top of the form and always visible.

The remaining attributes are then divided into groups that are related and need to be viewed together. For a Customers entity, you might combine those attributes that represent sales terms—standard discount and payment terms, for example—into one group, and contact information—purchasing officer, sales manager, and so on—into another. For a Products entity, you might combine technical specifications in one group and packaging-related attributes in another.

Having organized the attributes into groups, you have a couple of options. You could use a tab control on the main form with each group on a separate tab. This is the solution I use most often. Tab controls provide the most context for users—they know immediately that additional information is available and what that information is. If you have more than five or six groups, however, a tab control is unworkable.

In this case, you might have to move some or all of the groups to subsidiary forms. Subsidiary forms are also useful if the individual groups contain more attributes than you can comfortably fit on one tab. You could allow users to open the subsidiary forms from command buttons on the main form, in a structure similar to a switchboard. With too many command buttons, however, your form will once again become unworkable. A better solution in this case would be to have the subsidiary forms available from a menu.

Be careful to maintain context for users when using subsidiary forms. Users should always be sure to which instance of the entity the displayed details pertain. The easiest way to identify the entity is by having the subsidiary form repeat details from the main screen. It's not usually necessary to repeat the entire identifying group—just enough of the group to tie the subsidiary form to the master form.

Alternatively, you could make the subsidiary forms modal. This is one of the few places where modality can be justified in a system, since it helps maintain users' context. However, modal forms always constrain users, which is something you should avoid doing wherever possible. I use this technique only as a last

resort, when there absolutely isn't enough real estate to include the few attributes required to maintain context.

Rather than using multiple subsidiary windows, you could theoretically display the secondary information in multiple subforms (Frame controls, in Visual Basic) on the main form. I don't like this approach very much, as it's difficult to maintain the users' context. You must provide some mechanism for determining which subform is displayed. If you use a menu for controlling the display, there's no indication on the form itself that other information is available. If you use some control on the form, perhaps a set of radio buttons, it might not be immediately clear to the users why their form display keeps changing. I think it's preferable to use a tab control, which is an established mechanism, rather than inventing your own approach.

One-to-One Relationships

In most cases, forms that present information from two entities that have a one-to-one relationship can be handled just like forms that represent simple entities. You create a query that combines the appropriate fields from the two tables, and then you treat it as a single simple entity. If you have more attributes than can be comfortably displayed on a single form, the same techniques as for simple entities apply.

If the primary entity participates in multiple one-to-one relationships, the nature of the relationships determines the most natural layout. If the relationships can coexist, you can treat them as one big recordset and show the information on a single form or on multiple forms, as we discussed doing for simple entities.

Many times, however, the relationships are mutually exclusive, as when any given Product can be either a Beverage or a Cheese, but not both. This is a good time to use multiple subforms or frames, providing you have enough real estate. You needn't worry about users understanding that more related information is available in a given context; there isn't any information. In fact, using a tab control in this situation would be misleading.

If you have real estate problems, you'll need to use one of the techniques for grouping and displaying that we talked about for simple entities. If the controls representing the attributes of the subclass are placed on a tab, it's best to try to find some generic term for the tab label. It can be confusing for users if a tab label (or command button label) changes as they move through the table.

For the same reason, if users are able to move through the primary recordset, I try to avoid having the controls displaying the attributes of the subclassed entity on the first tab of the tab control. Since the controls for each subclass are different, the form display will jump as users step through the records. By

keeping the subclassed attributes off the first tab, you can keep the display stable and can incidentally provide some performance benefits by not recalculating the display unnecessarily.

One-to-Many Relationships

Many forms need to display entities that are linked in a one-to-many relationship. Determining the best layout for these forms is easy, as long as you remember that the form needs to display a one-to-many relationship, *not* a many-to-one relationship. When you're modeling complex relationships, it's often easier to think in terms of records rather than instances of entities. So in this case, you must be certain that the record on the one side must control the display of records on the many side, and not the other way around. Try to control the one-side record from the many-side record, and you'll tie yourself (and the system, and your users) in knots.

Having established that the record on the one side controls the form display, you need to decide how the records on the many side are to be displayed. You have two choices: you can display them all at once or one at a time.

Your choice is largely determined by the amount of detail users need to see for each many-side record. If you need to show only a few fields, you can usually display them all at once. The form shown in Figure 14-2, from the Northwind sample database, uses a subform to display four fields for each record on the many side.

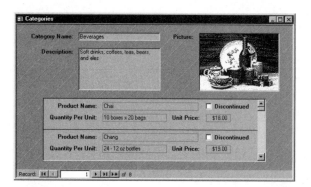

Figure 14-2. *This form displays the records on the many side of the relationship using a subform in continuous view.*

The vertical scroll bar on the subform indicates that not all the records are visible at any one time. For design purposes, this still counts as "all at once." In the next chapter, we'll look at some other ways to display multiple records.

I prefer the "all at once" form layout, since it provides the most context for users. You can always provide a mechanism for displaying additional details on a subsidiary form if you have real estate problems. But this style of layout isn't always appropriate or possible, and you might need to display the many-side records one at a time. Here, there are two issues you must address: making it clear to users that there are multiple records, and providing a mechanism for users to move between records.

The form in Figure 14-3 is identical to the one in Figure 14-2, except that the subform is shown in single record view rather than as a continuous form.

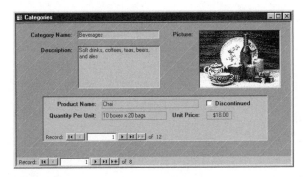

Figure 14-3. *This form displays the records on the many side of the relationship one at a time.*

The "video button" record selectors at the bottom of the subform are the default record navigation mechanism provided by Microsoft Access. As a rule, I stick to defaults wherever possible, but look at the result here: two record selectors are stacked on top of each other, with only their position to indicate which record selector is for the recordset in the subform and which is for the primary recordset. This isn't the end of the world, but it's not an optimal solution.

You can sometimes remove the record selectors from the primary form. This could be feasible for the form in Figure 14-3 if you provide a good interface for finding product categories. Users aren't all that likely to page through a maintenance form such as this one anyway, and a good find facility would almost certainly meet their needs.

Alternatively, you could replace one of the record selectors with some other movement mechanism—command buttons or a custom scroll bar, for example. However, using a different technique for moving through records can be difficult to handle because you're introducing inconsistency into the interface. It can be done, though, if you're careful about choosing a paradigm and sticking with it.

For example, you could decide to use something like the Forward and Back toolbar buttons in Microsoft Internet Explorer to control movement between records on the one side, and use the video button record selectors for moving between records on the many side. This will work as long as you use this paradigm consistently within the application. Thus even forms that represent simple entities, and therefore don't have many-side records, should use the Forward and Back buttons.

Occasionally, a form will display a primary table that has multiple one-to-many relationships, and you will need to display more than one of the tables on the many side of the relationships. I avoid these situations wherever possible. Multiple many-side tables on a form can be messy to design and even messier to implement, but sometimes you have no choice. If you must display multiple one-to-many relationships on a single form, the easiest solution is to use a tab control to separate the many-side displays. This solution provides a clear context for users. It can also improve performance, since the records for the tab control only need to be loaded when the control is displayed.

What you should try most earnestly to avoid is having a whole bunch of multirecord controls simultaneously visible. They would be slow and ugly, and their appearance on a single form implies a relationship between the entities on the many side that probably doesn't exist. In Figure 14-4, for example, it's unclear whether the listed phone numbers pertain to the company or the contacts.

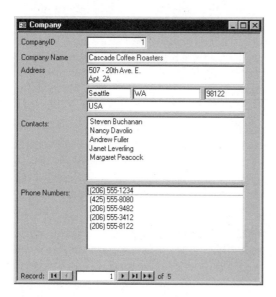

Figure 14-4. *It's unclear whether phone numbers on this form are for the company or the contacts.*

Hierarchies

Any one-to-many relationship is technically a hierarchy, but the term is usually restricted to relationships consisting of three or more recordsets: a one-to-many-to-many relationship, if you will. Hierarchical relationships occur frequently in data models, but they don't often need to be represented in forms.

In Figure 14-5, for example, the Customers to Orders to Order Details relationship is a three-level hierarchy.

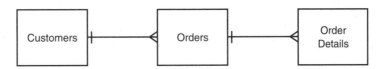

Figure 14-5. *This E/R diagram shows a three-level hierarchy.*

With this kind of structure, most applications would have a Customers form that, if it displays order information at all, shows it in a summary format. A separate Orders form would display the Orders and Order Details items. The Orders form would reference the Customers entity, of course, but would display the one-to-many relationship between Orders and Order Details only. Not many applications require a form that displays the details from all three tables.

However, it's difficult to know whether this tendency to avoid displaying hierarchical relationships is due to a lack of real need or to the difficulty of displaying them sensibly. Suppose, for example, that the client has requested the ability to review orders using the customer maintenance form. It would be easy to provide this functionality by displaying the records from the Orders table (the middle level) one at a time and the Order Details records all at once. Essentially, this would mean embedding the form shown in Figure 14-2 (on page 209) as a subform on the Customers maintenance form.

A one-at-a-time view of Orders records isn't really appropriate in these situations, however. Users are more likely to be asking, "How many orders has this customer placed?" or "What was their average order total?" than they are to be asking about specific products. Answering these common questions would be tedious if you represent the Orders records one at a time.

To avoid this problem, you might decide to display only summary order information on the Customers form and provide a mechanism for opening a subsidiary Orders form if users require more details. Unfortunately, this "summary with details" approach has some serious drawbacks as well.

If users want to review order details to determine what products the customer orders most often, they must endure the overhead of opening a second form.

Since the subsidiary Orders form usually displays an order in single form view, it's also difficult to compare the products ordered on multiple occasions.

Until recently, about the only viable alternative was to use a tree view control. Tree view controls are wonderful tools, but they are limited in the amount of data they can show at each level of the hierarchy, since all the data must appear on a single line. This restriction would make a tree view inappropriate for our example. Imagine trying to display all the customer details in a single line.

Fortunately, everything got a lot easier with the release of Access 2000 and Visual Basic 6. Both of these development tools provide a mechanism for nesting data shown in a multiple-record format. Access 2000 subdatasheets support the presentation of hierarchical data in an outline-like format, as shown in Figure 14-6.

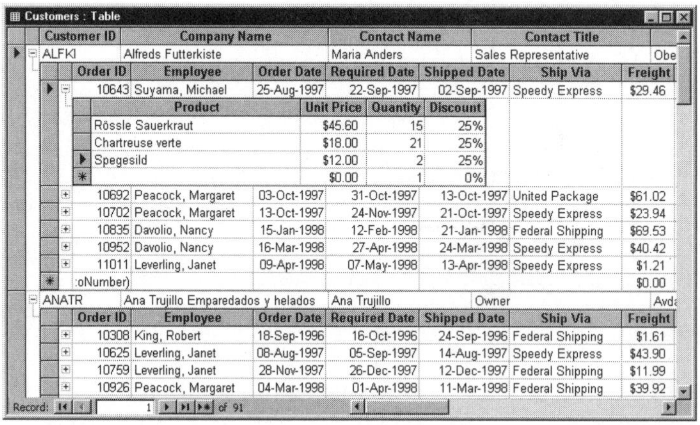

Figure 14-6. *Microsoft Access 2000 subdatasheets display hierarchical data.*

Subdatasheets aren't very pretty, but they work. Subdatasheets can be nested up to eight levels deep, but you can nest only a single recordset at each level. You couldn't, for example, create a subdatasheet that included both Addresses and Orders at the same level. The Visual Basic 6 Hierarchical Flexgrid control allows you the same sort of hierarchical display as subdatasheets, except you can nest multiple recordsets at each level.

Unfortunately, data displayed by the Hierarchical Flexgrid is read-only. If users need to edit the data, you must tie it to an additional set of controls, either on the same form or a secondary one. This can obviously lead to awkwardness in the user interface—it's always preferable to allow users to edit data in place.

A read-only display is often acceptable, however. Clients tend to use hierarchical data displays for review and management and to maintain data as part of a separate work process.

Many-to-Many Relationships

The final type of logical relationship that you might need to display in a form is the many-to-many relationship, which is represented by three or more tables in the database.

In the vast majority of cases, you can treat many-to-many relationships as though they were one-to-many relationships. For example, Figure 14-7 shows a many-to-many relationship between Customers and Products, with the Orders and Order Details tables acting as the junction tables.

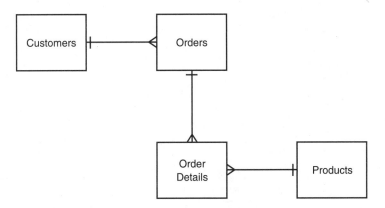

Figure 14-7. *Customers and Products have a many-to-many relationship.*

It's reasonable to display all the products a customer has ordered (in which case, you would treat the Customers table as the one side of the relationship) or all the customers who have ordered a product (in which case, the Products table is the one side). You can use the same presentation techniques as for any other one-to-many form. You need only address where to include data from the junction tables and how to handle duplicates on the many side.

Most junction tables contain only the primary keys from each side of the many-to-many relationship. As we saw in Chapter 3 and as shown in Figure 14-7, however, the relationship itself sometimes has attributes that are modeled as part of the junction table. If you need to include these attributes in your form, they should be displayed with the many side.

In our example, if the form is to display the products for each customer (the Customers table being the one side), the order date—which is a field in the Orders table—is clearly part of the product information, not the customer information. "Customer X bought product Y on the 15th and product Z on the 18th…" The order date would be part of the customer information if the display were the other way around, with Products being the one side: "Product X

was purchased by customer Y on the 15th and customer Z on the 18th...," as in this case the Customers table is treated as the many side.

It's quite likely that there will be duplicates, or at least partial duplicates, on the many side of the display. You must decide whether to display each item individually or to show summary information. For example, if you are listing the customers who purchased each product, you might choose to list the customer once for each product purchased; or you might just list each customer a single time, and show the total number of times the customer ordered the product and the total (and perhaps the average) quantity purchased.

You need to be careful here to avoid listing complete duplicates. It's of no use whatever to simply list a customer name 27 times if you're not providing any additional information, such as the order date. The only reason users might want to see this information is to determine the number of orders a customer placed, and the application should do this arithmetic, not the users.

Although treating a many-to-many relationship as a one-to-many relationship meets most requirements, there are times when you need to display the relationship fully. A product manager reviewing the customers who purchased a specific product might want to know what other products those customers purchased in order to develop "package deals," for example.

One relatively simple solution here is to treat the relationships as hierarchies and use subdatasheets or Flexgrid controls for display. The danger in this technique is that it isn't necessarily clear what the additional information represents. If you insert in a product listing a subdatasheet that lists only customer names, for example, it might not be immediately clear whether these are the names of customers who purchased a product or suppliers who are the source of the product.

If you're concerned about the potential confusion of a hierarchical display, or if the client doesn't commonly require hierarchical information, it might be better to provide the information in a secondary window, where you can make its meaning clear. Using a secondary window also allows you to provide summary information in addition to or in place of the straight details.

A product manager looking at other products bought by a customer might prefer a list of products purchased by all customers who bought the primary product to be organized according to the percentage of overlap—for example, all the customers who bought a widget bought a gizmo, but only 10 percent of these customers bought a doohickey. You can, of course, provide some of this summary information on the main form, but since the calculation is fairly complex (and therefore time-consuming), you are better off displaying it on demand in the secondary window unless it is frequently needed.

The two techniques for displaying all the data in a many-to-many relationship are not mutually exclusive. You can provide a list of customers for each product in a hierarchical display on the main form, and you can also provide a "top ten customers" display in a secondary window that users view on demand. As always, you must base your decisions on how you anticipate the form will be used.

SUMMARY

Having looked in Chapter 13 at how you can organize forms based on the tasks users perform, in this chapter we've examined how to structure the controls on the forms, based on the structure of the entities they display.

The choices you make in structuring your forms will be determined primarily by the entities that are to be represented on the form and—if more than one entity is represented—how the entities are related. Secondarily, the form's structure will be determined by the number of attributes to be displayed, since best practice dictates that no more than 25 to 30 controls or control groups should be visible on a form at one time.

In the next chapter, we'll move to the next level of user interface design: choosing individual controls to represent different kinds of data.

15

Choosing Windows Controls

In Chapter 14, we looked at various ways to structure forms based on how the entities represented in them are related. In this chapter, we'll look at how to match specific controls to certain kinds of logical data.

Two basic principles apply to choosing controls. The most important is to choose the control that best matches the way users think about the data—in other words, to match the users' mental model. Secondarily, you should limit user input to the narrowest possible range of values.

People who work with databases tend to think of data as textual values. If you open a recordset in datasheet view in Microsoft Access, as shown in Figure 15-1, all the fields are shown as text. But in fact only the CustomerName field has a Text data type. CustomerNumber is an AutoNumber field, DateOfFirstOrder is Date/Time, CreditLimit is Currency, and PreferredCustomer is Yes/No (Boolean).

CustomerName	CustomerNumber	DateOfFirstOrder	CreditLimit	PreferredCustomer
Alfreds Futterkiste	10060	9/4/98	$5,000.00	No
Ana Trujillo Emparedados y helados	10061	3/4/98	$2,000.00	No
Antonio Moreno Taquería	10062	1/28/98	$10,000.00	Yes
Around the Horn	10063	4/10/98	$15,000.00	Yes
Berglunds snabbköp	10064	3/4/98	$30,000.00	Yes
Blauer See Delikatessen	10065	4/29/98	$5,000.00	No
Blondel père et fils	10066	1/12/98	$20,000.00	Yes
Bólido Comidas preparadas	10067	3/24/98	$10,000.00	Yes
Bon app'	10068	5/6/98	$25,000.00	Yes
Bottom-Dollar Markets	10069	4/24/98	$10,000.00	Yes

Figure 15-1. *This datasheet shows several data types as textual values.*

When systems designers are manipulating data, we of course think about different data domains and don't try to join a date to a Boolean value. Nevertheless, there is a tendency to display values of different types the same way, usually

in text boxes. This approach works—you can display any data type in a text box—but it isn't doing your users any favors. You should consider a text box to be the control of last resort and use it only after you've determined that the other, more specific control types are inapplicable.

Looking at a field declared on the Date/Time domain, you might see a string of characters formatted in a specific way, but users see a date. Their mental process is not at all the same when changing a date as when changing a text string. If a user has mistyped a name, she might think, "The J in 'Jary' needs to be an M." If a user needs to change a date, however, she's more likely to think along the lines of, "Oh, that really should be a week from Monday." You can make users' lives easier by choosing a control that supports the way they think about the data.

You'll also make users' lives easier by limiting the values they can enter. Data limitation isn't the same issue as data validation, which we'll discuss in the next chapter. Data validation is an after-the-fact check performed by the system to ensure that the value entered is reasonable. Data limitation prevents users from entering an unreasonable value in the first place.

The place to start is, of course, limiting the type of data that users can enter. For choosing controls, data can be organized into four groups: logical data, sets of values, numbers and dates, and text. We'll look at each of these in this chapter.

| NOTE | It isn't possible for me to discuss the seemingly endless variety of widgets, gizmos, and gadgets available from third-party suppliers as ActiveX controls. I've limited my discussion to those provided by Microsoft Visual Basic and Access. However, I do encourage you to familiarize yourself with what's available. (The Microsoft Web site is a good place to start.) You'll find a lot of junk around, but a lot of seriously cool stuff, too—and you might find that a few hundred dollars spent on a third-party tool can save you weeks of development and testing. |

Representing Logical Values

Although you can display logical values in a text box, it's not a good practice. For example, a Customer table might contain a field called CreditApproved that you declared as a Boolean value (a Yes/No data type in Access). You *could* use a text box to display the field and then use data validation to check that users have entered "Yes," "No," "True," or "False." But allowing unlimited data entry like this is just begging for users to enter "Provisionally" or "Deadbeat." Unless you're prepared to accept and interpret these entries, you can do the users and yourself a favor by using a control that's limited to two values.

Both Access and Visual Basic provide two controls that do a better job: check boxes and toggle buttons, which are shown in Figure 15-2.

Figure 15-2. *Each check box and toggle button control is used to display a logical value.*

Most people are familiar with check boxes, and they're a good choice for representing most logical values. Toggle buttons are used less frequently. They're more effective for Boolean values that equate to "on" and "off" rather than to "true" or "false." The problem with toggle buttons is that in their "off" state they're indistinguishable from command buttons. Since users expect that pressing a button will cause some action to be performed, many might be hesitant to press a button labeled "Credit Approved," thinking that doing so will initiate the approval process rather than simply indicate that it has been completed. For this reason, I prefer to use toggle buttons in sets, like option buttons.

On the subject of option buttons (also known as radio buttons), please don't use these controls to represent single logical values. Nothing in the Microsoft Windows environment actually prevents you from doing so, but it's unnecessary (check boxes do just as well) and inappropriate. Option buttons are intended to represent a set of mutually exclusive choices. A single option button all by its lonesome looks peculiar.

Worse, if you're using option buttons to represent several logical values in the same area of the form, users are likely to erroneously believe that they are somehow related and that they can choose only a single option button at a time. They will also expect that selecting one option will automatically cause the others to be deselected. It's always disconcerting to users when a computer system doesn't behave as they expect.

Representing Sets of Values

A number of controls allow you to display sets of values on a form. The choice is largely determined by whether you need to capture a single value (albeit drawn from a range of values) or several.

Capturing a Single Value from a Set of Values

The acceptability of a given value is often determined by its existence in a list. For example, the CustomerNumber value in an Orders record might be valid if

and only if the customer number exists in the Customers table. Given that you want to limit the user input to the range of acceptable values wherever feasible, you'll want to present users with the list of Customers and allow them to choose one.

The controls most often used in this situation are the combo box and the list box, shown in Figure 15-3. The two have a few differences in functionality, the most important being that the combo box allows users to enter values that are not already in the list. As discussed elsewhere, this functionality can sometimes be used to create records for a linked entity. Even if entering new records isn't appropriate for your specific environment, the ability to find a value by typing it directly is preferred by most touch typists, who tend to find reaching for a mouse, or even looking at the screen, an inconvenience. For this reason, I prefer combo boxes in most situations.

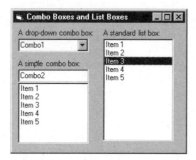

Figure 15-3. *Visual Basic provides three styles of combo boxes.*

Visual Basic allows combo boxes to be configured to display their lists all the time or only on demand. Access allows only drop-down combo boxes. (Additionally, list boxes in Visual Basic can display check boxes next to each value; Access doesn't support this functionality.)

The Windows Interface Guidelines for Software Design states that you should size simple combo boxes and list boxes to display between three and eight items. If you can't find the room on the form to do this comfortably, you should use a combo box with a drop-down list.

Even if you have the space to display the list permanently, you should use a drop-down combo box if the list is irrelevant once users make a choice. If you're providing a list of customers on an Orders form, for example, users don't care what other customers are known to the system once they've chosen the customer they want.

At times, it can be useful to allow users to see at a glance what values are possible, particularly if either the list itself or the value assigned to the record changes frequently. In a library system, for instance, in which titles are assigned

to a subject category from a list that is frequently updated and refined, users might want to see the most current list to determine whether a new category better defines a given book.

An extremely useful capability in both Visual Basic and Access is being able to display a value other than the one being stored in the table. If you're using a counter or identity value as the primary key in the Customers table, for example, you'll need to store this value as the foreign key in the Orders table, but there's no reason to make users look at it. In the Orders form, you can easily display customer names (from the Customers table) for users to choose from instead.

In Visual Basic, you do this by specifying a different value for the DataField and ListField properties. In Access, you use multiple columns—one for the customer name and one for the customer number—bind the control to the Orders customer number column, and hide the customer number column by setting its width to zero.

The ability of Access combo boxes to display multiple columns is extremely useful, and it has always seemed a pity to me that it's not possible in Visual Basic. In showing a list of customers, for instance, it's a good idea to include some additional information, such as the city in which they live, to further identify the customer. In Visual Basic, you can do this only by using a calculated field that concatenates the values as the ListField property setting. Somehow this never seems to work quite as well as Access combo boxes, particularly if some values are empty.

As useful as list boxes and combo boxes are, they aren't practical if the list contains too many values. With more than a couple hundred items, you'll need to find some way of limiting the list. You could have users select a letter of the alphabet, a sales region, or the state of residence, perhaps, and then filter the list items based on this selection.

If the list is very short—no more than five or six items—and if its values are fixed, you might want to use an option group rather than a combo box or list box. You can implement option groups using either option buttons or toggle buttons, as shown in Figure 15-4. Option buttons are the more usual choice.

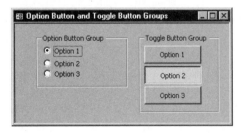

Figure 15-4. *Option buttons or toggle buttons contained in a group box can display short fixed lists.*

Although it's possible, at least in Visual Basic, to generate an option group at run time, it's not a good idea to do so. It's disconcerting to users for a form layout to change, as it will do if you're adding and deleting options on the fly. So unless the option list is permanent (or at least fixed until the next release), you're better off using a list box or combo box. The size of these controls stays the same when list items are added or removed, so it's not uncomfortable for users if the list items change.

Capturing a Set of Values

If you need to capture a set of values, you're working with the many side of a one-to-many relationship. As we saw in Chapter 14, the first decision you must make in these situations is whether you need to display and capture the records all at once or one at a time.

If you want to display and capture the many-side records one at a time in Access, you can use a subform in single-record view. Set the LinkChildFields and LinkMasterFields properties, and Access does the majority of the work for you. In Visual Basic, creating such a subform requires a little more work (OK, a *lot* more work), but in return you get slightly more control. Either way, this is a good technique if you have several field values to capture, and particularly if you want to use a variety of control types.

If you need to collect multiple values per record and want to display multiple records simultaneously, you might be able to use a datasheet in Access (as shown in Figure 14-2 on page 209) or a Grid control or Microsoft Hierarchical FlexGrid control in Visual Basic. Access datasheets are quite powerful (sometimes *too* powerful), and they allow several control types in addition to text boxes. Visual Basic grid controls are, frankly, a bit painful to implement, and Hierarchical FlexGrids allow data only to be displayed, not edited.

Fortunately, both Access and Visual Basic provide alternatives for when you want finer control over the form display. The Access subform control supports the display of subforms in continuous form view so that multiple records can be visible simultaneously. Visual Basic 6 introduced the DataRepeater control, which provides essentially the same functionality, although it's implemented quite differently. Either control is a good choice if you need to display multiple records and also need to use a control type—such as an option group—that isn't supported by a datasheet or grid control. Both controls allow each record to occupy multiple lines.

Another control that can be useful for displaying multiple records in some circumstances is the tree view control. The tree view control is most often used to display hierarchical data in outline form, but it can also be used to display selected details for each record. The tree view is not an effective mechanism

for editing this detail, but it can be very useful for negotiating records. Using a paradigm similar to Microsoft Windows Explorer, you can show details regarding the selected record in another section of the form.

Finally, in situations where users need to select a set of items from a list, a linked pair of list boxes can be a useful structure. This structure, shown in the Sample Fields and Fields In My New Table lists in Figure 15-5, is frequently used in wizards. (The screen shown is from the Access 2000 Table Wizard.) It's easy for users to understand list boxes linked in this way, but be warned, they're difficult to implement.

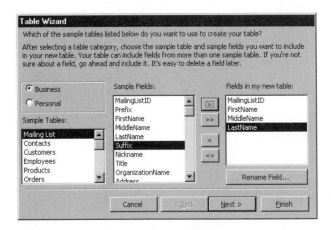

Figure 15-5. *The Access 2000 Table Wizard uses linked list boxes to allow users to choose fields for the new table.*

A pair of list boxes like this is convenient during initial data entry, but it's not an appropriate structure for subsequent editing and display, if for no other reason than that it takes up too much space. This is why the technique is most often used in wizards, where each bit of data entry can be handled on a separate screen. Once the initial data entry is complete, the user probably won't need to refer to the full lists of chosen and unchosen values, and you can more effectively use one of the controls listed previously or even a single multiselect list box.

However, because of the way selection works in multiselect list boxes, they can be dangerous. It's very easy for users to accidentally deselect all the currently selected items by single-clicking (rather than control-clicking) a new item. When the selections are bound to data, sorting out the record additions and deletions and reselections can be an absolute nightmare. A normal, single-select list box that only shows the items that have been selected is a better solution, perhaps in combination with a text box or combo box for adding items.

Representing Numbers and Dates

Numeric values and dates are most often presented in text boxes. As always, it's better to constrain the numeric values users can enter wherever possible. If the range of values is too broad, however, you might not be able to.

The Input Mask property in Access and the MaskedData control in Visual Basic provide a certain amount of control over numbers entered by means of a textbox—you can at least prohibit the entry of alphabetical characters. Access is also pretty smart about interpreting the data entered, but of course, this is after-the-fact data validation and not the best option if data limitation options are available.

Visual Basic 6 provides two new controls for entering calendar data, the MonthView control and the DateTimePicker control, shown in Figure 15-6. Access 2000 provides a calendar control similar to the MonthView control in Visual Basic.

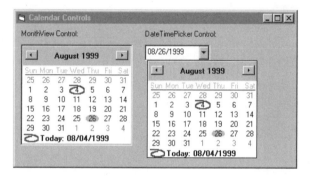

Figure 15-6. *The MonthView and DateTimePicker controls.*

You can think of these controls as calendar equivalents of list boxes and combo boxes—the DateTimePicker displays the calendar only on demand, while the MonthView displays it at all times. Both controls handle only dates, however, not dates and times. This can lead to some odd complications when they're bound to Date/Time fields, so you need to be careful during implementation.

Visual Basic and Access also provide the Microsoft UpDown control (sometimes called a spinner control) that can be used for entering both numeric and Date/Time data. Most users will be familiar with UpDown controls from having set the date and time in Windows, as shown in Figure 15-7.

UpDown controls are particularly useful if values are not incremented evenly—a date that can only be on a weekday, for example, or a numeric value that must be rounded to the nearest hundred.

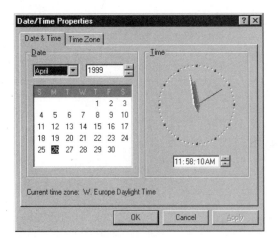

Figure 15-7. *Windows uses UpDown controls for controlling time values.*

A final set of Visual Basic controls that can be used for entering numeric data are slider controls and scroll bars, shown in Figure 15-8.

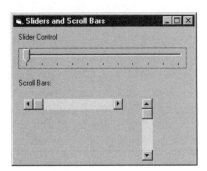

Figure 15-8. *Slider controls and scroll bars have limited value in database applications.*

These controls have a fairly limited value in database applications. They're essentially only graphic mechanisms for setting numeric values, and as such could theoretically be used to enter any numeric data. (You probably don't think of scroll bars as numeric tools—that's not their manifest model—but they actually return numeric values to the application in the background.)

I find them most useful when users can compare a set of values whose relative position is more important than their precise values—that is, "This field value

is more important than that field value." For example, I have occasionally used sliders for match checking, allowing users to set the relative importance or required tolerance of the fields to be compared in finding a match for a particular record.

Representing Text Values

Finally, we turn to those controls of last resort, text boxes. Text boxes aren't evil; they're just overused. Most data in a typical database is textual, and text boxes are the appropriate controls for representing those values. The exception is when the field is a foreign key, in which case a combo box or list box is usually a better choice, as described earlier.

The basic principles of choosing controls apply equally to text boxes: use them when they match the users' mental model, and employ whatever data limitation techniques are possible.

Data limitation is provided in Access by the Input Mask property of the text box control and by the MaskedData control in Visual Basic. Both features allow you to specify a pattern that controls the form of data entered. An American social security number, for instance, follows the pattern ###-##-#### (three digits, a dash, two digits, a dash, and four digits).

Input masks are useful in certain situations, but unfortunately these situations are infrequent, and it's easy to limit the data entry too much. Phone numbers are a good example: it's tempting to use an input mask for these values, but before doing so you must make sure that the system needs to accept phone numbers only from within the same country. Phone numbers in different countries often do not have the same format. Even within a single country, you need to think about possible variations—extensions and access numbers, for example.

Remember, your goal in providing an input mask is to make life easier for users. Preventing them from entering perfectly valid—but unexpected—values is a hindrance.

In addition to standard text boxes, both Access and Visual Basic support using a Microsoft Rich Textbox control for entering text that combines different typefaces and styles. Implementing a Rich Textbox control is more complex than using other controls because you must also provide an interface for setting the text properties.

In addition to the added complexity in the interface, a Rich Textbox control also adds some complexity to the data manipulation, since the text formatting is embedded in the control. For this reason, I recommend restricting the use of Rich Textbox controls to situations in which the added functionality is of tangible benefit to users. Furthermore, you should use them only for values that will be treated as "chunks" of text that are displayed in various places but are not searched or joined with other values.

For example, rich text can be useful for managing boilerplate paragraphs of text that are combined to produce standard letters. The actual paragraphs to be included would be stored as rich text but chosen by users on the basis of descriptive or categorical information stored as standard, unformatted text.

SUMMARY

In this chapter, we've examined the various types of controls you can use for displaying and capturing information. Your choice of controls should be based on matching users' mental model of the data and limiting the data entry to a valid range of values wherever possible.

In the next chapter, we'll look at what you can do when data limitation isn't possible, as we examine when and how to implement data validation.

16

Maintaining Database Integrity

Imagine that you're the owner of a small manufacturing company, and you've been working very hard to lure a customer away from a larger, better-established competitor. You finally convince the customer to give you a try, but you have to deliver the merchandise within 48 hours. You check with manufacturing and they can do it (just barely), so you break out the champagne.

Ten minutes later, there's trouble. It seems the accountant won't sign off on the order until the customer's credit has been approved, which will take a week, and without a signed order manufacturing can't proceed. What do you do? You'll probably start by explaining to the accountant that the situation requires bending the rules a little. If that doesn't work, you'll explain that requiring a credit check before completing an order is *your* rule, and because it's *your* company, you can break it as you see fit. If nothing else works, you'll sack the idiot and issue the paperwork yourself.

I have it on good authority that accountants are people and that they have families and mortgages like the rest of us, so the scenario I've just outlined isn't very likely. People don't just flatly refuse to carry out their boss's orders (or at least not very often). But computer systems do, regularly. They stamp their little electronic feet, throw little electronic tantrums, and refuse to comply with perfectly reasonable requests, all in the name of "maintaining data integrity." After telling you earlier in the book about what data integrity is, how to model it, and where to implement it, I'm now going to tell you something *really* scary: maintaining data integrity isn't very important. (I'll pause now and wait for the howls of protest to die down.) I'm not saying you should *eliminate* data validation. I'm saying that maintaining the integrity of the database is far less important than helping users, and you should design your system accordingly. Data does need to be valid *eventually,* but it doesn't necessarily need to be completely valid at the moment it's entered.

Stop for a moment and think about why your database system is being developed: to help people perform some task. Data validation that helps people perform tasks is good; it supports the system's goals. Data validation that prevents people from performing tasks in the order that makes sense to them, or from doing something perfectly reasonable, but unexpected, is bad. It's as simple as that. Your system should *never* prevent the user from entering data just because it isn't complete or you didn't anticipate it. Of course, doing this is sometimes easier said than done. In this chapter, we'll look at various types of integrity constraints and at how you can balance protecting the data from accidental errors with maintaining the reliability and usability of the system.

Classes of Integrity Constraints

In Chapter 4, we divided integrity constraints into six different types based on their logical levels in the relational model. In this chapter, we'll use a different organization. We'll separate integrity constraints into two classes: *intrinsic constraints* and *business constraints* (also known as *business rules*).

Intrinsic constraints govern the physical structure of the data and are derived from the relational model. The rule that prohibits users from deleting a record from the Customers table if any related records exist in the Orders table is an intrinsic constraint, since referential integrity is a function of the relational model. If a user deletes the customer record without deleting the dependent order records, the database is destabilized. If a customer record is added later that has the same primary key as the deleted customer record, the orphaned order records will be associated—incorrectly—with the new customer record. This can easily happen if you derive the primary key value from the customer's name.

Even if the primary key is never reused, orphan records can cause the database to return spurious results. Queries that calculate the total number of products sold over a given period of time will return different results depending on whether or not the Orders table is joined to the Customers table, for example. For a detailed listing of the number of each product sold to each customer, the Customers and Orders tables are usually joined using a natural join. Only the Orders records that have a matching record in the Customers table will be included in the calculation of total sales. The orphaned Orders records don't have an associated record in the Customers table, so they'll be left out of the calculation. For a summary sales listing that links the Orders table only to the Products table, on the other hand, these orphaned records will be included in the total sales calculation. Thus the system will provide two different answers to the question, "How much did we sell in June?" depending on how the question is phrased, which is clearly unacceptable.

Business constraints, on the other hand, are derived from the problem space. A rule that prohibits a customer record deletion from cascading to the Orders table unless all the relevant orders have been filled or canceled is a business constraint.

Business constraints say "we don't do that here," whereas intrinsic constraints say "it can't be done." In practice, the distinction between intrinsic constraints and business rules isn't always clear and isn't at all important. What is important is that one class of data integrity constraint derives from the problem space. You implement these constraints as a convenience to users, and you can safely ignore the constraints when doing so is convenient for the users. Deleting a customer who has open orders isn't convenient—it could very well be a disaster. But adding a sixth employee when a business rule says each manager can have only five employees *could* be convenient. In fact, not being able to enter that employee could be very inconvenient indeed.

The point is that overruling business constraints won't jeopardize the stability or reliability of the database. If a user deletes a customer record and also deletes associated outstanding orders, the system has lost important data but none of the remaining data is threatened. The relevant Customers and Orders records can be restored or reentered, and everything will be fine.

The two classes of data integrity constraints—intrinsic constraints and business constraints—must be handled differently by the system. Intrinsic constraints can't be ignored without jeopardizing the reliability of the data. Business constraints can and often should be overridden at the discretion of users. We'll examine each class of integrity constraint in detail in the following sections.

Intrinsic Constraints

The class of validation rules I'm referring to as intrinsic constraints control the physical structure of the database. This class includes the rules governing the type, format, and length of data; the acceptability of null values; range constraints; and entity integrity and referential integrity.

Data Type

Provided you've chosen appropriate control types, users normally don't run afoul of data type constraints. I've never known anyone to try to enter a date in the Amount Due field or enter text in a check box, unless he or she wasn't looking at the screen and accidentally hit the Enter key twice. Someone might, however, try to enter "eleven" into a text box that was expecting a numeric value, which is why the choice of data entry controls is so important, as we saw in the last chapter.

Format

Formatting doesn't usually pose a problem, particularly if you can reformat the entry as users leave the field (Microsoft Access makes this particularly easy) or provide an input mask to guide user input. Be careful not to impose data formats too rigidly, however. If the data entered doesn't quite fit the format you've defined, you might be better off to match the data to the format as best you can

and allow the user to fix it as they see fit. You don't want to do this if the invalid format indicates invalid data, but this situation is rare. A user who enters a telephone number as 9-9999-99999-99 could simply be dealing with a funky new phone system.

Length

Length constraints—particularly those on character fields—consistently cause problems. No matter how generous you've been, a perfectly valid entry that's too long to fit always seems to come along. You can sometimes avoid the length constraint problem by using Character fields, allocating the maximum field length (255 characters) and setting the field to a variable-length type. In Microsoft Access, all text fields are variable length. In SQL Server, you must explicitly set the field type to VARCHAR. Both engines will allocate space only for the characters stored, so no space is wasted.

Variable-length character fields aren't appropriate in all situations, however. First, a certain length might be required. For example, Social Security Numbers are always nine characters long. If a user has a 10-character Social Security Number, length isn't the problem; the data is invalid. Allowing it to be entered would be unwise. Second, because of the way SQL Server handles updates of records containing variable-length character fields, using them can result in slower performance. In most situations the performance hit is negligible, but in performance-critical applications that require updating the data frequently using fixed length fields is preferable. (There's no performance difference in *adding* data, only in *updating* it.)

Finally, although allowing very long field lengths can improve usability, it can sometimes wreak havoc with usability. Screen and report formats can get ugly (especially reports, because it isn't possible to scroll the data), and finding records that contain particular information can be a nightmare. When it isn't appropriate to allow long data values, try to provide conventions or policies for handling data that doesn't fit. If a customer name really is longer than the allotted space, you might work with users to establish reasonable conventions for shortening it, such as eliminating articles such as "The", always abbreviating "Company" to "Co", and truncating all the characters after the word "Company." This will ensure that "The Really, Really Long Name Company, Incorporated" will always be entered as "Really, Really Long Name Co" and not as "Really, Really Long, Inc" one time and "Really Long Name Company" the next.

Nulls

Missing values is the next area in which users often have trouble with intrinsic constraints. We've discussed null values at great length elsewhere, and I've tried to make it clear that I believe nulls should be allowed wherever values can reasonably be unknown in the real world, at least where doing so won't make

the data completely irrelevant to the system. If you choose to ignore this sage advice, however, you must consider how the system can assist the poor user who is trying to create a new record without all the data being available.

The issue here is *when* the data is needed. You know from analyzing the system's work processes that certain bits of information are required before a given task is completed. But that doesn't mean *all* the data required by *all* the tasks is required when the record is first created. You need new employees' bank details before you can pay them. So bank detail fields can't be null come payday. But just because the employee doesn't have the information handy when a user first creates the record, the database system shouldn't prevent a user from entering the rest of the employee's details or from performing other tasks. The user might need to produce a security card so that the person can get into the building. The bank details aren't needed for that task. The bank details will be needed *eventually,* just not necessarily on the first day of work. Don't let your system throw a tantrum; everything will be fixed up in time—the employee will see to that!

If you're unwilling to accept null values, even temporarily, the easiest way to handle this constraint is to provide some reasonable default value. One possibility is for the system to declare a single value as a default in the database schema. Alternatively, the system can present a selection of values to the user— perhaps "UNKNOWN", "NOT APPLICABLE", and "YET TO COME". Sometimes the system can calculate a reasonable default value on the fly.

Ranges

Specified ranges are the other attribute-level constraints—in addition to Null values—with which users often have trouble. Some range constraints are explicit in the data type—255 is the largest value that can be stored in a short integer, for example. When a data type determines a range constraint, you can't do much beyond explaining the constraint to users. If larger values are required, you must identify a data type with a higher range in the database schema. I do *not* recommend trying to have your application do this on the fly.

If you have defined the range constraint as a validation rule or CHECK constraint in the schema, or you have implemented the constraint in the application instead of in the schema, chances are that it's a business rule rather than an intrinsic constraint and you have a lot more room to maneuver. We'll examine business rules in the next section.

Entity and Referential Integrity Constraints

You'll remember that entity constraints ensure that each record in a table can be uniquely identified, while referential integrity constraints prohibit records from referencing records that don't exist in the same or another table. You must consider how to handle entity constraints and referential constraints without

unnecessarily imposing on the user. Entity and referential integrity constraints are most commonly handled by allowing users to select from a list of valid items. However, as shown in the last chapter, this isn't always possible, usually because the list would be too long to be practicable. When constraining users' entries in a list isn't possible or appropriate, check the data as soon as possible after it's been entered and notify the user of any problems. A record entry that appears to duplicate an existing record in the database is an entity constraint problem. The system's best response is to offer to display the existing record—or just the pertinent fields—to the user and allow the user to decide whether the new record really is a duplicate, as shown in Figure 16-1.

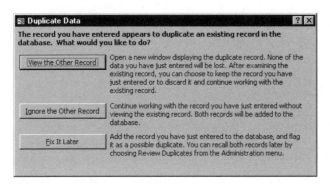

Figure 16-1. *This dialog box allows the user to decide whether the new record is a duplicate.*

Be careful not to overwrite the data the user has entered for the new record when you display the existing record. Display the existing record in a separate window, and allow the user to decide whether to overwrite the new record, as indicated in Figure 16-1. Notice, too, that the dialog box in Figure 16-1 allows the user to continue entering data without viewing the suspected duplicate. The user might already know about the other record, and you don't want to disrupt him any more than absolutely necessary. (Repeat after me, "The computer does *not* know best, the computer does *not*....")

The user who is trying to leave a primary key field blank presents another problem. That a primary key field value can't be empty is the best argument I know for using a system-assigned primary key. Using an AutoNumber field (an Identity field in SQL Server) ensures that users can do anything they require to the natural primary key fields without compromising entity or referential integrity. If using AutoNumber (or Identity) fields isn't appropriate in your system, you must ensure that users enter some value into each primary key field. Simple default values obviously couldn't be used, because the default would be accepted only once for each table. You *could* have the system calculate a value on the fly, but if you're

going to use an arbitrary value you might as well use an AutoNumber field. Your only other choice is to query users for an acceptable value.

When a referential integrity problem occurs, a user is usually trying to reference a record that doesn't exist. This can be accidental—the user might have misspelled a name, for example—or it can be more or less intentional. The user might not realize that the referenced record doesn't exist or might not have got around to entering the data yet. The dialog box shown in Figure 16-2 shows one way of handling this situation. This dialog box gives users four options: they can have the system add a new record and add the details now, they can have the system add a new record and update the record later, they can change the reference, or they can fix the reference later.

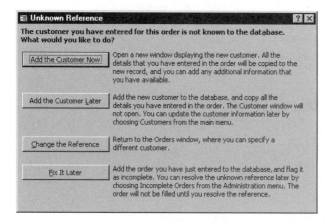

Figure 16-2. *This dialog box allows the user to choose how to handle a referenced record that doesn't (yet) exist.*

Note that overriding the constraint is not an option for the user. This constraint can't be overridden because doing so can make the database unstable, as we've seen.

If you were unable to have the dialog box present a list of valid items to users because the list would be too long, your dialog box can instead display a list of items that are close matches to the entered data. Any number of algorithms for performing these searches exists, from a simple SQL LIKE statement to a SOUNDEX search.

In some situations, it is not necessary to display a referential integrity validation dialog box at all. In fact, it's generally better to avoid doing so and thereby avoid disrupting users' work. If you can predict with reasonable certainty that users will want to add the new records and update the details later, *and* you have provided adequate facilities for undoing the system's actions if you've guessed wrong, the system can simply add the new record quietly, in the

background, without making a fuss. After the user completes the record, you might want to display a message in the status bar that the record has been added or display the message in a dialog box if you want the information to be more obvious. But whatever you do, don't interrupt users while they're entering the records if you can avoid it; it's unnecessarily rude and is scary for users.

The flip side of users trying to reference a record that doesn't exist is users trying to delete or change a referenced record. A user might be trying to delete a record for a customer that has outstanding orders, for example, or change the ProductID value for a product that is referenced in the OrderItems table.

The Microsoft Jet database engine supports cascading updates and cascading deletes that allow updates and deletes of referenced records to be handled without user intervention. You can implement the same functionality in SQL Server using triggers. If cascading updates and deletes make sense in your application, using them is by far the best solution. However, if only the users can decide the best course of action, be sure to explain to them the implications of their choice, as shown in Figure 16-3.

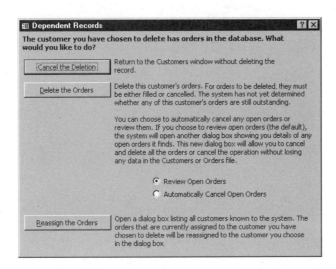

Figure 16-3. *This dialog box explains the implications of each option and allows users to choose.*

This dialog box lets users cancel the deletion, cascade the deletion, or reassign the dependent records to a different customer. Notice the dialog box warns users that open orders can't be deleted (which is a business rule) and provides the option of canceling the orders (essentially overriding the rule) or reviewing them.

You might also display the open orders, or all the customer's orders, on the validation dialog box. Your goal is to provide users with as much information as you can to allow them to make an informed decision.

Business Constraints

In the previous section, we looked at the intrinsic constraints that protect the structure and integrity of the database. You can do little to assist the user with data that violates an intrinsic constraint. Data must, at least eventually, be made to conform to the requirements of the relational model. Data that violates a business constraint, however, is a very different matter.

As I've said, you derive business constraints (better known as "business rules") from the problem space rather than from the relational model itself. Remember that a data model is just that—a simplified model of some part of the real world. As a system designer, you'll do your best to capture all the relevant aspects of the problem space in your model, but despite your best efforts you won't always succeed. Even if your model is perfect in every respect when it's first implemented, business conditions change. To be successful, your system must be able to handle the unexpected gracefully.

There are two reasons users might try to enter data the system isn't prepared to handle: either they entered the data by accident or reality doesn't match the system model. (Actually, there are three reasons if you count intentional sabotage, but that's *extremely* rare, and in any event business rules are not the best way to handle it.)

Accidental Entries

If users enter the unexpected data accidentally, your only concern is to make it as easy as possible for them to correct the problem. At the very least, this means you should explain exactly what the problem is and what needs to be done about it. Where you can, you should also provide reasonable alternatives that can be implemented directly by the system. The dialog box shown in Figure 16-4, for example, might be triggered when a user enters the month and day of a date field backwards. The dialog box makes a reasonable guess about what the user meant to enter and allows the user to select the revised date with a single click.

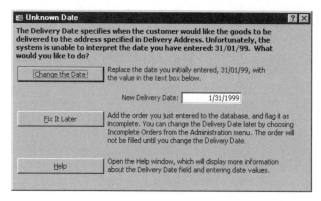

Figure 16-4. *This dialog box explains an entry error without issuing ultimatums.*

When users enter the data accidentally, it might be a genuine accident, or it might be that they don't really understand what was expected. The dialog box shown in Figure 16-4 goes some way toward explaining the purpose of the DeliveryDate field, but it also includes a Help button to allow the user to find more detailed information. We'll talk about user assistance in detail in Chapter 18.

Reality vs. the System Model

The second reason users might enter unexpected information is because reality doesn't match the system model. For example, users might be trying to correct a situation in which an order has already been delivered but for some reason wasn't entered into the system. The delivery date for this order will be earlier than the order date, which could break a business rule. If you don't provide users with some guidance, they'll enter any meaningless delivery date they can get the system to accept, and the integrity of your database will be compromised. So it behooves you to be as creative as possible in thinking of as many exceptions as you can and help the user resolve them consistently. Figure 16-5 shows a possible response to a user entering a DeliveryDate earlier than the OrderDate. This example assumes that the OrderDate is set to the current system date by default and that the user ordinarily can't edit the field.

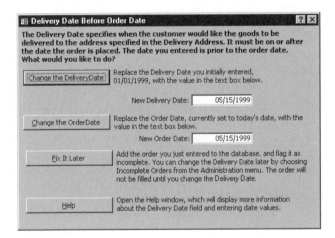

Figure 16-5. *This dialog box allows the user to backdate an order.*

Not all business rules can (or should) simply be overridden. Some business rules *can't* be broken, because the situation is impossible or because of statutory regulations, for example. But sometimes the question is not so much "whether" a rule can be broken as "by whom." In Figure 16-6, for example, a user has tried to enter information about a sixth employee reporting directly to a manager, in violation of the rule that no manager can have more than five employees.

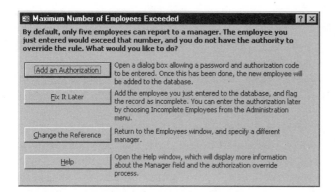

Figure 16-6. *This dialog box indicates that only someone with appropriate authority can override the business rule.*

The current user doesn't have the authority to override the rule. But the system makes available a secondary dialog box that allows a password and authorization code to be entered by someone who does have the authority—presumably a supervisor or manager. Because individuals in authority aren't always available on demand, the first dialog box also allows the user to save the current record and provides instructions for entering the authorization code at a later date.

Providing the ability to override business rules can add significantly to the usability of the system, but it does so at the cost of adding complexity to the data model. In this example, you must add a field to the Employees table to contain the authorization code and include in the integrity constraint a reference to the authorization code. You must also provide a mechanism for putting records in abeyance if the authorization is delayed. One approach is to add a single Boolean field to the Employees table to indicate that the record is not (yet) valid. This flag can be used to find the invalid records later, when the user is ready to resolve the outstanding problems, or to filter the records when producing reports. Sometimes it's useful to know why the record is invalid, and in this case you can use a code field—"MA" for "awaiting Manager approval" or "CC" for "Credit Check Outstanding," for example. This second approach provides more flexibility in handling the records. But using code fields can get complex if you have multiple possible code values for any given record, and in this case you can use a second table to contain the problem codes and relate it to the first table in a one-to-many relationship.

The changes required to hold records in abeyance might seem straightforward, and for the most part they are, but they can propagate through the system in unexpected ways. Should the records held in abeyance be included in reports, for example? An abeyance code field can be useful when deciding how to handle these reports, since it allows you to determine which records should be excluded from a particular report or query.

If records in abeyance *are* included in reports and queries, you must also consider whether they should be marked as unreliable in some way, perhaps by grouping them together under a separate heading. If you've determined that records held in abeyance, or a particular type of record held in abeyance, are not to be included in a report, you must then decide whether any associated records should be excluded. For example, if the problem is a record for an as-yet unauthorized sixth employee, should only that employee record be excluded or all the records for employees reporting to the same manager? All the issues we've discussed must be considered before you decide to include the ability to override a business rule. This ability increases the usability of the system, but the added complexity might not be justified. In simple systems it might be better to reject the record that doesn't comply with a business rule and handle the exception outside the computer system. If you decide to handle exceptional cases outside the system, be sure to say this on a data validation dialog box. Don't leave the user guessing how to proceed.

SUMMARY

In this chapter, I've taken the admittedly unorthodox position that database systems shouldn't necessarily enforce database integrity constraints. We've looked at two different classes of constraints: intrinsic constraints that govern the physical structure of the data and derive directly from the relational model, and business constraints that derive from the problem space. We've seen that allowing users to override intrinsic constraints is dangerous but that allowing records that violate business constraints to be held in abeyance and resolved at a later date often makes sense. We've also looked at several examples of how you might handle holding records in abeyance. In the next chapter, we'll look at various aspects of reporting on the data the system maintains.

17

Reporting

Only when the facts stored in a database system are combined in meaningful ways do they become information; before then, they are only trivia. In this chapter, we'll look at various issues involved in providing those meaningful combinations of facts—that information—to your users.

NOTE When I use the term "reporting" in this chapter, I don't mean only the production of printed reports. I'm using the word in a more general sense, to mean the provision of information based on data stored in the database. This information *might* be provided in the form of a printed report, but it might also be provided in a form or as a recordset shown in datasheet view.

In the days when computers cost much more than employees and computing time was an extremely scarce resource, database systems produced a few reports at regular intervals. If you wanted the system to do anything special, you could whistle for it. The backlog in the average MIS department was several years, so if you needed a report "just like this one, only sorted by Customer and subtotaled by State," you'd give it to your secretary, who would type it up for you.

These days, computers are cheap and plentiful and secretaries are extremely scarce resources. A user must now be able to tell the computer system, "I'd like a report just like this, but..." and *that* means your job as a database designer has gotten a little harder. But hey, it beats taking shorthand dictation, doesn't it?

You can take one of two general approaches to providing reporting functionality in a database system: attempt to predict all the possible reports in advance; or allow users to create them as needed. Most systems require a combination of both approaches.

The reports you can predict when designing the system can be created during implementation. I call these types of reports *standard reports*. You can also provide some mechanisms for users to create their own reports after the system

has been implemented. I call these types of reports *ad hoc reports*. We'll look at both types of reports in this chapter, but first we'll examine mechanisms for the sorting, searching, and filtering of data that reports require.

Sorting, Searching, and Filtering Data

When you're writing SQL statements, sorting, searching, and filtering data is relatively straightforward: you simply specify the appropriate criteria in either the WHERE clause or the ORDER BY clause. When you want to provide this capability to your users, however, you need to provide a buffer between them and the logic of the SQL SELECT statement.

The difficulty here is that SQL logic is a poor match to natural language. When a Sales Manager asks for a listing of all the company's distributors in Wyoming and Florida, she expects a list containing both the distributors in Wyoming *and* the distributors in Florida. But the SQL SELECT clause is WHERE State = "Wyoming" OR State = "Florida". Linguistically, the correct usage is "and," but in the formal syntax the correct term is "or." This is a huge problem for users—SQL is just close enough to natural language to be hopelessly confusing.

Teaching users how to write SQL SELECT criteria clauses is possible to do. In fact, I know of at least one well-respected database designer who does this regularly and, by all accounts, with great success. I think it's preferable to save yourself, the documentation writers, and (most importantly) the users the hassle of directly using SQL syntax by providing a more intuitive interface.

Fortunately, you're not on your own here. Microsoft Access provides examples of interfaces for constructing SQL criteria clauses. While it isn't always appropriate to copy one of these user interface mechanisms directly to your own systems, these mechanisms at least provide a place to start, which is how I'll treat them here. While the Microsoft Visual Basic interface doesn't support any of these mechanisms, you can implement most of them in Visual Basic code with a little work.

Sorting Data

Access provides an excellent sorting interface through the Sort Ascending and Sort Descending commands. Users click in the control by which they want the data sorted, and then select the appropriate command from the Records menu or on the toolbar. It's hard to think of a simpler interface.

Filter By Selection

When it comes to filtering data, the simplest interface Access provides is the Filter By Selection command and its partner, Filter Excluding Selection. The interface for these two commands works very much like Sort Ascending and Sort Descending. If a user either selects the contents of a field on a form or places the

insertion point in the field, and then chooses the Filter By Selection command, Access filters the form's underlying recordset to include only those records with a value that matches the selected field value exactly. In other words, the SQL WHERE condition is <fieldname> = <control value>.

If a user selects only the first part of a field's contents, Access limits the recordset to those records with a field value that begins with the selected characters. If a user selects the first three characters of the product name "Chartreuse verte", for example, the equivalent SQL WHERE clause would be WHERE [Product Name] LIKE "Cha*". In the Northwind sample database, this query returns records containing the product names Chartreuse verte, Chai, and Chang.

If a user selects any other characters within the field, Access returns all the records that contain the selection anywhere within the field. If a user selects "ar" in the above example, for instance, the equivalent SQL WHERE clause would be WHERE [Product Name] LIKE "*ar*". In the Northwind sample database, this would return the 10 records shown in Figure 17-1.

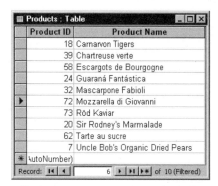

Figure 17-1. *These records are returned if a user chooses the Filter By Selection command and has "ar" selected in the Product Name field of a form or a datasheet.*

NOTE   We can't assume that Access is actually issuing SQL SELECT statements when a user chooses the Filter By Selection command. I think that this is the case, but I don't guarantee it. There's just no telling what those wizards on the development team are up to.

Filter By Form

Filter By Selection is a simple, elegant interface that's easy for users to learn, but it limits them to filtering on a single field. Users can issue additional Filter By Selection commands to progressively narrow the data set, but this can get tedious. For users who want a more powerful filtering interface, Access provides

the Filter By Form command. Figure 17-2 shows the Customers form from the Northwind sample database after a user has chosen the Filter By Form command from the Records menu.

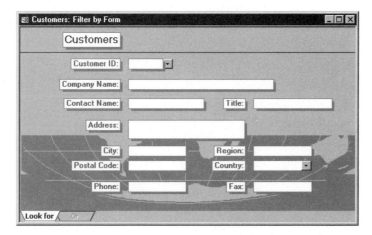

Figure 17-2. *The Filter By Form command allows users to filter information in multiple fields.*

In a Filter By Form window, users can set filter values for multiple fields on multiple tabs in the window. The values on the Look For tab will be combined with a logical AND, while those on separate Or tabs will be combined with a logical OR. This approach doesn't completely eliminate the differences between the linguistic and formal uses of AND and OR, but it comes pretty close.

By default, the Filter By Form window displays each text box from the source form as a combo box that contains all the current values for the field. You can turn this behavior off by setting the text box control's Filter Lookup property to Never. If the Filter By Form window displays a combo box, qualifying records must match the value a user selects exactly. If a text box is displayed—that is, if you set Filter Lookup to Never—users can either enter a value that must be matched exactly, or enter an expression such as LIKE "CHA*" or IS NOT NULL. Your decision on whether to use combo boxes in the Filter By Form window depends on the size of the underlying recordset (you don't want users to wait while Access populates a 100,000 item combo box) and the flexibility your users require.

Advanced Filter/Sort

Filter By Form, or an interface based on it, is sufficient for the majority of situations. However, if your users are familiar with Access's query design, or if you're using the Filter Lookup property to allow users to select values from a combo box in Filter By Form and also want them to be able to enter criteria expressions, the Access Advanced Filter/Sort window, shown in Figure 17-3, can be useful.

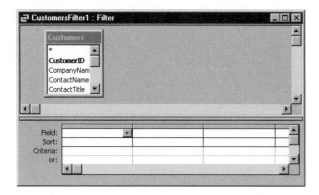

Figure 17-3. *Access displays this window if a user chooses Advanced Filter/Sort with the Customers form open in the Northwind sample database.*

The Advanced Filter/Sort window provides a subset of the functionality provided by the Design View for a query: It controls only the WHERE and ORDER BY clauses of the SELECT statement. It does not provide the ability to change the basic structure of the returned recordset by changing the field list or joining additional recordsets.

The Advanced Filter/Sort window is one filtering interface that I would *not* attempt to duplicate in Visual Basic. It could be done, I suppose, but it would certainly be a nontrivial exercise. If you need this functionality, you should probably choose Access as your development tool or find a third-party product to plug in to the system.

Microsoft English Query

If you choose SQL Server as your database engine, consider implementing Microsoft English Query. More than just a sorting and filtering interface, English Query provides a full-blown natural language interface to the database.

To implement English Query in your application, you will need to map the language of the problem space to the database schema by creating what English Query calls an "application file." Creating an English Query application file isn't difficult, but it isn't trivial, either. Like a good help file index, it requires spending a lot of time predicting the words users will use to reference the entities and attributes in the schema.

Once you create the application file, integrating English Query into your database application is easy. Your database application simply submits a user's natural language question to the English Query engine and receives a SQL statement in return. Well, in theory it's that easy. In reality, your application might receive an error message indicating that a user (creative little creatures that users are) has phrased the question in terms the engine doesn't understand.

In the right environment, English Query is a wonderful tool. If you have a complex database schema and a lot of novice users making inquiries, the natural language interface provided by English Query can be a superb solution.

Producing Standard Reports

Almost every database system has a certain number of reports that you can define in advance. You will have discovered most of these standard reports during the work process analysis, but it's worthwhile spending some time going over the database schema with users to consider whether any other reports would be useful to them.

Listing Reports and Detail Reports

For each entity in the system, consider using both listing reports and detail reports. A listing report is just a list of every instance of the entity—that is, every record in the table. Sometimes you can simply arrange these listings in alphabetical order. More often, you should group listings in some way. Customers might be grouped by state, region, or salesperson, for example. If you expect a report's source table to contain more than a few hundred records, provide users with the option of printing only a selected range of records. A salesperson is most likely going to want a list of only their own customers, for example, not of every customer in the system.

Whereas a listing displays a few details for every instance of an entity, a detail report shows all (or at least most) of the details about a specific entity. Again, you'll usually want to provide some way for users to select the records to print. A multiselect list box is often a good mechanism for selecting records because it doesn't require contiguous selections.

Remember to bear in mind the practical limitations of list boxes, however. If the table contains thousands of records, you must use a set of list boxes to allow users to progressively narrow the range of records. Alternatively, you could use some other type of control. You might consider using a text box similar in functionality to the one used by Microsoft Word in the Print dialog box to specify print ranges, for example. Parsing a range of records separated by a dash, or single records separated by commas, is not difficult to implement.

Summary Reports

A little more complicated to implement than listing and detail reports, but often more useful, are what I think of as "slice and dice" reports: summary data combined and compared in various ways. The percentage of sales by region or salesperson and the number of customers who purchase each product category are examples of this type of report.

Summary reports are good candidates for graphical representation, and Microsoft Graph and various third-party tools make the implementation of graphical reports straightforward. However, I recommend that you provide graphics in addition to textual data rather than instead of it. A text-based sales summary might not be the easiest thing in the world to look at, but it can be exported to a statistical analysis tool or a spreadsheet such as Microsoft Excel for further manipulation.

Form-Based Reports

In addition to the reports derived from the database schema, consider also the forms in the system as a source of useful reports. I provide the ability to print copies of the majority of forms in a database system as a matter of course. They're easy for you to implement and extraordinarily useful to users for checking their work or getting a quick printout to show to someone else.

Sometimes an entity detail report contains the same information as a form, and you can use the detail report rather than creating a new form report. Most often, however, entity detail reports contain additional information or are formatted differently than a form report. Reports based on forms are so cheap and easy to provide that I usually give my users both detail and form reports. The form-based report is the default printed when a user clicks the print button on the toolbar, and the detail report is available from a menu (and perhaps also from the toolbar).

Reporting Interfaces

Making reports available within the user interface is not very tricky. If you use Print Report as a command, you have three methods for making the command available to users: via a menu, a toolbar button, or a command button on a form. A command that prints a report must always make clear to users *which* report is to be printed.

Indicating which report will print is easy to do on a menu: you can use the report name as a Reports menu item. You can use the report name as a toolbar button's ToolTip or a command button's caption as well, but you should preface the name with the verb "Print". "Customer Listing" is sufficient as a menu item on a Reports menu, for example, but the corresponding ToolTip or command button caption would be "Print Customer Listing". In addition to being compliant with Windows guidelines, this text makes it clear to users that the system will print a report, as opposed to opening a window containing the report.

In addition to *where* you make the system's reports available to users (via a menu, a toolbar, or a command button), you must also consider *how*. A database system often contains dozens, even hundreds, of reports and listing them all in one huge umpteen-column menu is obviously not sensible. Fortunately, limiting the list of available reports to those that make sense within a user's

current context is usually easy to do. A user is unlikely to want to print a list of employee phone numbers in the middle of entering sales orders, for example.

If you think making all the system reports available at once is appropriate, you could provide a dialog box that presents a categorized list of the reports and allows users to choose the report they want to print. This approach can also be useful if users need to print multiple reports at once. By allowing them to select any number of reports at once on the report dialog box, you enable them to click the print button once and then go about their business.

For reports that are often printed as a set—such as month-end summaries—I use a variation of the dialog box list technique. I present a dialog box with all the reports that are usually printed as a set selected by default. Users can add any relevant reports that are printed only occasionally, or deselect a standard report, before sending the whole set to the printer.

Listing each report in a set imposes a little more overhead on users than batching the reports from a single menu item does, but I find that the additional flexibility for users is generally worth the single extra mouse click involved. A single report in a batch often needs to be reprinted because of a printer fault or because somebody spilled coffee on it. A dialog box that groups these report sets but allows each report to be printed individually eliminates the need to list each report on a menu, or worse, print an entire report set because there's a problem with only a single report.

Handling Printer Errors

Your system must always be able to handle printers messing up or printouts being messed up, and because of this, certain common printing situations can be very tricky to handle. A user might want to print all the invoices that haven't already been printed, for example. This common requirement is one of the most difficult for a system to handle gracefully because it can't know whether any given report has actually been printed. The system knows only that it sent the report to the print spooler, and that's not the same thing at all.

Some designers handle possible printer errors by displaying a message box after the reports have been sent to the printer, asking for confirmation that the reports printed successfully. This approach will work, but it requires that users stop using the system until they have the printouts in their hand. If the print job happens to be behind somebody's 1000-page manual in the printer queue, a user could be in for quite a wait. Furthermore, since most reports *do* print correctly the first time, the delay is unnecessary 99 percent of the time.

I prefer to handle printing problems as the exception that they are. To return to our earlier example, if the system needs to print only unprinted invoices, you'll need to add a field to the appropriate table anyway. If the system is relying on

user confirmation that the invoices have printed successfully, all that's required is a Yes/No or Boolean field. But it's easy enough to store a date or print job number instead. You can then add a command that allows users to record printing problems on either a print-job or an invoice-by-invoice basis.

If a report is printed no more than once a day, you can use the current date as a flag. It's safer, however, to generate a unique number for each print job and store that instead. If anything goes wrong, a user simply selects the appropriate print job and the system can set the fields containing that print job number back to Null. The records containing a Null will automatically be included in the next print job. Alternatively, the system can display all the records that were included in the problem print job and allow the user to select only specific records to be reprinted.

How does a user recognize a particular print job? You could include the print job number in a report footer, but I prefer to set up a system table that stores the name of the report, the print job number, the date on which the report was printed, and (if it is available) the name of the user who initiated the job. You can then present a descriptive list of print jobs to users rather than making them remember a meaningless number.

Sometimes more is at stake than whether a given record is included in the next print run. Accounting systems sometimes include report generation as part of end-of-month processing, for example. Once the month is rolled over, certain values will be reinitialized, and there might be no way (or at least no *easy* way) of regenerating the reports. I think this is an extremely poor design strategy.

Because of the unreliability of printing, I try very hard to keep report generation and record updates (other than "record printed" updates) as completely separate tasks, and I recommend you do the same. If the work process absolutely requires that updating a record be linked to printing a report, the safest approach is to hold up further system processing until the person printing the report confirms that the report has printed successfully.

Confirming a successful print job might be possible to do as a background process, so you don't hold up the system until the job is confirmed. You could, for example, place an icon in the status bar that, when clicked, displays the confirmation dialog box and completes the table update. Be sure to display a message to users explaining what they need to do.

Automatic and On-Demand Printing

Another consideration in producing standard reports is whether they should be printed on demand, automatically, or both. As a general rule, I make all reports on demand. The only exception I make is for a report that is clearly part of a work process, such as an invoice produced after a user enters a sales order. Such

an automatic report should be available on demand as well, in order to deal with those pesky printer problems.

Note that reports tied to a work process, such as invoices, can be printed one at a time or as a batch. For example, you can print each invoice as the corresponding sales order is entered or you can batch all the unprinted invoices and print them at the end of the data entry session. I've used both approaches successfully. I tend to print each invoice individually if users have a local printer and to batch print invoices on a network printer. You should probably make the choice configurable by users—printer setups are subject to change.

Some designers choose to have the system automatically produce reports that are printed at regular intervals—weekly or at the end of each month, for example—but I prefer to make these on demand as well. Having the system produce reports automatically is a complex task. The system must calculate when the report needs to be printed (allowing for weekends and holidays) and track whether the report has yet been printed on the correct date. If multiple people use the system, it must also determine which user or category of user should trigger the print job, and what to do if no users of that category log onto the system on the required date.

Compared with all the problems associated with automatic report generation, having the user select Print Weekly Reports from a menu at their convenience is trivial. In any event, you'll need to provide the menu item (or a reporting problem dialog box), since users will need to be able to regenerate the reports in case of printing problems.

Users aren't very likely to forget to print the weekly, monthly, or quarterly reports. However, there's no harm done if you allow users to specify the period for which the report is to be run, in case they do forget. By using the current period of time as a default value and allowing users to change the value, you enable them to easily correct any oversights. This technique also allows reports that are printed at regular intervals to be printed before the end of the current time period. To be able to check performance against budget while there's still time to do something about potential cost overruns can be useful.

Producing Ad Hoc Reports

The work processes a database system is intended to support are sometimes extremely well defined, and you can specify in advance all the reports the system must produce. More often, however, you will need to provide some level of flexibility for users to configure or design reports themselves.

Just how much flexibility is required must be determined by the needs of your users and will vary from system to system. The degree of flexibility can range from providing users with a full-blown report designer to simply allowing users to specify additional filter criteria for predefined reports.

Report Designers

Providing users with a report design tool is an easy option to implement if you can use a commercially available tool such as Access or a third-party control. (The new Microsoft Data Reports provided with Visual Basic 6 aren't really appropriate, since they require the development environment to be present on each user's machine.)

Report designers give users essentially unlimited freedom in designing whatever reports they need. Unfortunately, this flexibility has a price. It's not so much that the base cost of the reporting tool is high, although if you provide a full copy of Access to hundreds of users who otherwise don't need it, the base cost is certainly not insignificant.

The cost is more the result of having to train users to design reports using sophisticated tools. Not only must users know how to lay out the report using the report designer, they must also have at least a superficial understanding of the database schema to access the specific data they need. None of this is beyond the capabilities of the average user given adequate time and training. But these people already *have* a job, and building custom reports isn't it.

Customized Report Design

To make the report design process efficient for users, implementing a custom report design utility is often more appropriate than using a commercial tool. Theoretically, it's possible to provide a report design tool that has the same flexibility as the Access report designer and is customized to support the database schema of the system. Such an exercise would be expensive, however, and would not be justified in most situations. A more usual solution is to provide a set of predefined report layouts and allow users to specify the data to be displayed.

The Access Report Wizard is probably still too close to the implementation model for customized reporting, but it is an example of a useful approach to providing predefined layouts. The Report Wizard provides extensive formatting capabilities but avoids much of the complexity of report design by allowing users to select from a list of predefined report layouts and styles. Once the Report Wizard generates the report, users can further manipulate it using the Access interface.

Allowing users to specify the layout and style of a report separately provides a fine degree of control to users. Alternatively, you can combine layout and style in various ways to simplify the process. Most users require "custom" reports that are really only variations of standard reports. In other words, they need reports that are "just like this, but..." and what follows the "but" is either sorting or filtering criteria.

The taxonomy I use in my own work is therefore quite different from the one used by the Access Report Wizard. I divide an ad hoc report into two components,

which I call the "format" and the "criteria." The format rolls together the layout and style components of the report and also specifies the fields (and by extension the table or query on which the form is based) to print. It is, in fact, an Access Report or Visual Basic Data Report object that is modified at run time based on the criteria specified by the user. The criteria specify the sorting and filtering to apply to the format. I almost always provide the user with a means of storing and reusing criteria. We'll see how this works a little later. Allowing users to define grouping levels is sometimes appropriate as well, but as a general rule I have found this unnecessary.

Because users are specifying only two components, I use a dialog box for generating custom reports. A general structure for this dialog box is shown in Figure 17-4. (If you adopt this approach to ad hoc reporting, you should modify the sample to conform to the user interface of your system.)

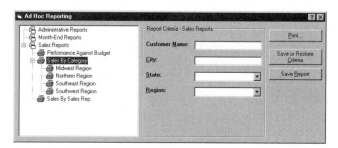

Figure 17-4. *I use this basic structure for providing ad hoc reporting to users.*

The dialog box is divided into three sections. In the left pane, a tree view control presents users with a list of formats to choose from. You could use a list box or even a set of radio buttons rather than a tree view control. In the example, the formats are grouped into categories. This technique is useful if you have a lot of formats. Grouping the formats into "Administrative Reports," "Month-End Reports," and "Sales Reports," for example, makes it easier for the user to find the report they want.

The third level of the hierarchy shown in Figure 17-4 are "reports." A report, in this context, is the combination of a saved criteria and format. Having specified "Southwest" for the Region in the criteria of a sales report format, for example, the user can save a report as "Southwest Region Sales." If you have complex criteria specifications, this capability can save users a great deal of time.

The middle pane of the dialog box allows users to specify the sorting and filtering criteria. You can sometimes use a single set of controls in the criteria pane for all formats, although it might be necessary to disable certain controls that don't apply to the format a user has chosen. Sometimes each format will require a completely different set of controls for establishing the criteria. In my work, I

tend to walk a middle path. As shown in Figure 17-4, I divide the report formats into categories, and it is the category that determines the criteria controls.

The right pane of the dialog box in Figure 17-4 contains a set of command buttons. The Print button displays a subsidiary dialog box allowing users to set print options, such as the number of copies or the printer. If these options aren't available, it's probably better to provide two command buttons, Print and Print Preview, and save the user the additional step of displaying a dialog box.

The Save Or Restore Criteria command button displays a dialog box that would be similar to that shown in Figure 17-5. This simple dialog box provides the same criteria controls displayed on the main custom reporting form in the middle pane. The criteria that users have already saved are shown in a list box in the left pane. Selecting a criterion in the list box displays it in the middle pane. The Save As… button first asks the user for a name and then saves the criterion specified, while the Restore button loads a criterion into the main form.

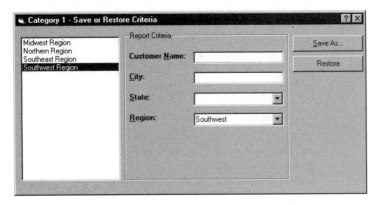

Figure 17-5. *This dialog box, called from the main custom reporting form, allows a user to save and restore report criteria.*

The ability to save criteria in this way is quite straightforward to implement. You simply need a table for each category, with fields for each control on the pane. In a multiuser situation, you need to decide whether to have the saved criteria be available to everyone or allow each user to maintain his own set. If the criteria are shared, the tables should be kept in the main database along with other shared data. If each user maintains his own set of criteria, the tables should be stored locally, in the front-end database (or a local database if your application is written in something other than Microsoft Access).

The two techniques are not mutually exclusive. You can easily provide both shared and user-specific criteria either by including the user's name in the criteria table or by displaying a UNION of the shared and local tables. I usually

include the user's name in a shared table because it makes it easier to support "roaming" users, who may use more than one computer to access the system.

Saving and restoring criteria allows users to save criteria on a category basis. The criteria thus saved can be applied to any report in that category (assuming that the reports share criteria specifications).

Sometimes, however, it's more appropriate to link the criteria with a specific report format, which is what the final command button in Figure 17-4 (on page 252) does. Again, this is straightforward to implement. You will need tables for each type of criteria (you can reuse the tables used for saving criteria if you've implemented that functionality) and a table that links the report formats and the criteria. The structure is shown in Figure 17-6.

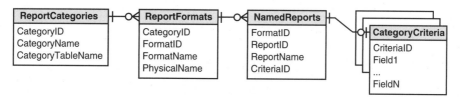

Figure 17-6. *This table structure allows users to save criteria and reports and has the added benefit of allowing reports to be added to the system at run time.*

The ReportCategories table contains a field called CategoryTableName. This allows the system to identify the specific criteria table that contains the criteria for that category of format. If all your reports have the same criteria structure, this field isn't necessary. On the other hand, if all your formats have different criteria structures, this field should be in the ReportFormats table.

The table structure shown in Figure 17-6 also allows the reports available within the system to be configured at run time, which is what the FormatName and PhysicalName fields in the ReportFormats table are all about. If your report formats are defined independently, either as objects in the database (as with Access reports) or as separate files (as with many third-party reporting tools), you can use indirection to enable adding reports to the system at any time. To do so, you base the list of formats shown in the form dialog box on the ReportFormats table rather than hard-coding the list.

To add a new report format, you need only create the format object (a report in Access, or a separate operating system file) and then add a record to the ReportFormats system table. The new format will automatically be available within the system without anyone having to touch core system functionality. The FormatName field contains the text to be displayed to the user, while the PhysicalName contains the actual name of the object and perhaps its file path if the objects are stored externally.

The approach to custom reporting described here, while simpler for users than a full-blown report design tool, is overkill for some applications. All your users might need is the ability to occasionally specify additional filter criteria for the predefined standard reports. You can often accommodate these simple criteria by adding a few controls for specifying the criteria to a custom print dialog box, rather than implementing a full custom reporting user interface such as the one I've described.

Standard Letters

A special type of custom report is the standard letter. Sometimes the text of standard letters is fixed, but more often users need to select from boilerplate paragraphs and have the system combine them to create the letter. Whether the text is fixed or not, I am of the opinion that a database report is not the best means of producing correspondence.

Although database report formatting capabilities are becoming increasingly powerful, they do not equal the formatting capabilities of a word processor specifically designed for this task. Furthermore, most users want the ability to add text to letters before they are printed, but allowing them to manipulate the database reports is not a good technique because any changes to the standard structure would be permanent.

By all means, use the database to maintain names and addresses, and even to store the boilerplate paragraphs. But outputting this data to a word processor, such as Microsoft Word, allows more sophisticated formatting and lets users manipulate the text before printing it.

Fortunately, sending standard letters to a word processor is becoming increasingly easy to implement. Gone are the days of struggling to send Dynamic Data Exchange (DDE) command strings to some uncooperative, poorly documented application. In Microsoft Word, for example, you can directly specify an Access table or query as the data source for a mail merge with a document. You can then use Visual Basic for Applications (VBA) to merge the document with the data from your database application and display the document to users for subsequent manipulation or send it directly to the printer.

In some circumstances, you might need to keep track of the standard letters that are created by the system. If you aren't allowing users to customize the letters before they print them, there's no need to store the letters themselves in the database. You need to store only the fact that a letter was sent, and perhaps the date and the name of the user who sent it. On the other hand, if users create the letters by combining boilerplate paragraphs, you can model this process using a complex entity, as shown in Figure 17-7.

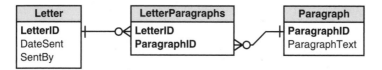

Figure 17-7. *This structure can store the paragraphs included in a specific letter.*

If the system allows users to customize letters before they are printed, it's better not to store the text of the letter in the database, since neither Access nor Microsoft SQL Server is particularly efficient at handling large amounts of text. You need to store only the location and name of the physical document file. This means the system must be prepared to handle the file being moved, renamed, or deleted, usually by asking users for assistance.

SUMMARY

In this chapter, we've looked at various aspects of providing information to users based on the data stored in the database. This usually means the production of printed reports, but it can also mean information provided by way of a form or a recordset shown in a datasheet.

We began by examining the techniques provided by Microsoft Access for sorting and filtering data. Even if your application isn't being implemented in Access, these techniques provide useful examples of the kind of functionality that you might want to provide.

We examined various kinds of standard reports that might be provided by the system, including listing and detail reports, summary reports, and reports based on the forms in your system. We then looked at how reporting can be integrated into the user interface of the system and some of the issues involved in handling reporting errors. The production of ad hoc reports was discussed in some detail, and I presented the technique that I use for providing this functionality. Finally, we looked at the production of standard letters by combining the data management functionality of a database with the advanced formatting capabilities of a dedicated word processor.

In the next chapter, we'll turn to the subject of user assistance and look at the explicit forms of user assistance that can be incorporated into the user interface of your database system.

18

User Assistance

In a sense, everything we've talked about in Part 3 of this book comes under the heading "user assistance." Your goal in architecting the user interface and choosing windows structures and controls should always be to assist users in accomplishing their tasks. Most of the discussion of data integrity in Chapter 16, for example, was couched in terms of your system helping users avoid accidents without getting in their way. In this chapter, we'll look at more explicit forms of user assistance that you can incorporate into the user interface.

In Chapter 12, we discussed three categories of people who will be using your systems. Beginning users need to know *what* the system does. Intermediate users need to know *how* to perform specific tasks, and expert users want to know how to perform tasks *quickly*. Different types of assistance are appropriate for each level of user. The introductory screens and guided tours that are so helpful to beginners will get in the way of intermediate users and drive advanced users to distraction.

You must therefore consider not only the support mechanisms that you will provide for each type of user, but also the best way for the various mechanisms to coexist. The introductory dialog box that you display for beginners on application startup, for example, can contain a "Don't show me again" check box that enables more advanced users to get the dialog box out of the way. The ToolTips and status bar messages that support intermediate users usually don't cause problems for more advanced users, but you might consider providing a mechanism for turning off ToolTips and status bar messages just to be sure. We'll discuss the customization of the user interface for different types of users in greater detail later in this chapter.

In addition to the coexistence of support mechanisms, consider how your system can help a user move from one level of competence to another. You can rely on the system documentation, but it's not a very effective mechanism, for reasons we'll examine later. A better technique is to assist users from within the user interface itself.

Most systems of even moderate complexity will provide multiple paths to each command. For example, saving changes to a record might be accomplished by choosing Save from the File menu, clicking a toolbar button, or typing Ctrl-S. Each of these paths is called a *command vector*, and each command vector is appropriate for a different level of user.

Beginning and intermediate users tend to rely on menus to remind themselves of what functionality is available; intermediate users will make greater use of toolbar buttons; and experts will use the shortcut accelerator keys. To assist users in moving from one user level to another, you can consistently display all of these vectors for each command throughout the system.

Figure 18-1 shows the default File menu in Microsoft Access 2000. Note that the Save item shows all the command vectors for the command. The mnemonic keyboard access Alt-F-S is indicated by the underlined capital letter S in the word Save. (The F in the File menu name is also underlined.) The icon used for the command on toolbars is also shown, as is the Ctrl-S accelerator. By displaying all the command vectors on the menu, the user interface itself helps users learn faster ways of performing tasks.

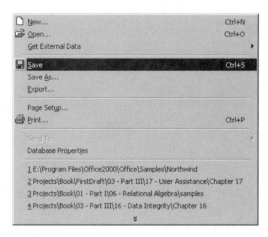

Figure 18-1. *The default File menu in Access 2000 displays all the command vectors for the Save command.*

NOTE	Microsoft Visual Basic doesn't allow toolbar icons on its intrinsic menus, although there are several third-party ActiveX controls available that do support icons on their menus. The menu creation paradigm in Access 2000 allows you to include icons; however, the selection of built-in icons is so ridiculously small that you'll almost certainly have to use the Button Editor to draw your own icons. Both Visual Basic and Access make it easy to create accelerators that are automatically displayed on the menu.

Displaying multiple command vectors doesn't present any coexistence problems because it is a passive mechanism. All user assistance mechanisms can be divided into *passive mechanisms* that form part of the user interface, *reactive mechanisms* that are invoked in response to some user action, and *proactive mechanisms* that attempt to anticipate a user's needs. We'll discuss each of these mechanisms in turn in this chapter and end with a brief discussion of training materials and user customization.

Passive Assistance Mechanisms

Passive assistance mechanisms include all the clues, pointers, and explanations that you embed in the user interface to guide users in their tasks. Unlike reactive assistance mechanisms, passive assistance mechanisms don't require users to do anything—hence the name.

Control labels, menu names, and even the titles of your forms and dialog boxes are passive assistance mechanisms, and therefore you should give due consideration to how you name these elements. Choose names that describe as clearly as possible the action to be performed or the data to be entered.

In addition to names, many other passive mechanisms are available. We'll examine just three: mnemonic access keys, ToolTips, and status bars.

Mnemonic Access Keys

Mnemonic access keys provide direct functionality and passive assistance to users. Because they allow users to navigate through the system quickly, mnemonic access keys provide direct functionality. Because they are always underlined in control labels, access keys also provide passive user assistance. Any user with even moderate experience with Microsoft Windows will be familiar with the "Alt-underlined character" paradigm.

You should provide mnemonic access keys for all menu items and all controls. Choose which letter to use as the access key in the following order of priority:

1. The first letter of the menu item or control label.

2. A distinctive consonant in the menu item or control label.

3. A vowel in the menu item or control label.

Defining access keys is trivial to do in both Access and Visual Basic: you precede the access key character in the label with an ampersand (&). In both environments, the system will underline the character in the label and handle the navigation for you. (To display an ampersand character instead of an underlined character in a label, by the way, you use two ampersands. "Nuts & Bolts" will be displayed as "Nuts _Bolts," but "Nuts && Bolts" will be displayed as "Nuts & Bolts.")

ToolTips

The ToolTip for the Save button on the Access Form View toolbar is shown in Figure 18-2. Not terribly exciting, is it? The principle behind ToolTips is straightforward: they function as labels for toolbar buttons and other controls that don't have labels.

> **NOTE**   When a ToolTip is used for any control other than a toolbar button, it's called a control tip. ToolTips and control tips work the same way, and for convenience I'll call both of them ToolTips in this section.

Figure 18-2. *ToolTips indicate the purpose of controls that don't have labels.*

Unexciting and straightforward as ToolTips might be, their impact on the usability of the system is immense. If you've ever had to choose icon images to represent system functionality, you know how difficult it is for an icon to convey information. Choosing an icon for "Save" isn't too hard (at least it isn't now that we've all seen the disk icon used in Microsoft Office), but what about an "Open Customer Form" button? You might use a little figure, but what if you also need images for opening the Employees and Vendors forms? Your visual metaphors can get a little tenuous.

Fortunately, ToolTips take off a lot of the pressure to find a self-explanatory icon. Given half a chance, most people are pretty good at making up little stories to associate an image with an idea—that's the principle behind one method for remembering peoples names—and ToolTips give them that half a chance.

So you're using the little fish icon in Access to represent Customers. (What *did* Access designers have in mind?) That a fish represents the Customers form is never going to occur to users the first time they see your toolbar, but the ToolTip will explain the icon's meaning. Provided you reinforce the association by using the image everywhere customers are referenced—the menu, the forms, and the documentation—users will adjust with no problems.

To implement ToolTips in either Access or Visual Basic, you simply set the appropriate property. The ToolTip text should be short—just a word or two.

Remember that the ToolTip functions as a label: its purpose is to *remind* users of what the control represents, not to *teach* them how to use it.

If the control duplicates a menu item, use the same word or phrase in the ToolTip as in the menu item. If the control doesn't duplicate a menu item, use the noun or verb that best describes the control's functionality and distinguishes it from other controls. If a toolbar contains three buttons that open the Customers form, Suppliers form, and Employees form, for example, you could use the ToolTips "Customers", "Suppliers", and "Employees". If, on the other hand, one button represents opening the Customers form and a second button represents printing a customer list, you would need to use the ToolTips "Open Customer Form" (or perhaps "Maintain Customers") and "Print Customers" to distinguish between the two buttons.

A note on images: in associating images with ideas, as in all other areas of user interface design, consistency is critical. Each image that represents an entity in the system should be used wherever your system references the entity, as should each image associated with a verb. In my own work, I select a range of images for each category—entities and verbs—and combine images from the two categories where necessary. If I were to associate an X image with the delete action, and a person's profile image with the Customers table, for instance, I would superimpose one image on the other to indicate "Delete Customer," as shown in Figure 18-3.

Figure 18-3. *Once you have associated images with verbs and entities, combining them can be very expressive. If the X is used consistently to indicate "delete" and the profile image to indicate "Customer," it will be clear to most users that this image means "Delete Customer."*

Status Bars

A status bar is a common mechanism for providing passive assistance to users. Displayed at the bottom of the window, a status bar can display modal information such as the state of the Num Lock key, the Caps Lock key, and the extend selection mode. The status bar also displays messages for users. Figure 18-4 shows an Access status bar. Note that the Categories form is maximized, so the status bar at the bottom of the window appears to be part of the form. However, the status bar is actually part of the Access window itself.

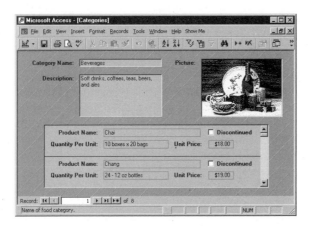

Figure 18-4. *The status bar is at the bottom of the main window.*

Access makes it easy for you to display descriptive information in the status bar for each control on a form by setting the control's StatusBarText property. If you don't explicitly define the StatusBarText property for a control bound to a field, that field's Description value (which you specify in the table's Design view) will be displayed in the status bar. You can't, to the best of my knowledge, set the status bar text from code in Access, however, so there is no way to use status bar text for an extended description of a menu item or for general messages to users.

In Visual Basic, you control the text displayed in a status bar by explicitly setting the Text property of the appropriate panel of a StatusBar control. You can therefore use the status bar to display explanatory messages throughout the system, not just to describe the active control as in Access. A trade-off for this additional flexibility is that you must always set the text in code, and there is no way to tie text to a control and have Visual Basic display it automatically. Admittedly, this extra work can get tedious, but it's a fairly small price to pay for the expanded functionality.

The greatest advantage of a status bar is that it doesn't intrude on users. Unlike a message box, the status bar doesn't capture keyboard input or require explicit user dismissal. In fact, in Access (and Visual Basic as well, if you provide the functionality) a user can choose not to display the status bar.

In Visual Basic, you can use the status bar to display extended descriptive information to users or to keep them informed about processes that are operating in the background. You can also use the status bar to display error messages, although you must allow for the possibility that users won't have the status bar visible. It's dangerous to use status bar text for anything users *must* see. Even if the status bar is visible in the main window, users might not notice a message displayed there.

Displaying messages in the status bar does have its uses, however. If, as I recommend in Chapter 16, you suspend rather than reject records that violate integrity constraints, the status bar is a good place to explain the situation and how to resolve it. I sometimes display the "problem" field contents in red, and when the user selects the field, describe the problem in the status bar and suggest how to fix it. Because space in the status bar is limited, however, I also make available a dialog box with more extensive instructions, usually having it appear when a user presses a function key.

Reactive Assistance Mechanisms

Reactive assistance mechanisms, unlike the passive mechanisms we've been discussing, are displayed only as a response to some action by a user. Intermediate or advanced users are more likely to use reactive mechanisms than beginners, who might not know how to invoke them or even that they exist. For this reason, they're not particularly good mechanisms for the kind of "what's this all about, then?" assistance that beginning users require.

Most reactive assistance is provided as some form of online help. Several paradigms for providing this type of online assistance exist, and we'll look at two in this section: traditional online help and the newer What's This tips. Although not often considered in that light, error messages are also a kind of reactive assistance, and we'll look at them at the end of this section.

Online Help

Traditional online help is essentially a transfer of printed documentation to the computer, and as almost always happens when a real-world object or activity gets computerized, this transfer makes some things easier and some things harder. Online help is more accessible than printed documentation, and the ability to display cross-referenced material with the click of a mouse is certainly a benefit. On the other hand, online help is a lot more difficult to browse, and you can't take it with you to the lunchroom when you go to get a cup of coffee.

Careful design of the help system can go some way toward ameliorating the disadvantages of online help. (It's still only as portable as the computer is, however.) Designing and writing help systems is a huge topic, most of which lies outside the scope of this book. All I can do here is give you some general guidelines, point out a few peculiarities of writing help for database systems, and refer you to the Bibliography for more detailed information.

The first and most important consideration when designing online help for your system is that no matter how tightly linked the help might be to your system, you should never consider it an *integral* part of the user interface. That is, your system must be able to stand on its own and never force users to resort to online help (or any other documentation, for that matter) to complete a task.

Remember that beginning users might not understand what online help contains, so they might not think to press F1 when they get confused. You should consider online help as a support for the user assistance provided within the system itself, not as a replacement for it. It's all too common for designers to think that having an online help system relieves them of the burden of making the system self-explanatory. In my experience this is a mistake and leads to ugly, unusable software.

The second consideration when designing online help is what type of support you want it to provide. Online help topics can be roughly divided into two types: task-oriented and function-oriented. Task-oriented topics tell users how to complete a specific task, such as how to print an invoice or schedule a meeting. Function-oriented topics provide detailed information regarding a specific function (such as the Print command on the File menu) or control (such as the CustomerID text box on a form). The two types correspond roughly to Users Guides and Reference Manuals in printed documentation.

Both task-oriented and function-oriented help have a role in supporting database systems. If your system supports many work processes, or if the work processes it supports are complex, task-oriented help can be of considerable assistance to users by providing a kind of roadmap to the procedures. It's still important to provide support and guidance within the system itself, though. It's not acceptable to merely present users with an alphabetical list of forms like the one in the Access Database window and rely on online help to tell them in which order the forms must be completed. (Well, it's not acceptable if you're working for me, anyway.)

Ideally, task-oriented topics should not include conceptual or introductory material. Remember, this isn't the right tool for teaching your users what the system does. The only purpose of task-oriented help topics is to provide a summary of the "how" of a procedure, not to explain the "what" or the "why."

Using multiple help topics for complex subjects will keep the topics readable on the computer screen. If the work process being explained is complex and has multiple paths, it's best not to try to explain all paths in a single topic. Just explain the simplest or most usual path in the main topic and provide links to topics explaining the variations.

Whereas task-oriented topics concentrate on the "how" of using your system, function-oriented topics concentrate on the "what" and the "why." For database systems, most function-oriented topics will refer to data items and controls rather than functions per se. Few database systems will require topics such as those provided by Access help, for example, where it's necessary to explain the precise syntax of the Mid$ function.

Systems *do* require topics that explain the purpose of every entity and attribute in the system and the constraints that pertain to each of them. They might also

require topics to explain the use of various control types used by the system—how to navigate through a tree view control, for example, or how to pick a date using a calendar control.

In planning these data-oriented topics, it's important to think about why users would ask for help. If a user is looking at an Orders form text box with the caption "Desired Delivery Date," it's *really* unlikely he would press the F1 key because he doesn't understand that this is the date the customer would like the goods delivered. If this is all your topic tells users, it's worse than useless—it's an irritating waste of time.

So why *might* the user have pressed F1? Maybe he doesn't understand why the date is already filled in—so explain the default and how to override it. Or maybe the customer has told him to have the goods delivered "any time after the first of the month"—so explain that he should enter the earliest date or whatever rule applies in your environment. The better you are at thinking about the questions users might really be asking, the more effective your help system will be.

What's This Tips

What's This tips are much like task-oriented online help except for how they are invoked. What's This tips are invoked by clicking the question mark icon in the window's title bar and then clicking a control within the window. Figure 18-5 shows the What's This topic for the Windows In Taskbar check box in the Options dialog box in Access 2000.

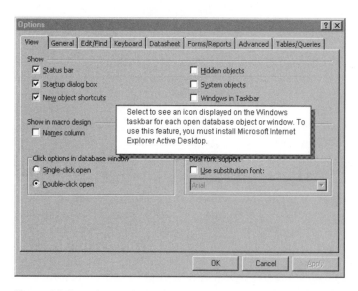

Figure 18-5. *What's This tips are displayed in dialog boxes by clicking the question mark button in the title bar and clicking a control.*

I like the idea of What's This tips a lot because they are so tightly integrated with the user interface of the system. I've seen novice users stumble upon What's This tips on several occasions. I've never seen novice users find online help by pressing F1 by accident, and I imagine it might be a little scary if they did, what with strange windows opening up all over the place.

For simple systems, a good set of What's This topics might be all the help you need to provide, particularly if the system doesn't support a lot of complex work processes. What's This topics must be fairly short, however, since they're displayed on top of the associated window and can't be scrolled. If you need to explain complex constraints, you simply won't have the space and you'll need to back up the What's This topic with one or more longer online help topics. (Be sure to add "Press F1 for more details" or words to that effect to the end of the What's This topic.)

The specific question a What's This topic attempts to answer is—as you've probably guessed from the name—"What is this thing?" Think of a What's This tip as a paragraph-long control caption. Because of space constraints, you usually can't be highly creative in responding to the questions you think users might be asking. But with a little thought, you can do better than just providing a reworded control label.

Describing the Desired Delivery Date as "the date on which the customer desires delivery of the goods" is just as evil in What's This tips as it is in online help. At the very least, try saying "the earliest date on which the goods are to be delivered. This value defaults to three days after the order date, but you can change this value by clicking the field and typing a new date. Press F1 for more details."

Audible Feedback

Audible feedback—using a computer tone to describe some system state—is an extremely powerful mechanism for assisting users, but designers can use its power for good or evil. The "Beep, you blew it" dialog box that's displayed when the system detects a "user error" is a prime example of using audible feedback for evil purposes. Users do not enjoy having attention drawn to their mistakes, and a beep not only draws a user's attention to the problem, it also notifies anyone within earshot. Besides, the default beep is a *really* annoying sound.

Turn audible feedback on its head, however, and it can be a wonderful tool. Instead of having the system blow a computer raspberry at a user when it gets confused, try having the computer emit a soft sound (I think of it as a purr) when something goes right. Say that during data entry the system is checking each field as the user exits the corresponding control. If the data complies with all relevant constraints, the system can issue a soft "I'm OK" sound. (The sound shouldn't be very loud.) If any problems occur, the system makes no sound but

instead displays a message in the status bar. Silence is sufficient notification of the problem, and the user will check the screen.

The best analogy for this positive feedback technique (for which I am indebted to Alan Cooper) is the keyboard. As you press each key, the keyboard makes a soft click. You're probably not consciously aware of the sound, but if it were to stop, you'd notice it immediately and investigate the problem.

The example of the keyboard ought to calm any fears you might have regarding the cacophony of a room full of data entry operators. As I've said, the "I'm OK" sound needn't be obtrusive to be effective. I've successfully used positive audible feedback in a system designed for a call center with over 100 users in a single room.

Error Messages

Most people don't consider error messages as a means of providing assistance to users, which is a pity. But then, most error messages *don't* assist users, they chastise instead. Instead of treating error messages as an opportunity to point out users' faults, treat them instead as a plea for users' assistance. The system has got itself into trouble, and it needs user help in getting out.

A well-behaved person, when requesting another's assistance, doesn't make cryptic statements or issue demands. A well-behaved person doesn't try to imply that it's someone else's fault that she is confused or in trouble. A well-behaved person explains a problem as clearly as possible, requests assistance politely, tries not to impose any more than necessary, and takes pains to explain the implications of her requests.

A well-behaved computer system ought to do no less. In fact, because computer systems are deserving of less respect than people, they ought to do more. (Groveling is not inappropriate here.) When issuing "error" messages, the system has an obligation to:

- Explain the situation clearly, in terms users will understand.

- Request assistance politely, without implying that users are at fault.

- Not impose on users by asking them to do anything the system could reasonably do for itself.

- Describe the implications of any action users might take.

The system will sometimes get itself hopelessly confused, or some environmental factor such as a shortage of memory or a disk failure will at times make it impossible for the system to continue operation without assistance from the user.

When these events occur, you have little choice but to display a message to the user. This is a wonderful opportunity not only to get the assistance the system needs, but also to provide the user with the information *she* needs to help the system stay out of trouble in the future.

By explaining the situation clearly and not using confusing jargon, the message you display to users will allow them to resolve the problem right away. Having understood the problem the first time, a user will be in a position to avoid having the same problem in the future—assuming the situation is avoidable. Invalid data entry formats are avoidable; hard disk failures generally aren't.

By explaining the implications of users' choices instead of presenting some option chosen more or less at random by a confused and disconcerted user, the system is far more likely to receive the most sensible response. Remember that a lot of things that seem perfectly obvious to you won't be obvious to the user. Don't talk down, of course, but don't be afraid of stating the obvious.

Wording the message politely and not imposing on users are just good manners. Remember when your mother told you that you'd catch more flies with honey than you would with vinegar? If users perceive your system as generally polite and helpful, they'll be inclined to forgive that one weird GPF that you never were able to track down. (Nobody's perfect.)

Proactive Assistance

Passive and reactive user assistance are relatively well-understood categories of user support, although they become increasingly sophisticated as our knowledge of computer-human interaction grows and new implementation tools become available. The final category, proactive assistance, is very much the new kid on the block and very few systems currently implement it.

The principle behind proactive user assistance is simple: the computer system monitors users' actions and acts proactively to assist, either by making suggestions for more efficient use of the system or by undertaking tasks on the users' behalf. The Microsoft Office Assistant gives proactive assistance by offering users tips based on their actions.

One type of proactive assistance currently receiving a great deal of attention is the intelligent agent. An intelligent agent is a piece of software to which users can delegate a task. Intelligent agents are most often implemented as a specialized Web user interface that answers such requests as "Find me the best price for this item" or "Suggest a book that I might like to read." But nothing restricts them to the Web environment. You might, for example, implement an agent that assists students in organizing a class schedule based on their preferences—"Don't schedule any math before noon, and I prefer language courses in the evening."

Microsoft provides two tools for creating interfaces based on animated characters, the Microsoft Office Assistant and the Microsoft Agent. Most people are familiar with the little bouncing paperclip representing the Microsoft Office Assistant (the character can be changed by a user), but not everyone realizes the Office Assistant has a programmable interface. The Office Assistant is available only within Microsoft Office applications, however, and can't be distributed with the Access run-time engine.

If you're working in Access (or in any other development environment that can use Microsoft ActiveX controls, including Visual Basic), you might want to download the Microsoft Agent SDK from the Microsoft Web site. It's quite a bit more powerful than the Office Assistant.

Microsoft Agent is a very cool toy. You can design and animate your own characters in addition to the ones provided in the SDK. Microsoft Agent also supports speech recognition, which has fascinating potential for database applications. I'd love to see a Microsoft Agent interface to the Microsoft English Query tool (which provides natural language processing of SQL queries) included in Microsoft SQL Server 7.0. Imagine representing the database itself as a Microsoft Agent character.

Be forewarned, though. Neither the Office Assistant nor Microsoft Agent provides any direct support for you to monitor and react to user actions. They provide simple interfaces to sophisticated character interactions with users, but when it comes to actually implementing the intelligence in your intelligent agent, you're strictly on your own.

User Training

The requirements for user training are no different for database systems than for any other type of software. Initial user training can be provided by documentation, classroom instruction, or the computer. And of course these options aren't mutually exclusive.

If you decide to implement computer-based training mechanisms, remember to be clear about both the scope and the audience of the project. Beginning users are primarily interested in what the system does and only secondarily interested in how to do it.

The scope of training aimed at beginning users varies with the complexity of the system and with the budget. Many systems require only an introductory screen or two explaining the system. More complex systems will benefit from more extensive training mechanisms—perhaps a guided tour or even formal computer-based training with exercises and quizzes and whatnot.

Intermediate users are primarily interested in how to perform specific tasks, and in many cases task-oriented help can meet their requirements. In fact, the

distinction between "help" and "training" is somewhat arbitrary. Complex systems, however, might require the same kind of formal computer-based training implemented for intermediate users as for beginning users.

Whatever the scope of the training you implement, keep the training reasonably separate from the system itself. Users should certainly be able to initiate the training from within the system's user interface, perhaps from an item on the help menu. But the existence of training materials should never interfere with normal use of the system.

SUMMARY

In this chapter, we've examined three types of explicit user assistance: passive assistance that is built into a system's user interface, reactive assistance that occurs as a result of some user actions, and proactive assistance that is initiated by the system itself.

We began by looking at three types of passive assistance: mnemonic access keys, ToolTips, and status bars. We then examined reactive assistance, which is usually implemented in the form of online help or What's This tips but can also include audible feedback and *should* include error messages. Finally, we looked briefly at the new area of proactive assistance and user training.

GLOSSARY

abstract entity An entity that models relationships between other entities.

ad hoc report A report that is configured by the user after implementation of the application.

aggregate function A SQL function that returns summary values.

alternate key A candidate key of a relation that is not used as the primary key of a table.

application The forms and reports with which the user interacts.

attribute A column in a relation.

base relation A relation that is instantiated as a table in the database.

binary relationship A relationship having two participants.

Boolean expression An expression that results in either True or False.

business constraint A constraint derived from the problem space.

business rule An integrity constraint that originates in the problem space rather than from relational theory.

candidate key One or more attributes that uniquely identify a relation.

cardinality of a relation The number of rows in a relation.

cardinality of a relationship The maximum number of instances of one entity that can participate in a relationship.

Cartesian product A relational operation that combines every record in one recordset with every record in a second recordset.

cascading update The automatic updating of entities in a foreign relation when the corresponding entity in the primary relation is changed.

closure The principle that all operations on a relation result in a relation and can be used for further manipulation.

command vector A path to the execution of a command in a user interface, for example a menu item or a toolbar button.

composite entity A single entity in the problem space that is modeled by one or more relations.

composite key A candidate key composed of two or more attributes.

concrete entity An entity that models an object or event in the real world.

database The combination of the database schema and the stored data.

database application The forms and reports with which the user interacts.

database constraint An integrity constraint that references multiple relations.

database schema The physical layout of tables in a database.

database system The combination of the database application, database engine, and database.

data integrity The rules used by a database to ensure that the data is, if not correct, at least plausible.

data model The conceptual description of a problem space in relational terms.

declarative integrity A method of defining integrity constraints by explicitly declaring them as part of a table definition.

degree of a relation The number of columns in a relation.

degree of a relationship The number of participants in a relationship.

derived relation A virtual relation that is defined in terms of other relations.

domain The range of values from which an attribute can be drawn.

domain constraint An integrity constraint that determines the range of possible values for a domain.

entity Anything about which the system needs to store information.

entity constraint An integrity constraint that ensures the validity of the entities being modeled by the system.

equi-join A join between two tables on the basis of equality.

field The physical representation of an attribute in a database.

foreign relation The relation that receives the primary key of the other participant in a relationship.

full outer join An outer join that returns all fields from both participants.

inner join A join that returns records only when the result of an operation is True.

integrity constraint A data integrity rule.

intrinsic constraint A constraint that governs the physical structure of the database.

junction table A table that represents a relationship in the database.

left outer join An outer join that returns all fields from the first recordset listed in a SELECT statement.

lossless decomposition The ability to divide relations in such a manner that they can be recombined without loss of information.

natural join A special case of an equi-join in which the join is performed on the basis of equality, all common fields participate in the join, and only one set of common fields is included in the result set.

orphan entity A weak entity that is not related to an entity in the primary relation of a relationship.

outer join A join that returns all the records of an inner join plus all the records in either or both of the other participants.

participant An entity that is associated to another in a relationship.

passive user assistance A user assistance mechanism that is an intrinsic part of the user interface.

primary key The candidate key of a relation that is used to uniquely identify the records in a table.

primary relation The relation whose primary key is stored in the other participant in a relationship.

proactive user assistance A user assistance mechanism that attempts to anticipate the users' needs.

problem space The portion of the real world that is to be modeled by a database application.

procedural integrity A method of enforcing data integrity by creating procedures that are executed automatically when a record is updated, inserted, or deleted.

query A derived relation in Microsoft Access.

reactive user assistance A user assistance mechanism that is triggered by some action by the user, such as an invalid entry or the request for online help.

record The physical representation of a tuple.

recordset The generic term used in Microsoft Access to mean the physical representation of a relation.

referential integrity The integrity constraints that ensure that relationships between entities remain valid.

regular entity An entity that can exist without participating in a relationship.

relation A logical construct that organizes data into rows and columns.

relational difference A relational operation that returns the records of one recordset that are not matched in another recordset.

relational divide A join that returns all the records in one recordset that have values that match all the corresponding values in the second recordset.

relational intersection A relational operation that returns the records two recordsets have in common.

relational union The concatenation of two recordsets.

relation body The tuples comprising a relation.

relation heading The definition of the attribute and domain at the top of a relation.

relationship An association between two or more entities.

right outer join An outer join that returns all fields from the second recordset listed in a SELECT statement.

scalar value A single, nonrepeating value.

schema The physical layout of tables in a database system.

simple key A candidate key composed of a single attribute.

standard report A report that can be defined and implemented as part of the database application.

table The physical instantiation of a relation in the database schema.

task A discrete step in a work process.

ternary relationship A relationship having three participants.

theta-join Technically, any join based on a comparison operator, but normally restricted to joins based on operators other than equality.

three-valued logic A model for logical evaluation that allows the values True, False, and Null as results of expressions.

transaction integrity An integrity constraint that controls the validity of multiple operations on the database.

tuple A row in a relation.

type-compatible domains Domains that can be logically compared.

unary relationship An association between a relation and itself.

update anomaly Problems with data manipulation resulting from a poorly designed data model.

view A derived relation in Microsoft SQL Server.

weak entity An entity that can exist only if it participates in a given relationship.

work process Something that is to be done using the database application.

BIBLIOGRAPHY

Part I — Relational Database Theory

Date, C. J. *An Introduction to Database Systems*. 7th ed. Reading, Mass.: Addison-Wesley Publishing Company, 1999.

Date, C. J. and Huge Darwen. *Foundation for Object/Relational Databases: The Third Manifesto*. Reading, Mass.: Addison-Wesley Publishing Company, 1998.

Fleming, Candace C. and Barbara von Halle. *Handbook of Relational Database Design*. Reading, Mass.: Addison-Wesley Publishing Company, 1989.

Teorey, Toby J. *Database Modeling & Design*. 3rd ed. San Francisco: Morgan Kaufmann Publishers, 1999.

Part II — Designing Relational Database Systems

Gilb, Tom and Susannah Finzi. *Principles of Software Engineering Management*. Reading, Mass.: Addison-Wesley Publishing Company, 1988.

Haught, Dan and Jim Ferguson. *Microsoft Jet Database Engine Programmer's Guide*. 2nd ed. Redmond, Wash.: Microsoft Press, 1997.

McConnell, Steve. *Rapid Development*. Redmond, Wash.: Microsoft Press, 1996.

Pressman, Roger S. *Software Engineering: A Practitioner's Approach*. 3rd ed. New York: McGraw-Hill, 1992.

Sommerville, Ian. *Software Engineering*. 6th ed. Reading, Mass.: Addison-Wesley Publishing Company, 1996.

Soukup, Ron. *Inside Microsoft SQL Server 6.5*. Redmond, Wash.: Microsoft Press, 1997.

Part III — Designing the User Interface

Cooper, Alan. *About Face: The Essentials of User Interface Design*. Foster City, Cal.: IDG Books Worldwide, 1995.

Heckel, Paul. *The Elements of Friendly Software Design*. New York: Warner Books, 1991.

Mandel, Paul. *The Elements of User Interface Design*. New York: John Wiley & Sons, 1997.

Microsoft Corporation. *The Windows Interface Guidelines for Software Design*. Redmond, Wash.: Microsoft Press, 1998.

Shneiderman, Ben. *Designing the User Interface: Strategies for Effective Human-Computer Interaction*. Reading, Mass.: Addison-Wesley Publishing Company, 1980.

INDEX

Special Characters

A

T

U

V

W

Rebecca M. Riordan, with 17 years' experience in the field, has earned an international reputation for designing and implementing computer systems that are technically sound and reliable, and that effectively meet her clients' needs.

She works as an independent consultant specializing in the design of database and work support systems. She was awarded MVP status by Microsoft in 1998 for her support in internet newsgroups.

Rebecca lives in Amsterdam, The Netherlands, with her husband and two cats. She can be reached at rebeccar@ibm.net

The manuscript for this book was submitted to Microsoft Press in electronic form. Galleys were prepared using Microsoft Word 2000. Pages were composed by Microsoft Press using Adobe PageMaker 6.52 for Windows, with text type in Garamond and display type in Futura Medium. Composed pages were delivered to the printer as electronic prepress files.

Cover Graphic Designer
Girvin Strategic Branding & Design

Cover Illustrator
Glenn Mitsui

Principal Interior Graphic Artist
Rob Nance

Principal Compositor
Barbara Levy

Principal Proofreader/Copy Editor
Roger LeBlanc

Indexer
Lynn Armstrong

Masterful instruction.
Your pace.
Your place.

Master the tools of your trade with in-depth developer training—straight from the source. The award-winning MICROSOFT MASTERING series is now available in ready-anywhere book format. Work at your own pace through the practical, print-based lessons to master essential development concepts, and advance your technique through the interactive labs on CD-ROM. It's professional-level instruction—when and where you need it—for building real-world skills and real-world solutions.

Serve up
powerfully scalable
business solutions

U.S.A. **$59.99**
U.K. £56.49 [V.A.T. included]
Canada $89.99
ISBN 0-7356-0517-3

With the innovations in Microsoft® SQL Server™ 7.0, organizations like yours get a powerfully enhanced tool for turning enterprise information into business results. In this essential companion to version 7.0, two of the most knowledgeable authorities on SQL Server technology step inside the reengineered SQL Server engine to reveal how underlying system structure and behavior affect application development. Use this in-depth, expert investigation—plus the ready-to-load evaluation copy of SQL Server 7.0—to understand how to create high-performance data warehousing, transaction processing, and decision-support applications that scale as far as your vision for the enterprise.

mspress.microsoft.com

Build
collaborative
solutions
that **bridge**—and **extend**—
enterprise
resources.

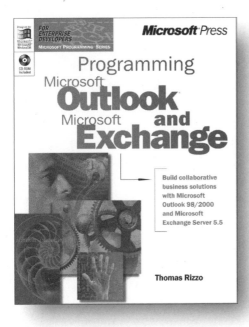

Microsoft Press

Programming
Microsoft
Outlook
Microsoft **and**
Exchange

Build collaborative
business solutions
with Microsoft
Outlook 98/2000
and Microsoft
Exchange Server 5.5

Thomas Rizzo

Build and run core business services across the enterprise using Microsoft's powerful messaging and collaboration tools— Outlook® 98, Outlook 2000, and Exchange Server 5.5. This book offers detailed guidance—plus a full cache of code and other resources on CD—to help you build open, extensible solutions for tracking, messaging, workflow, knowledge management, and real-time collaboration.

U.S.A.	**$49.99**
U.K.	£46.99 [V.A.T. included]
Canada	$74.99
ISBN 0-7356-0509-2	

Microsoft®

mspress.microsoft.com

MICROSOFT LICENSE AGREEMENT

Book Companion CD

IMPORTANT—READ CAREFULLY: This Microsoft End-User License Agreement ("EULA") is a legal agreement between you (either an individual or an entity) and Microsoft Corporation for the Microsoft product identified above, which includes computer software and may include associated media, printed materials, and "online" or electronic documentation ("SOFTWARE PRODUCT"). Any component included within the SOFTWARE PRODUCT that is accompanied by a separate End-User License Agreement shall be governed by such agreement and not the terms set forth below. By installing, copying, or otherwise using the SOFTWARE PRODUCT, you agree to be bound by the terms of this EULA. If you do not agree to the terms of this EULA, you are not authorized to install, copy, or otherwise use the SOFTWARE PRODUCT; you may, however, return the SOFTWARE PRODUCT, along with all printed materials and other items that form a part of the Microsoft product that includes the SOFTWARE PRODUCT, to the place you obtained them for a full refund.

SOFTWARE PRODUCT LICENSE

The SOFTWARE PRODUCT is protected by United States copyright laws and international copyright treaties, as well as other intellectual property laws and treaties. The SOFTWARE PRODUCT is licensed, not sold.

1. **GRANT OF LICENSE.** This EULA grants you the following rights:

    a. **Software Product.** You may install and use one copy of the SOFTWARE PRODUCT on a single computer. The primary user of the computer on which the SOFTWARE PRODUCT is installed may make a second copy for his or her exclusive use on a portable computer.

    b. **Storage/Network Use.** You may also store or install a copy of the SOFTWARE PRODUCT on a storage device, such as a network server, used only to install or run the SOFTWARE PRODUCT on your other computers over an internal network; however, you must acquire and dedicate a license for each separate computer on which the SOFTWARE PRODUCT is installed or run from the storage device. A license for the SOFTWARE PRODUCT may not be shared or used concurrently on different computers.

    c. **License Pak.** If you have acquired this EULA in a Microsoft License Pak, you may make the number of additional copies of the computer software portion of the SOFTWARE PRODUCT authorized on the printed copy of this EULA, and you may use each copy in the manner specified above. You are also entitled to make a corresponding number of secondary copies for portable computer use as specified above.

    d. **Sample Code.** Solely with respect to portions, if any, of the SOFTWARE PRODUCT that are identified within the SOFTWARE PRODUCT as sample code (the "SAMPLE CODE"):

    i. **Use and Modification.** Microsoft grants you the right to use and modify the source code version of the SAMPLE CODE, *provided* you comply with subsection (d)(iii) below. You may not distribute the SAMPLE CODE, or any modified version of the SAMPLE CODE, in source code form.

    ii. **Redistributable Files.** Provided you comply with subsection (d)(iii) below, Microsoft grants you a nonexclusive, royalty-free right to reproduce and distribute the object code version of the SAMPLE CODE and of any modified SAMPLE CODE, other than SAMPLE CODE, or any modified version thereof, designated as not redistributable in the Readme file that forms a part of the SOFTWARE PRODUCT (the "Non-Redistributable Sample Code"). All SAMPLE CODE other than the Non-Redistributable Sample Code is collectively referred to as the "REDISTRIBUTABLES."

    iii. **Redistribution Requirements.** If you redistribute the REDISTRIBUTABLES, you agree to: (i) distribute the REDISTRIBUTABLES in object code form only in conjunction with and as a part of your software application product; (ii) not use Microsoft's name, logo, or trademarks to market your software application product; (iii) include a valid copyright notice on your software application product; (iv) indemnify, hold harmless, and defend Microsoft from and against any claims or lawsuits, including attorney's fees, that arise or result from the use or distribution of your software application product; and (v) not permit further distribution of the REDISTRIBUTABLES by your end user. Contact Microsoft for the applicable royalties due and other licensing terms for all other uses and/or distribution of the REDISTRIBUTABLES.

2. **DESCRIPTION OF OTHER RIGHTS AND LIMITATIONS.**

    - **Limitations on Reverse Engineering, Decompilation, and Disassembly.** You may not reverse engineer, decompile, or disassemble the SOFTWARE PRODUCT, except and only to the extent that such activity is expressly permitted by applicable law notwithstanding this limitation.

    - **Separation of Components.** The SOFTWARE PRODUCT is licensed as a single product. Its component parts may not be separated for use on more than one computer.

    - **Rental.** You may not rent, lease, or lend the SOFTWARE PRODUCT.

    - **Support Services.** Microsoft may, but is not obligated to, provide you with support services related to the SOFTWARE PRODUCT ("Support Services"). Use of Support Services is governed by the Microsoft policies and programs described in the

user manual, in "online" documentation, and/or in other Microsoft-provided materials. Any supplemental software code provided to you as part of the Support Services shall be considered part of the SOFTWARE PRODUCT and subject to the terms and conditions of this EULA. With respect to technical information you provide to Microsoft as part of the Support Services, Microsoft may use such information for its business purposes, including for product support and development. Microsoft will not utilize such technical information in a form that personally identifies you.

- **Software Transfer.** You may permanently transfer all of your rights under this EULA, provided you retain no copies, you transfer all of the SOFTWARE PRODUCT (including all component parts, the media and printed materials, any upgrades, this EULA, and, if applicable, the Certificate of Authenticity), **and** the recipient agrees to the terms of this EULA.

- **Termination.** Without prejudice to any other rights, Microsoft may terminate this EULA if you fail to comply with the terms and conditions of this EULA. In such event, you must destroy all copies of the SOFTWARE PRODUCT and all of its component parts.

3. **COPYRIGHT.** All title and copyrights in and to the SOFTWARE PRODUCT (including but not limited to any images, photographs, animations, video, audio, music, text, SAMPLE CODE, REDISTRIBUTABLES, and "applets" incorporated into the SOFTWARE PRODUCT) and any copies of the SOFTWARE PRODUCT are owned by Microsoft or its suppliers. The SOFTWARE PRODUCT is protected by copyright laws and international treaty provisions. Therefore, you must treat the SOFTWARE PRODUCT like any other copyrighted material **except** that you may install the SOFTWARE PRODUCT on a single computer provided you keep the original solely for backup or archival purposes. You may not copy the printed materials accompanying the SOFTWARE PRODUCT.

4. **U.S. GOVERNMENT RESTRICTED RIGHTS.** The SOFTWARE PRODUCT and documentation are provided with RESTRICTED RIGHTS. Use, duplication, or disclosure by the Government is subject to restrictions as set forth in subparagraph (c)(1)(ii) of the Rights in Technical Data and Computer Software clause at DFARS 252.227-7013 or subparagraphs (c)(1) and (2) of the Commercial Computer Software—Restricted Rights at 48 CFR 52.227-19, as applicable. Manufacturer is Microsoft Corporation/One Microsoft Way/Redmond, WA 98052-6399.

5. **EXPORT RESTRICTIONS.** You agree that you will not export or re-export the SOFTWARE PRODUCT, any part thereof, or any process or service that is the direct product of the SOFTWARE PRODUCT (the foregoing collectively referred to as the "Restricted Components"), to any country, person, entity, or end user subject to U.S. export restrictions. You specifically agree not to export or re-export any of the Restricted Components (i) to any country to which the U.S. has embargoed or restricted the export of goods or services, which currently include, but are not necessarily limited to, Cuba, Iran, Iraq, Libya, North Korea, Sudan, and Syria, or to any national of any such country, wherever located, who intends to transmit or transport the Restricted Components back to such country; (ii) to any end user who you know or have reason to know will utilize the Restricted Components in the design, development, or production of nuclear, chemical, or biological weapons; or (iii) to any end user who has been prohibited from participating in U.S. export transactions by any federal agency of the U.S. government. You warrant and represent that neither the BXA nor any other U.S. federal agency has suspended, revoked, or denied your export privileges.

DISCLAIMER OF WARRANTY

NO WARRANTIES OR CONDITIONS. MICROSOFT EXPRESSLY DISCLAIMS ANY WARRANTY OR CONDITION FOR THE SOFTWARE PRODUCT. THE SOFTWARE PRODUCT AND ANY RELATED DOCUMENTATION ARE PROVIDED "AS IS" WITHOUT WARRANTY OR CONDITION OF ANY KIND, EITHER EXPRESS OR IMPLIED, INCLUDING, WITHOUT LIMITATION, THE IMPLIED WARRANTIES OF MERCHANTABILITY, FITNESS FOR A PARTICULAR PURPOSE, OR NONINFRINGEMENT. THE ENTIRE RISK ARISING OUT OF USE OR PERFORMANCE OF THE SOFTWARE PRODUCT REMAINS WITH YOU.

LIMITATION OF LIABILITY. TO THE MAXIMUM EXTENT PERMITTED BY APPLICABLE LAW, IN NO EVENT SHALL MICROSOFT OR ITS SUPPLIERS BE LIABLE FOR ANY SPECIAL, INCIDENTAL, INDIRECT, OR CONSEQUENTIAL DAMAGES WHATSOEVER (INCLUDING, WITHOUT LIMITATION, DAMAGES FOR LOSS OF BUSINESS PROFITS, BUSINESS INTERRUPTION, LOSS OF BUSINESS INFORMATION, OR ANY OTHER PECUNIARY LOSS) ARISING OUT OF THE USE OF OR INABILITY TO USE THE SOFTWARE PRODUCT OR THE PROVISION OF OR FAILURE TO PROVIDE SUPPORT SERVICES, EVEN IF MICROSOFT HAS BEEN ADVISED OF THE POSSIBILITY OF SUCH DAMAGES. IN ANY CASE, MICROSOFT'S ENTIRE LIABILITY UNDER ANY PROVISION OF THIS EULA SHALL BE LIMITED TO THE GREATER OF THE AMOUNT ACTUALLY PAID BY YOU FOR THE SOFTWARE PRODUCT OR US$5.00; PROVIDED, HOWEVER, IF YOU HAVE ENTERED INTO A MICROSOFT SUPPORT SERVICES AGREEMENT, MICROSOFT'S ENTIRE LIABILITY REGARDING SUPPORT SERVICES SHALL BE GOVERNED BY THE TERMS OF THAT AGREEMENT. BECAUSE SOME STATES AND JURISDICTIONS DO NOT ALLOW THE EXCLUSION OR LIMITATION OF LIABILITY, THE ABOVE LIMITATION MAY NOT APPLY TO YOU.

MISCELLANEOUS

This EULA is governed by the laws of the State of Washington USA, except and only to the extent that applicable law mandates governing law of a different jurisdiction.

Should you have any questions concerning this EULA, or if you desire to contact Microsoft for any reason, please contact the Microsoft subsidiary serving your country, or write: Microsoft Sales Information Center/One Microsoft Way/Redmond, WA 98052-6399.

Designing Relational Database Systems

WHERE DID YOU PURCHASE THIS PRODUCT?

CUSTOMER NAME

Microsoft®Press

mspress.microsoft.com

Microsoft Press, PO Box 97017, Redmond, WA 98073-9830

Designing Relational Database Systems

FIRST NAME

MIDDLE INITIAL

LAST NAME

INSTITUTION OR COMPANY NAME

ADDRESS

CITY

STATE

ZIP

(   )

E-MAIL ADDRESS

PHONE NUMBER

U.S. and Canada addresses only. Fill in information above and mail postage-free.
Please mail only the bottom half of this page.

For information about Microsoft Press® products, visit our Web site at mspress.microsoft.com